# DEMOCRACY WITHIN REASON

Miguel Ángel Centeno

# DEMOCRACY WITHIN REASON

Technocratic Revolution in Mexico

Second Edition

The Pennsylvania State University Press
University Park, Pennsylvania

Library of Congress Cataloging-in-Publication Data

Centeno, Miguel Ángel, 1957–
   Democracy within reason : technocratic revolution in Mexico /
Miguel Ángel Centeno.—2nd ed.

    p.      cm.
   Includes bibliographical references and index.
   ISBN 0-271-01701-5
   1. Mexico—Politics and government—1988–   2. Salinas de Gortari,
Carlos.   3. Government executives—Mexico.   4. Political leadership
—Mexico.  I. Title.
F1236.C46   1997
320.972—dc21
                                                     96-47836
                                                       CIP

Published by The Pennsylvania State University Press,
University Park, PA 16802-1003

Para Tía Ana, con todo mi cariño.

# Contents

## IDEOLOGY

## CONCLUSION

# Preface

Answers are enticing. Often it makes no difference whether an answer is right or wrong, as long as one exists. The more precise and decisive, the better; all the more so if the problem is complex. I remember my enchantment with linear programming during my first year in business school. One could enter as many variables as necessary, assign appropriate prices, choose what to maximize or minimize, write a few lines of instructions, and magically the most intricate management problem was reduced to a single quantity. The tools of modern management and economic analysis could dispel doubt, calm anxiety, and guarantee efficiency.

After my initial fascination I started wondering who chose what to maximize or minimize. As in Douglas Adams's novels, the significance of the answer "42" depends on the question. It was only after starting graduate school that I realized that power was not about producing solutions but about which questions were posed and how answers were verified. While studying the debt crisis in Latin America, for example, I read that populist policies were not viable and that proposals to share the costs of the crisis were clearly demagogic. What was important was responsibility, realistic appraisals, and truly feasible solutions. But, responsible to whom? Feasible for what? I found it difficult to accept that all these requirements coincidentally shifted most of the sacrifice toward the poor. Why would the debtor countries be so willing to take on such a burden? With all the talk of free riders in contemporary academic parlance, it struck me that the Latin American debtors behaved quite irrationally in paying their bills.

Perhaps the leaders of these countries were simply stooges of international finance? Having met many of those on Wall Street who supposedly had concocted this complex conspiracy, however, I found it difficult to believe that they had the intelligence or the skills to do so. The key to the "new dependency" of the debt was not the circulation of capital or commodities but the flow of knowledge. Those policy makers who had decided to pay back the debt, no matter the cost, simply could not imagine challenging the dictates of a model of international behavior. Much like medieval Ptolemists constructing evermore complex corollaries to explain the distance between theory and observation, the financial experts in both creditor and debtor countries tried to shape the world to meet their own expectations. As long as one asked the right questions, the model would work.

This book began as a study of the men and women who came up with these answers, the means by which they achieved power, and the consequences for their countries. While searching for a case study with which to examine financial policy making, I was struck by the particular characteristics of the Mexican state. Among the leaderships of regimes that could be loosely classified as bureaucratic-authoritarian, the Mexican elite was unique in that it achieved power without the apparent assistance of the military. How was it possible that these men and women, with no popular support, little or no charisma, and no military allies had been able to impose a regime of sacrifice? Who were these people and what was their vision of Mexico? Large parts of this book were written in order to answer these questions.

At the time I thought the answer would only be of historical interest since the Mexican technocrats would not remain in power for long. Like many others I thought that I had witnessed the last gasp of the Mexican regime in 1988. Whether Carlos Salinas had managed to win or steal the presidency did not matter since the regime was obviously on its last legs. In a proposal I wrote late in 1988 I mentioned that, unlike the Communist Party of the Soviet Union, the PRI did not have the resources to stay in power and that Salinas, unlike Mikhail Gorbachev, could not expect to survive while undermining his own political base.

Four years later and not quite so certain of my predictive powers, I arrived in Moscow to teach Russian students about the Mexican version of perestroika. From the Russian perspective the Mexican model could appear quite attractive. Among the ruins of one absolute dogma many sought yet another model, equally perfect in its logical closure. The new Mexican miracle certainly compared favorably to the chaos and uncertainty of the Russian transition. If one defined success as the ability to remain in power while overseeing radical social change, the achievements of the Mexican regime were truly outstanding. The trick was in the definition of success. Given the right question, Mexico seemed the perfect answer.

One obvious question was whether glasnost had doomed perestroika. Many Russians appeared to think so. In Moscow I often heard that perhaps Russia could not afford democracy. Democracy was fine, but perhaps it should be momentarily delayed. Russians should once again wait for the withering of the state. To some, Salinas seemed a smarter version of Gorbachev, having focused on the economy before democracy. I was struck by how easy it was to see democratic procedures as an unaffordable luxury and how the willingness of a population to express anger at suffering and declining standards of living could be seen as an obstacle to needed change. Russians were not alone in this opinion. The assumption in much of the academic literature was that reasonable solutions required reasonable governments, and democracies had an unfortunate habit of producing quite unreasonable results. Democracy was a perfectly respectable objective, but only within reason.

If this book reflects my biases (and undoubtedly it does), one is clear and explicit: a preference for democracy over wisdom. Contemporary Moscow is one obvious example of what happens when an elite vanguard insists on the inevitability of its model. Both the now-discredited Leninist model and the fashionable technocratic alternative share the same distrust of their own population and the same inflated sense of their own virtue. That the Salinas government has produced almost miraculous results is indisputable, but Moscow, in its time, was also said to represent the future. Precisely because it appears to represent such a wonderful solution, a perfect answer to those who seek a way to make a leap into "modernity," it is important to understand the origins, characteristics, potential, and limitations of the Mexican model. This book is an attempt to define these.

The book is not an attempt to defend democracy since I believe it is impossible to do so except on its own terms. If the question of the transition to the market is posed in terms of effectiveness, stability, and speed, the answer will most likely be authoritarian. The advantages of not having to worry about opposition when imposing unpopular policies do not need belaboring. The ability of an all-powerful state to create economic miracles was more than adequately proven in both Germany and the Soviet Union in the 1930s; the potential costs were also made patently clear. Rather, the book is concerned with the specific organization, personnel, and doctrine of the Mexican technocratic state and the relationship between these and specific policy choices. It is about who asked what questions and how their answers shaped Mexico's response to the revolution of the market in the 1980s.

Chapter 1 summarizes the economic, political, and economic situation in Mexico in the 1990s, as well as providing some historical background for those unfamiliar with that country. Chapter 2 then proceeds to discuss the academic literature on transition to the market and provides a summary of my argument. Both of these chapters have been written from a comparative perspective. The following chapters are more oriented toward those interested in the specifics of the Mexican case but are organized so that they may be read in isolation. In deciding how to tell the story of the Mexican technocratic revolution, I had to choose whether to privilege the narrative or the analysis thereof. I have tried to do justice to both by essentially telling the same story from three different angles, or at three different analytical levels.

Chapters 3 and 4 define the institutional arena in which the technocratic revolution took place. The first describes the centralization of power within the bureaucracy and its relationship with the military, the ruling party, and international and domestic capital. Chapter 4 discusses the structure of that bureaucracy, particularly the role of the presidency and the rise in importance of the planning and finance sectors. The next two chapters define who led the revolution and their relationships to their predecessors. Chapter 5 provides a detailed description of the dominant elite and their social origins, educational background, political activity, and professional experience. Chapter 6 analyzes the maintenance of a complex system of interlocking political networks of patron-client relationships and their role in the empowerment of the new elite. Chapter 7 and Chapter 8 turn to a discussion of the ideology of the revolution. Chapter 7 describes the hegemony of new economic and social principles in policy making. Chapter 8 analyzes the specific methods used to design and implement these and the implications for democratic participation. With the last chapter I turn to more speculative analysis oriented to promoting comparative discussion and debate. My conclusion proposes some alternative scenarios for Mexico's future and suggests some guidelines for the study of regimes undertaking similar transitions.

With this summary in mind I would like to note what this book is not. As I finished the last revisions I realized that in my efforts to bring the state back in, I tended to keep society out. I still feel that politics and policies do matter to anyone interested in analyzing the transition to the market. But I also realize that there are many actors missing from my study. All scholarly enterprises must have limits, and the walls of the state are those of this book.

I would like to thank the following institutions for providing assistance in the research and writing of this book. The Yale College Financial Aid office helped begin it all quite a few years ago. I would also like to thank all my employers in the years between college and graduate school for understanding and supporting my dream to return to academia. More recently I have depended on the generosity of the National Science Foundation, the Yale University Graduate School, the Fulbright-Hays office at the Department of Education, the Spencer Foundation, the John F. Enders Foundation, the Center for U.S.-Mexican Studies at UCSD, Princeton University, and the Council for International Exchange of Scholars.

I also owe a great deal to my teachers. First to Frank Snowden who introduced me to both Marx and Weber so long ago. In graduate school Woody Powell, Chick Perrow, David Apter, Scott Boorman, Robert Kaufman, Barbara Stallings, Charles Lindblom, and Matthews Hamabata were wonderful teachers and supporting mentors. John Bailey, Roderic Camp, and Daniel Levy were also kind enough to offer their assistance at critical stages. I especially want to thank Sylvia Maxfield, Paul DiMaggio, and Juan Linz. Each of them contributed more than they know to this book, and I only hope that the end result justifies their faith and efforts.

For listening to my endless harangues about technocracy, Mexico, and the general injustice of the universe, I want to thank my friends and colleagues whose patience appeared to know no bounds. In New Haven these included María José Moyano, Alberto Vourvoulias, Miriam Smith, Bill Reese, and Emmanuel Lazega. I only wish Konrad Stenzel could have read this book—I have no doubt it would have been a much better one had he done so. Kimberly Carson supported this project through some of the most difficult periods, and I am especially grateful to her. In Mexico so many helped that they must remain anonymous. I owe a great deal to the over seventy academics, politicians, and journalists who answered my questions. My deepest thanks go to the Gameros family, and especially to Manolo, for introducing me to their fantastic country. The fellows and staff at the La Jolla Center made finishing my thesis an almost pleasant experience. I owe my sanity and much more to Joe Foweraker, Oton Baños, Juan Molinar, Arturo Sánchez, Peter Smith, Wayne Cornelius, Graciela Platero, Jeff Weldon, Luin Goldring, and Carol Zabin. Thanks also to Christa Beran and Mitch for their wonderful hospitality. In Princeton I was again very lucky to find a great group of colleagues: Frank Dobbin, Michèle Lamont, Gene Burns, Michael Jiménez, Ben Ross Schneider, Viviana Zelizer, John Waterbury, Marvin Bressler, Donna DeFrancisco, Blanche Anderson, and Cindy Gibson. I also had wonderful students who not only taught me a lot but also laughed at all my jokes. Thanks as well to Ernest Mastria for keeping me in the present. And since I promised, thanks to Carol Swegle for the most honest comment an academic ever heard: "That sounds great Miguel. I wish I could say that I will be interested enough to read it."

Many of those listed above read parts or even all of previous versions of this book and I hope they will recognize some of their contributions and forgive my stubbornness and many errors. I especially want to thank Dale Story and Nora Hamilton whose suggestions helped me clarify the final version of the argument. Sandy Thatcher at Penn State Press has been the ideal editor and deserves more thanks than I can give here. Cathy Thatcher also did a wonderful job on copyediting.

Finally, and most important, I want to thank my family for allowing me the luxury of doing what I love for a living. Arturo Girón and Debby Anker saved me from more than one disaster and always seemed to believe that I would make it. Deborah Kaple has given me more than I ever thought possible; finishing this book is an especially happy occasion since it means we can spend much more time together. But none of this would have been possible without the sacrifice and love of Ana Pintado, and I hope she will not mind that I have dedicated the book to her. Gracias, Tía Ana.

*Note to the second edition:* The Postscript has been added to bring the story up to date as of mid-1996. A few minor editorial corrections, but no substantive changes, have been made in the rest of the text.

# List of Abbreviations

| | |
|---|---|
| Banobras | National Bank of Public Works and Services |
| CEN | National Executive Committee (PRI) |
| CEPES | Center for Political, Economic, and Social Studies (PRI) |
| CNC | National Peasant Confederation |
| CNOP | National Confederation of Popular Organizations |
| CONASUPO | National Company of Basic Products |
| CTM | Workers' Confederation of Mexico |
| DF | Federal District |
| FCE | Economic Culture Foundation |
| FDN | National Democratic Front |
| FLACSO | Latin American School for Social Sciences |
| GATT | General Agreement on Tariffs and Trade |
| Icap | Institute for Political Training (PRI) |
| IEPES | Institute for Political, Economic, and Social Studies (PRI) |
| IMF | International Monetary Fund |
| IMSS | Mexican Social Security Institute |
| INAP | National Institute of Public Administration |
| INEGI | National Institute of Statistical and Geographical Data |
| Infonavit | Institute of the National Fund for Workers' Housing |
| ISSSTE | Institute for Social Security and Services for Public Employees |
| ITAM | Autonomous Technological Institute of Mexico |

| | |
|---|---|
| LFOPPE | Federal Law of Political Organizations and Elections |
| Nafinsa | National Development Bank |
| NAFTA | North American Free Trade Agreement |
| NICs | Newly Industrializing Countries |
| PAN | National Action Party |
| PARM | Authentic Party of the Mexican Revolution |
| PCM | Mexican Communist Party |
| Pemex | Mexican Petroleum Company |
| PFCRN | Party of the Cardenist Front for National Reconstruction |
| PGD | Global Development Plan |
| PIRE | Immediate Program for Economic Reorganization |
| PMS | Mexican Socialist Party |
| PNDI | National Plan of Industrial Development |
| PNR | National Revolutionary Party |
| PPS | People's Socialist Party |
| PRD | Party of the Democratic Revolution |
| PRI | Revolutionary Institutional Party |
| PRONASOL | National Solidarity Program |
| SAHOP | Ministry of Housing and Public Works |
| SAHR | Ministry of Agriculture and Water Resources |
| SCT | Ministry of Communications and Transport |
| Secofi | Ministry of Commerce and Industrial Development |
| Sedesol | Ministry of Social Development |
| SEDUE | Ministry of Urban Development and Housing |
| SEMIP | Ministry of Energy, Mines, and Parastatals |
| SEP | Ministry of Education |
| Sepafin | Ministry of National Patrimony and Industrial Development |
| SHCP | Ministry of the Treasury |
| SPP | Ministry of Programming and Budget |
| STPRM | Revolutionary Syndicate of Petroleum Workers of Mexico |
| UNAM | National Autonomous University of Mexico |

# INTRODUCTION

# 1

## Salinastroika

In the fall of 1991 progovernment rallies in Mexico featured a new cheer—"*Uno, dos, tres, Salinas otra vez*"[1]—and newspaper columns openly discussed the possibility of Carlos Salinas running for a second term as president. Given the importance of the principle of no reelection in the Mexican political iconography, even the hint of such a radical shift raised a few eyebrows.[2] Much of the discussion in the restaurants, political salons, and offices of the capital revolved around whether Salinas had approved, gently supported, or even had knowledge of an orchestrated campaign (the idea that this was a spontaneous demonstration of support was never seriously considered). While the possibility of a reelection had been dismissed by late 1992, the mere airing of such sentiments indicated the fantastic political success of the first half of the Salinas *sexenio*.[3]

The Salinas *sexenio* represented a revolution in Mexico comparable to that presided by Lázaro Cárdenas in the 1930s.[4] While it did not involve a total social transformation such as the classic revolutions of 1789, 1910, and 1917, or even 1989, it certainly changed both the organiza-

1. Interview, Mexico City, December 1991. The phrase translates literally into "One, two, three, Salinas one more time," but may be best understood as the Mexican equivalent of "Four more years."

2. See discussion in *El Universal* (Mexico City), February 16, 1992.

3. Literally, sexenial. This is the common term used to define Mexican presidential administrations.

4. See Nora Hamilton, *The Limits of State Autonomy: Post-Revolutionary Mexico* 1982; Arnaldo Córdova, *La política de masas del cardenismo*, 1973; and the Colegio de México's *Historia de la revolución mexicana*.

tion of and the policies advocated by the state.[5] The economic ramifications included the strengthening of the position of private capital vis-à-vis labor and the integration of Mexico into a global market. Its effects were felt by the Church and by lay social organizations, by peasants and industrial workers, by the domestic bourgeoisie and the urban marginalized, and perhaps most of all by the country's political class.

The revolution was technocratic in that it was directed from above, by a state elite committed to the imposition of a single, exclusive policy paradigm based on the application of instrumentally rational techniques.[6] The answers provided by the theoretical models of economics dominated those provided by political negotiation. The legitimacy of popular participation was accepted only as long as it would support the correct policies. Election results would be respected, but only as long as they supported the right candidate. Discussion was welcomed, but only within preset constraints and assumptions. Democracy was desirable, but only within reason.

The main instrument of this revolution was not the ballot box or the mass demonstration or even the barrel of a rifle but bureaucratic control over economic and political resources. The regime sought to "modernize" Mexico through the creation of an economic and political system where administrative and productive efficiency were paramount. The democratic spirit of the original revolution was replaced by a faith in the rule of expertise; the institutions created to balance the needs of the various social sectors were replaced by calls for solidarity.

The transformation of Mexico during the late 1980s has been compared to similar efforts by Mikhail Gorbachev. By late 1989 it was already common to hear references to *salinastroika*.[7] Yet, some noted that Mexico had yet to experience glasnost.[8] Obviously, Mexican society had a much shorter distance to travel to democracy than the former Soviet Union, but the efforts at economic reform were far ahead of any political openings. It is precisely this imbalance that makes the last de-

---

5. Theda Skocpol, *States and Social Revolutions*, 1979, p. 4.

6. Miguel Ángel Centeno, "The New Leviathan: The Dynamics and Limits of Technocracy," 1993.

7. The term even made it to Moscow, where it was hailed as a much more successful variant of political and economic change. The new Russian magazine *VIP*, for example, included a glowing review of the Salinas presidency (no. 8, Winter 1992, p. 2).

8. Lorenzo Meyer, "Aquí, perestroika sin glasnost," *Excelsior* (Mexico City), December 13, 1989.

cade in Mexico so interesting. The true triumph of *salinastroika* is not necessarily the macroeconomic success claimed by the government but the political stability that allowed the creation of Calles to survive that of Lenin.

Perhaps most impressive, the government has survived without the help of the military or significant increases in the use of systemic terror. This is not to deny the often-used intimidation tactics or the presence of state-sponsored violence, but the Mexican state has not engaged in either the pervasive surveillance nor the organized terror and repression of other authoritarian regimes. While Salinas had not turned Mexico into a democracy, there had been no Tiananmens. As with the utopian dreams of the futurists of the 1920s or the cinemagraphic visions of Fritz Lang, the technocratic revolution appeared bloodless and pristine. The Mexican regime was touted as a model for reform that the new nations of Eastern Europe should try to emulate.[9] More than one reformer in various parts of the world must have looked enviously on the Mexican regime's ability to remain in power as it transformed the social and political bases of its support.

The final section of this chapter describes the limits and accomplishments of the technocratic revolution. These can only be understood, however, in light of Mexican history and especially the conditions under which Salinas assumed power. The following two sections provide this background.

# The Institutionalized Revolution

For the first fifty years following its independence from Spain in 1821, Mexico endured political dislocation and economic stagnation.[10] The

---

9. See, for example, the comments of James Baker in the *Washington Post*, September 10, 1991.

10. Any attempt to summarize the history of a country in a few pages must necessarily involve simplification and superficiality. The few pages that follow are intended as a summary for readers not familiar with Mexico who may need a general guide before starting the book. Those who already know the basic outline of Mexican history and who are familiar with the language and structure of Mexican politics may wish to skip this section. For an excellent narrative account of Mexican history, see Ramón Eduardo Ruiz, *Triumphs and Tragedy*, 1992. See also Alan Knight, "The Peculiarities of Mexican History," 1992. Bibliographic details on the various periods or events discussed may be found in the text.

country was ruled by forty-five administrations during this period and failed to develop even a rudimentary industrial infrastructure. It also suffered a series of foreign attacks and invasions, the most dramatic one resulting in the loss of over half of its territory to the United States. (This historical fact often is ignored by Americans when confronted by Mexican nationalism.)

The chaos and uncertainty of this period came to an end with the Porfirio Díaz dictatorship, commonly known as the Porfiriato (1875–1911). During this administration of "order and progress," the central government finally established its authority over the entire country while supporting considerable industrial development. The economic model was based on what today would be called "outward development" oriented toward the export of primary commodities largely in the hands of foreign firms. These and roughly 250 elite families (controlling nearly 80 percent of the national territory) enjoyed access to the presidential office and expected that their rights and interests would be considered. For the majority of the population, however, the Mexican variant of positivism provided few benefits and explicitly excluded their political participation.

The combination of political deinstitutionalization, economic development, and continued social exploitation during the Porfiriato produced the first great social revolution of the twentieth century. Opinions on and analyses of the Revolution (the accepted custom of capitalizing the term reflects its central importance in Mexican history) differ radically. Some see it as a liberal battle of a nascent middle class, others as the culmination of a century of peasant resistance; some focus on the regional elements, others on the manner in which it helped to unite the country; some even challenge the extent to which it was revolutionary. Each interpretation also has a corresponding actor in the great drama: Francisco Madero representing the political reformers and social conservatives; Emiliano Zapata leading a peasant army demanding agrarian reform; Pancho Villa with his rancheros whose goals are still the subject of debate; and the constitutionalists of Venustiano Carranza and Alvaro Obregón whose victory in the bloody civil wars of 1911–1919 gave birth to the contemporary Mexican state.

The legacy of this victory is contradictory and paradoxical. On the one hand, the 1917 Constitution may be seen as marking the birth of the first socialist state. On the other, the regime created by Obregón and his successors may also be seen as continuing the model of Don Porfirio, emphasizing the continuity of central authority and the role of private property in economic development. During the first ten years of its existence, the regime faced a series of challenges ranging from political assassination and Catholic counterrevolution to the animosity of foreign firms and their governments. With regard to the latter, if the regime was not able to completely and securely establish its economic autonomy vis-à-vis the "colossus of the North," it was successful at maintaining its political independence and certainly did not have to fear a return of gunboat diplomacy after the 1930s.

The challenges of rebellion and political instability were more definitively resolved toward the end of the decade under the leadership of Plutarco Elías Calles, who created a new political body with the National Revolutionary Party (Partido Nacional Revolucionario, PNR) in 1929. This precursor of today's Institutional Revolutionary Party (Partido Revolucionario Institucional, PRI) succeeded in uniting all the various players who agreed to a set of formalized rules to govern the political game so that if none could be sure of its domination, all could be guaranteed a role.

What had been essentially an interelite settlement became much more during the presidency of Lázaro Cárdenas (1934–1940). During his *sexenio* Cárdenas created the corporatist apparatus that would link the state and the party to both peasants and the working class and, if not necessarily assuring that their interests would be represented, guaranteed that neither would mount an independent challenge to the regime. These years also saw perhaps the last gasp of the "radical" element of the Revolution with the acceleration of agrarian reform and especially the support the communal landholdings known as *ejidos,* the defense of labor's rights, and the nationalization of the oil industry in 1938.

Four critical elements of the order established by Calles (and later modified by his successor) serve to distinguish the Mexican version of the "party-state" and help define Mexican political life to this day. First, the prohibition on reelection combined with the massive concentration of power in the presidency helped to guarantee that no single individual would be able to dominate. Instead the state was ruled by an orderly succession of temporary monarchs. Each could attempt to shape future polices through the *destape* or unveiling of his successor, but time and again each president failed to maintain his influence after the proscribed six years. Second, partly by design, partly due to the struggle inside the elite during the 1930s, the state bureaucracy was able to establish its hegemony over both the military *and* the party. Each of the latter was able to provide the security and mass support required by the regime without being able to constrain the actions of the central bureaucracy. Third, the regime was successful in establishing links to the legacy of the Revolution, thereby simultaneously providing a basis for legitimacy and constraining the nature of opposition demands, whether of the right or the left. In short, in a pattern to be envied by almost all Latin American countries, the Mexican state by 1940 appeared to have resolved the problems of succession, praetorianism, governmental autonomy, and mass legitimacy. Cárdenas's successors Manuel Ávila Camacho (1940–1946) and Miguel Alemán (1946–1952) added the final defining characteristic of the Mexican regime: an implicit alliance between state and private capital that provided the foundation for the so-called "miracle" of the 1950s and 1960s.

As Mexico prepared to host the Olympics in 1968, it appeared to have it all. The rhapsodical descriptions of the Korean miracle during the 1988 Olympics parallel those heard twenty years earlier. Mexico enjoyed both political stability and economic growth. Yet there were already signs of stress. The dramatic urbanization and industrialization of the past two decades created strains in the political legitimacy of the regime as it had to deal with the consequences of both its failures and successes. The economic growth had failed to benefit significant parts of the population, especially in the countryside, and many began to question the relevancy of the revolutionary rhetoric espoused by the state. The boom had also created a relatively large urban middle class who, like its Korean counterpart twenty years later, began to demand a larger role in the political life of the country. Both trends, along with an international environment that encouraged political activity in the universities, produced a confrontation between the government and students beginning in August 1968. The government's decision to adopt a hard-line approach to the protests led to the killing of several hundred demonstrators in the Plaza of the Three Cultures in Tlatelolco. While the students were cowed by this unprecedented use of violence and the government appeared to have reestablished its political stability, the legitimacy of the regime and the reputation of the president, Gustavo Díaz Ordaz (1964–1970), never recuperated. Simultaneously, the success of the industrialization model faced new obstacles, especially a worsening trade deficit and the limitations of its overprotected industry. The next twenty years were an attempt to recapture the magic of the Mexican miracle.

# Inauspicious Beginnings

Mexicans refer to the years 1970–1982 as the "tragic dozen," during which dreams of greatness and autonomy were continuously shattered. During the first three years of the decade, President Luis Echeverría (1970–1976) attempted to resuscitate the popular support of the regime, but this produced strains with the previously acquiescent private sector as well with foreign firms. This opposition, combined with the disruption of the oil shock of 1973, forced Echeverría to abandon many of his policies in favor of a more conservative approach perhaps best exemplified by his choice of a successor. José López Portillo (1976–1982) appeared to be saved from the difficult choice between political stability and economic growth by the discovery of massive oil deposits. The first four years of his *sexenio* witnessed an unprecedented boom as petrodollars fueled economic growth and purchased the loyalty (or at least the compliance) of most segments of the Mexican population. But the boom was more a product of massive borrowing than anything else, and by 1981 Mexico was facing an even worse economic crisis than in the early 1970s. Despite such measures as the bank nationalization of 1982 and an increase in the president's nationalist and populist rhetoric, his *destape* of Miguel de la Madrid signalled yet another swing in the political pendulum toward a more conservative direction.

The *sexenio* of Miguel de la Madrid (1982–1988) coincided with the "lost decade" for much of Latin America. The Mexican economy shrank and the population continued to grow, producing a decline in per capita wealth. While most experienced a fall in income, those at the bottom faced a disastrous collapse that was reflected in worsening measures of social development and public health. The economic collapse and the pressures of repaying the debt contributed to worsening public deficits with accompanying inflation and capital flight. By the end of de la Madrid's term the economy was shrinking, the deficit consumed nearly a fifth of GDP, and inflation was on the verge of hypervelocity.[11]

Simultaneously, the political legitimacy of the regime was at a historical low. Instead of the promised "moral renovation" and political reform, the government of Miguel de la Madrid limited itself to the arrest of a particularly odious figure who had no strong constituency support-

---

11. Stephen A. Quick, "Mexico's Macroeconomic Gamble," 1989, pp. 7–8.

ing him (ex-Mexico City Police Chief Durazo) and the imprisonment of an expolitical rival of de la Madrid's whose corruption paled next to that of ex-President López Portillo (Jorge Díaz Serrano). The local and congressional elections of 1983, 1985, and 1986 were marred by obvious fraud and intimidation. With its half-hearted reforms, the de la Madrid administration simultaneously alienated the traditional wing of the party and frustrated those who had hoped that the president would begin the long-delayed political democratization of the regime. In the May Day parade of 1984, dissident labor organizations unfurled banners attacking government policies, and molotov cocktails were thrown at the Presidential Palace.[12] The government had also lost the support of significant sections of the middle class. During the ceremonies opening the soccer World Cup in July 1986, de la Madrid's speech was drowned out by the whistling (the Mexican equivalent of booing) of 100,000 spectators.[13]

The earthquake of September 17, 1985, not only demolished a considerable part of the capital but also did irreparable damage to the government's prestige. Instead of taking advantage of what could have been a marvelous opportunity for the president to establish a personal link with the population and restore the legitimacy of the system, de la Madrid appeared confused by and, to some, even indifferent to the suffering of thousands of citizens.[14] On less symbolic grounds the government and the army demonstrated that they were, at best, incapable of managing the response to the disaster and, at worst, quite capable of profiting from it. While Mexicans had come to expect a *mordida* (demand for bribe) from policemen or clerks in government offices, the rumors of international supplies being sold in the black market further fueled dissatisfaction. The failure of the government also gave rise to grass-roots organizational and coordination efforts, many of which came to replace the traditional PRI patronage machines as the political centers in poor neighborhoods.

12. Carlos B. Gil, *Hope and Frustration: Interviews with Leaders of Mexico's Political Opposition*, 1992, p. 47.

13. The high ticket prices assured that the stadium audience was largely drawn from the richest quarter of the population.

14. One acquaintance described the image shown on TV of de la Madrid walking around the ruins by saying: "He looked liked he was more concerned with getting his jacket dirty than anything else." Another, a longtime bureaucrat in the PRI headquarters, could not imagine that the group around the president could think of nothing better than having him walk around a few destroyed buildings or give a speech that even by de la Madrid's less than charismatic standards was a political disaster. A still unresolved question is why de la Madrid did not use the earthquake to provide a "breather" in debt servicing.

Overall, the population no longer believed that the government was capable of responding to the economic, social, and political crises it was facing. The percentage of the population who thought the government was doing a good job declined from 45 percent to 29 percent from 1983 to 1987, while the number who thought it was doing a bad job increased from 12 percent to 29 percent.[15]

The selection of the PRI's presidential candidate for 1988 was seen as the most critical point in the history of the regime since the departure of Lázaro Cárdenas. Several academic analysts and political participants agreed that this election probably represented the last instance of an outgoing president being able to impose his choice of successor without popular participation.[16] For these authors the delegitimation of the regime and its failure to grow out of the debt had weakened the government to a historically unprecedented extent.

In the accepted wisdom of that time the political and economic crises had generated so much popular discontent that no matter the choice, the new president would have to oversee a dramatic transformation in the Mexican political system, either by relying more explicitly and directly on repression or by accepting a loss of the monopoly over power that his predecessors had enjoyed. Such a transformation would require an exceptional person who could combine a multitude of talents. In the words of a prominent Mexican political analyst, "[(In the 1980s)] Mexico needs a new political class capable of mixing archaic traditions and anticipated modernities, to be at home in both Harvard and Teziutlan, with doctorates from Nanterre and votes in Ecatepec."[17] Could the regime produce "this paragon, this charismatic politician and brilliant economist" who would lead the country out of its problems?[18]

On October 4, 1987, it was still uncertain which of the leading candidates would be selected. That morning, after some false rumors that cost several members of the elite whatever political careers they may have had, the PRI announced that its three sectors "in consultation with their members" had agreed to present Carlos Salinas de Gortari as their candidate. Carlos Salinas was the Minister of Programming and Budget and the technocratic candidate *par excellence*. Widely admired for his analytical

15. Miguel Basáñez, *El pulso de los sexenios: Veinte años de crisis en México*, 1990, p. 100.
16. Abraham Nuncio, ed, *La sucesión presidencial en 1988*, 1987.
17. Héctor Aguilar Camín, "La transición política," *Nexos* 51 (March 1982), pp. 9–14.
18. Government economist and PRI member quoted in the *New York Times*, February 2, 1987, p. 4A.

brilliance, he was also known for his impatience with those who disagreed with him and his disdain for the traditional party elite. The accolades for the party's "unanimous choice" came from practically all sectors, each describing Salinas as the obvious selection from the very beginning and praising his "nationalism, patriotism, serenity, and commitment to the future of his country."[19] The enthusiasm, however, was not quite universal, and the divisions in the party became increasingly obvious.

Partly because of his association with the harshest policies of the regime (people referred to him as Salinas de *Cortari*—a pun on the Spanish word for cutting), partly because of personal appearance and lack of charisma (a favorite nickname was "Atom Ant"), he was considered the least popular of all the possible presidential choices.[20] Certainly he was intensely disliked by Fidel Velázquez of the Mexican Workers Confederation (Confederación de Trabajadores de Mexico, CTM)—the corporatist labor arm of the government—by other leading labor bosses such as the oil workers' Joaquín Hernández Galicia ("La Quina"), and by large segments of the political administrative apparatus. From various interviews with PRI bureaucrats it appears that there was little real support for Salinas among the rank and file that managed the political machinery. Most of them would have preferred one of their own, or at least a compromise choice.[21] They felt that the selection of Salinas was a clear and direct announcement that the PRI they had known was dead. One respected *político* went as far as to say that the "reactionaries had taken over the PRI."[22]

The left wing of the party, which was already in the process of a complete break with the system, was even more adamant, repudiating "[t]he shamelessness with which this comedy of errors culminated in the selection of a single candidate. . . . This is nothing but a disguised reelection which will perpetuate the rule by a counter-revolutionary clique . . .

19. The need to ensure such "unanimous" approval often produced comical results. For example, the governor of the state of Campeche, knowing that the presidential announcement was coming but not privy to its contents, arrived in Mexico City with signs and slogans supporting each of the six most likely candidates as "his personal choice." *Proceso*, no. 571, October 12, 1987, p. 6.

20. In a poll taken by *El Norte*, the leading newspaper of Monterrey, only 7 percent chose Salinas while the majority preferred Manuel Bartlett and Alfredo del Mazo (quoted in *New York Times*, October 5, 1987, p. 8). A survey taken in the spring of 1988, which the author helped organize for the state TV network IMEVISION, demonstrated that his public image had not improved in the intervening six months.

21. See also Tomás Brito Lara, *La sucesión presidencial de 1910 en 1988*, 1988.

22. Rodolfo González Guevara, quoted in *Proceso*, no. 570, October 5, 1987.

controlled by international financial interests."[23] Considering that the speaker had been a prominent member of the elite who had served in both the presidential cabinet and in the National Committee of the PRI, the new candidate faced a serious crisis of confidence within his own political apparatus. This produced the first break in the PRI monolith in over thirty years with the defection of large numbers of *priístas* who supported the candidacy of the dissident Cuauhtémoc Cárdenas.

The Mexican private sector, on the other hand, was ecstatic.[24] In the months prior to the announcement the preferences of the bourgeoisie (at least that wing of it attached to the PRI) had been relatively clear.[25] When PRI chief Jorge de la Vega met with a group of businessmen in May 1987, the latter had emphasized the need to stay the course with the de la Madrid economic policy and indicated its support for its creator, Salinas. On June 11, Agustín Legorreta, head of the Consejo Coordinador Empreserial (the most important Mexican business association), made his support for Salinas even more explicit: "[P]opulist decisions have hurt the country; it is necessary to return to economic orthodoxy. . . . the next *sexenio* must continue the policy of privatization as part of a strategy of modernization."[26] As many observers had noted, parts of the private sector, having supported the opposition National Action Party (Partido Acción Nacional, PAN) for many years, had decided they could support the PRI as long as it was properly "breaded."[27] According to Pablo González Casanova, "the choice of the official candidate is the result of private sector forces associated with the multinationals which desire the development of a privatizing, monetarist, and free-trade PRI."[28]

23. Porfirio Muñoz Ledo, quoted in Manuel López Gallo, *El elegido,* 1989, p. 30.

24. *El Financiero* (Mexico City), October 6, 1987, p. 1. A few days after the *destape,* however, the Mexican stock market began the crash that would lead to the loss of 70 percent of its value by the end of the year.

25. While the opposition National Action Party (Partido Acción Nacional, PAN) did enjoy the support of large elements of capital (especially in the north), the PRI could still count on the backing of most large industrialists and financial groups, particularly those with links to the international economy. See Sylvia Maxfield, "International Economic Opening and Government-Business Relations," 1989; and her *Governing Capital: International Finance and Mexican Politics,* 1990.

26. Alejandro Ramos, José Martínez, and Carlos Ramírez, *Salinas de Gortari: Candidato de la crisis,* 1987, p. 50.

27. Play on words with PAN, which means bread in Spanish. Founded in 1939, the PAN for many years served as the leading organized opposition to the PRI.

28. Quoted in Alejandro Ramos et al., *Salinas de Gortari: Candidato de la crisis,* p. 302.

The foreign press was in general delighted with the choice but all emphasized that, in the words of one observer, the selection of Salinas "elevated to power a generation more technocratic than political."[29] Perhaps the most to the point comment came from the *Wall Street Journal* which said that the choice would "overjoy business groups and sadden the unions."

What was possibly the most remarkable aspect of the selection was that precisely at the moment of greatest crisis, when all observers considered him to be one of the weakest presidents in many years, de la Madrid was able to impose a relatively unpopular choice on the party and government. Moreover, de la Madrid had chosen the candidate who most resembled himself and who had played the leading role in defining economic policy over the past six years.[30] Facing popular rejection of their economic vision and the approaching collapse of the political system that had given them power, the ruling elite had chosen the one person who seemed to be the least likely candidate to save the status quo. The presidential election confirmed the traditional political class's worst fears.

Salinas's performance on the stump confirmed everyone's misgivings about the ability of a technocrat to manage a political campaign. The popularity of the opposing candidates Cuauhtémoc Cárdenas and the PAN's Manuel Clouthier and their access to considerable resources, as well as well-managed political organizations, made his task even harder. On election night, July 6, 1988, the computers of the Federal Election Commission had an unexplainable breakdown that resulted in the delay of the results for nearly a week. It is likely that the problem had little to do with technical difficulties and much more to do with the results in the capital where Cárdenas was beating Salinas by *at least* a 2–1 margin.[31] While Salinas had probably intended to reduce the degree of electoral

29. See the coverage in the *New York Times, Washington Post,* and *London Times* on October 5 and 6, 1987. The tone of the coverage (despite the cautionary notes about technocrats not knowing about politics) was extremely patronizing and bordered on racist, hinting that Mexico could now move forward under the leadership of a moderate and "cool-headed" Harvard graduate (as opposed to "hot-blooded" and probably corrupt traditional Mexicans?). A month after the selection *The Economist* chose to remind its readers that "Harvard-Educated Economist" was *not* the new president's middle name.

30. Labor boss Fidel Velázquez remarked that the party should be careful not to break the constitutional prohibition against reelection.

31. The official results in the capital were 22 percent for the PAN, 27.3 percent for the PRI, and 48.2 percent for the Cardenista coalition. *Cuadernos de nexos* 128 (August 1988): 3. For analysis of the election see Jaime González Graff, *Las elecciones de 1988,* 1989; and Juan Molinar Horcasitas, *El tiempo de la legitimidad,* 1991.

fraud, he was not prepared to lose the election. As the figures from other regions began to come in, he and de la Madrid called upon the very traditional and corrupt apparatus that they so despised to assure Salinas's victory. While the final results will always be disputed, it is possible that Cárdenas won the election by a narrow margin.[32] Certainly Salinas did not obtain a majority, and the decision to limit this figure to 50.4 percent (the lowest ever for a PRI candidate who normally could count on 70–75 percent of the vote) indicated that the electoral alchemists were aware of the limits to credulity of both national and international audiences.

The electoral disaster of July 1988 was followed by continuing challenges to the legitimacy of the regime. During the last months of his administration de la Madrid faced the most rebellious Congress in decades. The new Congress was more than willing to break the traditional decorum with shouted insults, accusations of treason and fraud, and calls for a new election. A prominent intellectual noted that the Mexican system was in a crisis because presidential authority had been robbed of its "magic aura," was caught in a bureaucratic morass, challenged by increasing provincial autonomy, and had failed to solve immediate problems.[33] By the time the new president took office on December 1, 1988, many agreed with one prominent political columnist who said that "Salinas is the weakest president since [the 1930s]."[34]

## Salinas Triumphant

Similar descriptions of the feebleness of the Mexican regime and predictions of the dire consequences of calling an uncharismatic technocrat to the rescue tended to dominate writing on Mexico toward the end of the decade. This contrasted with the much more positive appraisal of Gorbachev and the Soviet regime. Certainly few people in 1988 would have bet that Salinas would survive Gorbachev, much less the Soviet

---

32. According to PRD numbers (Partido de la Revolución Democrática, *Radiografía del fraude*, 1988), Cárdenas received 42 percent of the vote and Salinas 36 percent.

33. Héctor Aguilar Camín, "El canto del futuro," in *Nexos, México Mañana* (Mexico City: Nexos, 1988), p. 58.

34. Juan José Hinajosa, quoted in *Latin America Weekly Report* (*LAWR*), December 8, 1988 (WR-88-49), p. 10.

Union itself. Yet, the contrast between the fate of the two men by the summer of 1991 could not be starker.

The Salinas administration's economic accomplishments are very impressive.[35] Inflation declined from 159 percent in 1987 to 12 percent in 1992.[36] Consequently, the peso enjoyed a rare period of relative stability. The public sector deficit, which accounted for 17 percent of GDP in 1987, had turned into a surplus by 1991.[37] After a decade of economic decline the Mexican GDP had grown at an average of 3.9 percent during the first three years of the Salinas *sexenio*. Thanks to renegotiations in 1989, Mexico had lowered its external debt from $107 billion (U.S.) to $91 billion (U.S.) and achieved annual savings in debt service of $2 billion (U.S.). The goal of privatizing the Mexican economy also appeared to be well under way. Accelerating the policies begun by his predecessor Miguel de la Madrid, Salinas ordered the sale of some of the largest government enterprises, including the national banking system, the telephone company, and other profitable manufacturing and service industries. In response to these changes and with the stimulus of new lending approaching $20 billion (U.S.), the repatriation of capital totaling over $8 billion (U.S.), and the elimination of restrictions on ownership, private investment had increased by 25 percent during the *sexenio*.[38] Finally, thanks to the practical dismantlement of protectionist barriers, one could now purchase practically any imported good at prices not much higher (and sometimes lower) than across the Rio Grande. The torrential flood of imports (including both capital goods and consumer items) did result in an ever increasing trade deficit that

35. I should make clear that my references to Salinas do not imply a "great-person" explanation of recent events in Mexico. Salinas is merely the most visible symbol of a new elite with new ideologies who took over the Mexican state in the 1980s. Nevertheless, the personal characteristics of the president and his immediate circle did play a role in the shaping of government policies and attitudes and I will refer to these when appropriate.

36. *LAWR*, December 5, 1991 (WR-91-47), p. 10; *The Economist*, Mexico Survey, February 13, 1993, p. 1. There are, however, serious doubts regarding the relevance of these inflation figures for the bottom half of the population as the prices of basic items have increased at a much faster rate: for example, the price of tortillas increased by 130 percent during the first eighteen months of the Salinas *sexenio* (*LAWR*, October 18, 1990 [WR-90-40], p. 4). For this summary I have also relied on Andrew Reding and Christopher Whalen, "Fragile Stability: Reform and Repression in Mexico under Carlos Salinas," 1992.

37. Part of this surplus reflected a one-time infusion of $5.5 billion (U.S.) from the sale of parastatals (Tom Barry, ed., *Mexico: A Country Guide*, 1992, p. 124). The budget changes, however, were not merely cosmetic.

38. Reding and Whalen, "Fragile Stability"; *LAWR*, March 21, 1991 (WR-91-11), p. 10; *LAWR*, January 9, 1992 (WR-92-01), p. 2.

was estimated to reach $20 billion (U.S.) in 1992, but the inflow of capital enabled the country to meet its obligations.[39]

There were also significant social changes. The rupture with the Church, which dated back to the nineteenth century, was partly healed as constitutional changes returned civil rights to the clergy, recognized the Church's legal existence, and removed many of the anticlerical clauses in the 1917 Constitution. Reversing a long-standing commitment to at least rhetorical support of agrarian reform, the president declared the end of land distribution. Constitutional amendments also threatened the continued existence of the centerpiece of the government's agricultural policy, the communal *ejidos*. Although the effect of these changes were only beginning to be seen, many already spoke of a rural revolution that would completely change the face of Mexican agriculture.[40]

The traditionally uneasy relationship with the United States has been transformed into a close (if not necessarily equal) partnership. Salinas initially attempted to diversify Mexico's trade relations by establishing better links with Japan and Western Europe. After a frustrating first year his administration appeared to have accepted the inevitability of a close alliance with the United States. Salinas spoke to an admiring U.S. Congress, and the two countries were about to create a North American common market. The success of the North American Free Trade Agreement (NAFTA) was increasingly seen as the key to the Salinas economic program, making the Mexican government extremely dependent on the approval of the United States.

Salinas had also challenged the domestic political order. Beginning with the 1988 elections and continuing through gubernatorial contests, the Institutional Revolutionary Party recognized opposition victories in what had previously been safe monopolies of the ruling party. Salinas also dismantled the corporatist structure of the party and curtailed the power of leading labor bosses or *caciques*.

There were, however, significant limits to the reform. The recognition of opposition victories in the states of Baja California (Norte) and Chi-

---

39. The need to finance this deficit through high enough interest rates to attract foreign investors did appear to have a dampening effect on economic growth beginning in 1992 (*The Economist*, Mexico Survey, February 13, 1993, p. 7).

40. At the time of writing this book, little academic analysis has been published on the consequences of the new agricultural policy. David Myhre and Wayne Cornelius of the Center for U.S.-Mexican Studies at the University of California, San Diego, will hopefully soon be publishing the results of the research project they are coordinating with the participation of several U.S. and Mexican social scientists.

huahua, the disavowal of elections in San Luis Potosí and Guanajuato, and the replacement of governors in Tabasco and Michoacán seemed to reflect the president's power and search for international legitimacy rather than a newfound respect for democratic norms. In local, provincial, and national elections the process was still dominated by fraud and corruption. Despite the opposition victories, the government party still controlled the vast majority of leading positions. And if the PRI appeared weaker, there were rumors that this would not lead to a more competitive electoral environment but to the replacement of the old party by a new one of the president's own creation, ready and able to maintain the power of the new political elite.

Salinas also increased the power of the presidency and imposed an ideological hegemony on what had always been a philosophically heterogeneous political apparatus. Interest mediation through the traditional corporatist sectors of the party was not replaced by a more direct popular participation, and the departure of leading labor bosses did not bring about a democratization of the unions.[41] Beginning with the 1988 election there was an increase in the reports of harassment and intimidation of journalists and opposition figures.[42] According to human rights organizations, torture remained endemic. The appearance of groups such as "Peasant Torch" in the countryside was more reminiscent of Guatemala than the "modernized" polity Salinas sought to portray.[43]

Most important, the economic reforms had yet to benefit the majority of the population.[44] The cuts in government budgets, the decline of

41. In the Oil Workers Union, for example, Joaquín Hernández Galicia, "La Quina," was replaced by Sebastian Guzmán Cabrera. In the Teachers Union Carlos Jonguitud Barrios was removed in favor of Elba Esther Gordillo. Both new leaders were imposed by the president and neither was known for their commitment to union democracy. Similar changes occurred in the Musicians Union and that of government employees.

42. Even prominent and internationally renowned figures such as Jorge Castañeda were targeted. On the press see *Proceso*, nos. 767–771, June–July 1991. According to opposition forces over one hundred militants have been killed in the past three years (Partido de la Revolución Democrática, *Three Years of Political Repression in Mexico*, 1991).

43. Americas Watch, *Human Rights in Mexico: A Policy of Impunity*, 1990; Amnesty International, *Mexico: Torture with Impunity*, 1991. Violence was not only used against opposition figures but also against defenders of the traditional order who chose to reject the president's changes (*Washington Post*, October 25, 1991).

44. While one study found that five of the world's two hundred richest persons were Mexican, 47 percent of the country's population was living in abject poverty (*LAWR*, February 7, 1991 [WR 91-5], p. 4). From 1950 to 1987 the share of income earned by the bottom 20 percent had declined from 6.1 percent to 2.4 percent while that of the top quintile had increased from 60 percent to 65.5 percent (Basáñez, *El pulso de los sexenios*, p. 116). The latest census

industries unable to compete in the new open market, and the changes in the agricultural policies had also resulted in terrible social costs. [45] Those lucky enough to have a job (estimated unemployment in 1990 was 18 percent with 25–40 percent suffering from underemployment) had seen their earnings drop precipitously as the minimum wage in 1991 had lost two-thirds of its purchasing power since 1982.[46] In 1990 over 70 percent of Mexico's families did not earn enough to purchase the basic market basket of consumption goods.[47] The results were predictable: nutrition levels had declined both in terms of aggregate caloric intake and in the quality of foodstuffs, malnourishment had doubled since 1974, half of rural children were hungry, one-third of the population did not have access to medical care, and public health indicators showed the reappearance of diseases previously eradicated.[48]

And yet Carlos Salinas remained perhaps the most popular president in decades. According to a *Los Angeles Times* survey over 60 percent of the population approved of his performance.[49] The mid-term elections of 1991 indicated that the ruling PRI had staged a dramatic comeback from the political debacle of 1988. Winning over 61 percent of the vote nationwide, it retook parts of the center of the country it had lost to the left opposition National Democratic Front (Frente Democrático Nacional, FDN, later the Party of the Democratic Revolution, PRD). Perhaps most important, the PRI appeared to have honestly won a plurality in Mexico City. Despite the many reported cases of fraud and voter intimidation, observers held that electoral irregularities were not as serious as in previ-

---

found that labor's participation in personal income had declined from 36 percent in the mid-1970s to 23 percent in 1990. The INEGI income survey for 1989 reported increasing inequality throughout the 1980s.

45. On the relationship between government policy and worsening social conditions, see David Barkin, *Distorted Development: Mexico in the World Economy,* 1991.

46. Barry, ed., *Mexico: A Country Guide,* pp. 96–98. Over 5 million Mexicans made the minimum wage, and a large number probably earned less. Official figures of unemployment are much lower than those cited but are based on a minimal definition of employment.

47. David Barkin, "Salinastroika and Other Novel Ideas," paper available through CARNET.MEXNEWS computer bulletin board, August 1992.

48. Barry, ed., *Mexico,* pp. 95, 234–236. According to *LAWR,* 5 percent of children died before reaching their first birthday (February 8, 1990 [WR–90–05] p. 10).

49. October 11, 1991. Even taking into account the underrepresentation of the marginalized and those worse hit by the Salinas policies, the results reflected a real popularity in the shantytowns and in the countryside. A poll published in *Este País* (August 1991) showed very similar figures.

ous contests and that, while the actual PRI vote might have been smaller, the results reflected real support for the government's policies.[50] Despite the worries of 1988 and the lack of initial confidence in his administration, it appeared that Salinas had won not only an economic battle but also a political one.

Salinas now received the accolades that international opinion had previously saved for Gorbachev.[51] Many ex-Soviet officials must have asked themselves how their Mexican counterparts had done it. It seemed that the Mexican elite had managed the impossible: they had overseen a radical transformation of the economy, resulting in traumatic social costs, while simultaneously dismantling the traditional political order. Most impressively, they were still in power.

During the past decade the Mexican regime survived a bout with hyperinflation, several years of economic decline, the collapse in the price of its major commodity, natural catastrophes, a variety of political scandals, and a strong and popular electoral challenge. By the middle of the Salinas *sexenio* prices were (relatively) stable, the economy was growing and was no longer so dependent on oil revenues, Mexico had regained the confidence of international capital, and the political stability of the regime was no longer so fragile. This last point was perhaps the most impressive accomplishment. De la Madrid and Salinas had managed to impose draconian cuts on the state budget, with subsequent losses of jobs and subsidies, while simultaneously maintaining political stability and expanding the degree of government control. The harsh living conditions of the population had produced the strongest challenge to the regime since 1968, but this had apparently been successfully defused by 1992. The key to the Mexican success seemed deceptively simple: perestroika before glasnost, economic efficiency before social justice, international support before national sovereignty. The next chapter will discuss the various potential explanations for the success of *salinastroika*.

50. *LAWR*, August 29 (WR-91-33) and September 5 (WR-91-34), 1991.
51. The normally phlegmatic *Economist* referred to him as possibly one of the greatest men of the twentieth century (Mexico Survey, February 13, 1993, p. 4).

# 2

---

# The Technocratic State

*Salinastroika* was part of a global revolution of the market. In the developing world, states reduced public subsidies, competed for links with the developed economies and investment capital from multinationals, and sought to prove their "fiscal responsibility." The collapse of communism in the ex-Soviet Union and in Eastern Europe and the continuation of economic reform in China even after Tiananmen appeared to seal the victory of neoliberal policies.

These changes elicited a great deal of academic analysis that sought to explain the conditions under which states could impose the new economic order.[1] How did the case of Mexico fit into these models? The following section discusses the impact of international forces. The second analyzes the relationship between democracy and economic restructuring, while the final section discusses the importance of institutional arrangements inside the relevant states.

## The International Environment

A prominent theme in these studies is the relative influence of domestic and international forces on the definition and implementation of eco-

---

1. The literature on this topic is immense and growing. For a review of the issues see Joan Nelson, ed., *Fragile Coalitions: The Politics of Economic Adjustment*, 1989; Adam Przeworski, *Democracy and the Market: Political and Economic Reforms in Eastern Europe and Latin America*, 1991; Stephan Haggard and Robert Kaufman, eds., *The Politics of Economic Adjustment: International Constraints, Distributive Conflicts, and the State*, 1992; Miguel Ángel Centeno, "Between Rocky Democracies and Hard Markets," forthcoming.

nomic policy. Much of the argument that emphasizes international conditions is a logical extension of dependency theory and world system approaches. In a globally integrated economy where asymmetrical distributions of power make the survival of some states conditional on their acceptance by others or where the legitimacy granted by multilateral institutions is vital to the viability of an economy, such an emphasis on external constraints is logical.

There are three channels through which this leverage is exercised roughly corresponding to the economic, political, and social environments in which the reforming states operate.[2] The influence of the economic and political spheres are fairly obvious. The general economic health of the world economy clearly helps determine the possibilities available to developing countries. The international boom that lasted until 1973 provided a critical opportunity for the export-oriented economies of East Asia.[3] Conversely, a weak international economy and domestic pressures to protect markets in the developed countries make it more difficult for new players to enter the game, as the countries of Eastern Europe are rapidly finding out.

There is also an element of coercion involved. Countries that play the game dictated by either creditors or other potential sources of capital are rewarded with investments or new loans. Exporters of primary materials may find that the international markets are only open to those producers that respect a certain set of rules. In the most extreme interpretations of this situation, reforming governments have lost their autonomy over economic policy and must follow the dictates of external powers. But even in less dramatic cases the promise of extra capital or the threat of curtailment has an obvious effect on government decisions.[4]

While it is unlikely that external military threats would be used to enforce an economic restructuring, those regimes that are willing to impose certain policies may find that their political survival is supported or

---

2. Barbara Stallings, "International Influence on Economic Policy: Debt, Stabilization, and Structural Reform," and Miles Kahler, "External Influence, Conditionality, and the Politics of Adjustment," in Haggard and Kaufman, eds., *The Politics of Economic Adjustment*.

3. Nelson, ed., *Fragile Coalitions*, p. 5.

4. The unofficial embargo on Chilean copper during the Allende years is one example of economic warfare. Note, however, that such an international influence need not originate in a conspiracy among creditors or consumers but can simply reflect the supply and demand of a product or the LIBOR rate. The connection between the onset of the debt crisis and the imposition of adjustment programs is obvious. Of perhaps equal importance is the disappearance of an alternative financial source after the collapse of the Soviet Union.

even guaranteed by external factors. Regimes that enjoy little political support or that feel threatened by internal opposition may be willing to surrender control over their economic policy in exchange for such patronage. External powers may also use their leverage with internal oppositions to either increase or lower the volume of protest facing a government.[5]

The type of mechanisms discussed above would probably come into play only in crisis situations where the start or the fate of a reform program was already in doubt. The third, or social channel, is perhaps the most important since it operates in a much greater number of cases and has had a much more pervasive influence on policy making. The social mechanisms can be divided into two interacting parts: social learning and social networks.[6] The former refers to the socialization of decision makers regarding the appropriate rules for international relations and economic policy; the latter defines the mechanisms through which these rules are taught and passed on.

The world system of states helps determine what are legitimate goals, correct priorities, and acceptable costs and benefits. The isomorphism of political and bureaucratic rationalities supports particular methods for achieving objectives and provides an often critical source of external legitimacy.[7] Moreover, the international environment also provides the "intellectual lenses" through which policy makers perceive situations, thereby determining the acceptable range of political and economic alternatives.[8] One of the most outstanding characteristics of the shift toward markets in the less-developed countries in the last decade has been the crisis in the intellectual confidence of the ideological left and center.[9] After nearly two decades as the leading paradigm in both policy and

5. This can take the form of direct subsidies to opposition forces or opening and closing channels for voices or exits by leading adversaries. Nicaragua is an obvious example of military force being used to weaken states that offer a social or economic alternative to the orthodoxy. The provision of military support may also allow core states to exercise considerable political influence such as that of France in its African excolonies. Mobutu's Zaire is another example of economic policy being dictated by foreign technocrats in exchange for military support.

6. Kahler, "External Influence, Conditionality, and the Politics of Adjustment."

7. John Meyer, "The World Polity and the Authority of the Nation-State," in A. Bergesen, ed., Studies of the Modern World-System, 1980, pp. 109–137.

8. Miles Kahler, "Orthodoxy and Its Alternatives: Explaining Approaches to Stabilization and Adjustment," in Joan Nelson, ed., Economic Crisis and Policy Choice: The Politics of Adjustment in the Third World, 1990. See also Peter Hall, The Political Power of Economic Ideas: Keynesianism Across Nations, 1989.

9. North American Congress on Latin America, "The Latin American Left: A Painful Rebirth," 1992.

intellectual circles, dependency theory failed to explain the divergent fates of the Asian and Latin American economies.[10] The economic, social, and environmental disasters of Eastern Europe and the apparent anomie of the "third way" in Scandinavia further disarmed the left. In its place there arose a new orthodoxy of markets and free trade; to paraphrase Richard Nixon's famous remark concerning Keynes, it appeared that everyone was now a "Chicago boy." The often-noted strength and importance of *dirigiste* states in the development of Japan and the so-called "dragons" did not appear to detract from the appeal of the new orthodoxy that called for a dismantling of protectionist barriers and a radical curtailment of the role of the public sector in the economy.[11] This new orthodoxy not only helped shape the education of elites but also provided intellectual legitimacy for those who sought to dismantle the state apparatus.

The social and professional relationships that the leading elites established also played a major role in defining the new policy paradigms. The existence of this international network linking IMF analysts, private investors, bank officials, and government technocrats was not the figment of the conspiratorial imagination of those who sought to understand the new wave. Publications that naturally supported the new policies recognized its importance: "A continental network of Harvard, Chicago, and Stanford grads are back [in Latin America] atop businesses and ministries spreading the new market mind-set. They're using old school ties to reach across Latin America's borders, signing joint ventures and free-trade agreements with fellow alumni."[12] Not only creditors and multilateral agencies, lecturers and seminar presenters, media pundits and intellectual authorities, but even the exroommates of the new elites approved the new policies.

How relevant were these international factors in assuring the success of *salinastroika?* Salinas has obviously benefited from the apparent U.S. decision to politically and economically underwrite his project. The reasons for this may include geopolitical considerations, the ability of the U.S.-educated Mexican elite to establish working relationships with their

10. Peter Evans, "Class, State, and Dependence in East Asia: Lessons for Latin Americanists," in Frederic C. Deyo, *The Political Economy of the New Asian Industrialism,* 1987, p. 203.

11. On this debate see Gary Gereffi and Donald L. Wyman, eds., *Manufacturing Miracles: Paths of Industrialization in Latin America and East Asia,* 1990.

12. *Business Week,* June 15, 1992, p. 51.

American counterparts, and the fact that the Salinas policies are well in tune with American goals.

This support has included making financial resources available through the banks and new direct investment. The United States even seemed ready to help Mexico track parts of the capital that had "flown" out of the country in the 1970s and 1980s. Salinas was also helped by the continued availability of an "exit" for excess labor and political dissidents via the Rio Grande. The U.S. government also appeared quite willing and able to uphold Salinas's claims for legitimacy during the critical months of late 1988. Support for PAN accusations of fraud or, less likely, acceptance of Cárdenas's claims to have been the winner of July 1988, could have been fatal to the stability of the Mexican government. Such a dependence has its obvious risks. Should NAFTA fail to be ratified or should it not provide the expected economic bonanza, the Mexican government will have to face not only a possible economic depression but also a drastic decline in its political legitimacy and stability. Under such conditions the autonomy of the Mexican regime vis-à-vis the United States and international business in general may be further constrained by the need to make a deal at any cost.

Perhaps the most important international factor was the intellectual legitimacy of the Salinas reforms both within policy-making and academic circles and in general world opinion. As the leader of the left opposition in 1988, Cuauhtémoc Cárdenas was an extremely attractive figure, the perfect David taking on a disreputable Goliath. But he never enjoyed the adulation of Walesa, Havel, or Aquino. Part of the reason is that the U.S. government preferred its rebels to either invoke vague commitments to democracy without undue reference to social structures or to question the merits of socialism, not capitalism. Perhaps more important, Cárdenas sounded anachronistic. By the time of the July election it was becoming evident that the intellectual Cold War between statists and free-marketers was drawing to a close with one clear winner. Salinas, with his calls for individual responsibility, fiscal discipline, entrepreneurship, and free trade was perceived by much of the international community as the progressive figure battling a traditional and corrupt machine. Much like American politicians who campaigned against Washington from inside the Beltway, Salinas legitimated his regime by an assault on the very system that put him in power.

The Salinas elite was also familiar with the international territory in which it operated. The impressive educational and professional pedigrees of the new elite assured that they could communicate with those who had control over the resources the government required. They spoke the same language as their European and American counterparts across the bargaining table. This made it possible to establish (or in some cases continue) relationships of trust that quickened the flow of funds and gave the Mexican government much needed leeway. Even if his government had agreed to the same terms, it is difficult to imagine that the banking syndicates would have given Cárdenas the same terms provided Salinas, nor is it likely that George Bush would have risked the negotiation of NAFTA or foreign investors the future of billions of dollars.

A favorable international climate, however, is not decisive. Even those who emphasize the international environment recognize that there are limits to its explanatory power.[13] Few political figures since World War II enjoyed the popularity of Mikhail Gorbachev, or Vaclav Havel, who was the intellectuals' ideal politician. Yet both men were out of a job as of mid-1992. If external resources were so critical, Venezuela would not be nostalgically recuperating from a failed coup, nor would Taiwan have enjoyed the success of the past decade. Political support and leverage are important but they could not guarantee an efficient Zairian state or the Shah of Iran's throne.

Despite the obvious relevance of external influences, it is important to avoid a mechanistic determinism in explaining the success of *salinastroika*. The development of the Mexican technocratic revolution is the result of the convergence of two forces: international and domestic. The international environment certainly provided support, but the determinant factor was a set of institutional changes within the organization of the state. A process as complex as *salinastroika* could not develop spontaneously from a supportive environment beginning in 1988 but was based on a decades-long transition within the Mexican state.

## Democracy and the Market

Adding to the radical nature of the 1980s, many of the new governments that were attempting to impose economic adjustments were democrati-

---

13. Haggard and Kaufman, eds., *The Politics of Economic Adjustment*, pp. 14–18.

cally elected.[14] With the defeat of Pinochet the last of the authoritarian regimes that had arisen during the 1960s and 1970s disappeared from Latin America. In Africa the democratic wave led to a peaceful transition in Zambia, serious challenges to dictatorships in Kenya, Zaire, and the Ivory Coast, and even to the promise of freedom in South Africa. The democratic reforms were no less evident in Asia. In 1992 South Korea was to elect its first nonmilitary president in thirty years, the Guomindang experienced its worst electoral performance since 1949, while the octogenarians of the PRC (People's Republic of China) now had to contend with popular forces and demands. Finally, the fall of the Iron Curtain and the break-up of the Soviet Union produced over twenty new governments, some of which were led by elected representatives.

What is the relationship between the marketizing of the economy and the democratization of political life? How could states manage the "cruel choices" assumed to be inherent in such a relationship?[15] How could they manage an equilibrium between the rights of citizenship and those of property, between economic growth and political liberty?[16] Could the two revolutions coexist or did one have to precede the other? If the second was the case, what model best assured success: Should democracy come before economic change as in Eastern Europe until 1992, or should an economic base be established first as in the Asian NICs (Newly Industrializing Countries) or Pinochet Chile?

During much of the 1950s and 1960s the accepted view in social science was that "all good things go together" and that democracy was compatible with growth.[17] For the past two decades, however, the predominant opinion has held that democracy and economic growth via markets are often in conflict. This struggle follows from the contradiction already noted by T. H. Marshall (and by de Toqueville before him) between the equality of citizenship and the inequality of property.

14. See Guillermo O'Donnell, Phillipe Schmitter, and Laurence Whitehead, eds., *Transitions from Authoritarian Rule: Prospects for Democracy,* 1986; and Larry Diamond, Juan Linz, and S. M. Lipset, eds., *Democracy in Developing Countries,* 1989.

15. Karen Remmer, "Democracy and Crisis: The Latin American Experience," 1990; Stephan Haggard, *Pathways from the Periphery: The Politics of Growth in the Newly Industrializing Countries,* 1990, pp. 256–264; Atul Kohli, "Democracy and Development," in John P. Lewis and Valeriana Kallab, eds., *Development Strategies Reconsidered,* 1990; Centeno, "Between Rocky Democracies and Hard Markets"; and Martin Staniland, *What Is Political Economy?* 1985.

16. See Przeworski, *Democracy and the Market,* Chapter 4.

17. For a summary of this perspective, see Robert Packenham, *Liberal America and the Third World: Political Development Ideas in Foreign Aid and Social Science,* 1973.

Democracies are seen as having a myriad of faults.[18] Democracies tend to encourage consumption at the expense of investment, thereby slowing economic growth. Pluralism in general reduces efficiency, creates more divisions, and retards decisions. Popular participation may even make democracies ungovernable. Politicians will tend to outbid each other in their efforts to purchase the support of a population whose expectations are far above what the society can deliver. Democratic governments will fall victim to a populist vicious circle in which participation begets equality, slower growth, class conflict, and implosion, leading to a harsher authoritarian regime. In short, according to many observers democracies can only coexist with the difficult stages of development as long as the population is completely docile and passive.

Perhaps the most difficult problem facing democratic regimes attempting economic restructuring is that popular participation makes it difficult to impose the pain associated with the transition. The path to the market, whether in the eighteenth century or in the 1990s, is a "valley of tears,"[19] and the population is likely to seek some comfort through its votes. While it is difficult to separate the costs of the economic reforms from those caused by the crises that helped bring them about, adjustment programs as imposed in the 1980s do have considerable social consequences, particularly for those at the bottom of the socioeconomic ladder, but also for the middle classes and parts of the domestic bourgeoisie.[20] In Eastern Europe, for example, the elimination of guaranteed employment and consumer subsidies have, at least temporarily, led to a decline in the standards of living of large parts of the population. In Latin America and Africa these changes have been even more drastic. Since they often entail high social costs, economic adjustment programs often enjoy little popular support and can tax even the most flexible institutional arrangements. Even in such situations where only a minor-

---

18. The problems cited in the text may be found in the following: Samuel Huntington, *Political Order in Changing Societies*, 1968; Samuel Brittan, "The Economic Contradictions of Democracy," 1975; Mancur Olson, Jr., *The Rise and Decline of Nations: Economic Growth, Stagflation, and Social Rigidities*, 1982; Michel Crozier, Samuel Huntington, Jaji Watanuki, *The Crisis of Democracy: Report on the Governability of Democracies to the Trilateral Commission*, 1975; Karl de Schweinitz, *Industrialization and Democracy: Economic Necessities and Political Possibilities*, 1964.

19. Giuseppe di Palma, *To Craft Democracies: An Essay on Democratic Transitions*, 1990.

20. See Howard Handelman and Werner Baer, ed., *Paying the Costs of Austerity in Latin America*, 1989; William L. Canak, ed., *Lost Promises: Debt, Austerity, and Development in Latin America*, 1989.

ity stands to lose, the accrued power from its previously privileged position represents a considerable obstacle to the new regime. Where the social costs affect the majority, political opposition in a democratic setting may be insurmountable.

Yet some have argued that democracies are no less able to manage economic reforms than authoritarian regimes.[21] According to this perspective the analysis of the relationship between democracy and market reforms requires much more precise regime categories than are often utilized. Some emphasize the difference between established and new democracies and claim that the former are much better able to overcome the obstacles involved.[22] The relative strength or political capacity of the state is also considered to be a better measure of capability for reform than regime type.[23]

It is interesting, however, that one rarely hears the case for democracy actually *helping* the process of economic adjustment. Eastern Europe may yet represent an exception to this rule, as a democratic revolution was necessary in order to depose the *nomenklatura* opposed to the market. There is also the argument that since democracies tend to assure a more equal distribution of wealth and income, they are better able to create domestic markets and thus foster long-term development.[24] Yet, given the low levels of participation and access to power by the very poor, it is even doubtful whether democracies can actually minimize the worst costs of such transitions.[25] At best, the case seems to be made that democracies are capable of avoiding the "populist temptation" whereby support is maintained through material incentives that derail economic reform.

Moreover, it would appear that those democratic regimes that are best able to cope with the political traumas of economic adjustment are those in which power is heavily concentrated, in which interest groups have

21. See Dietrich Rueschemeyer, Evelyne Huber Stephens, and John D. Stephens, *Capitalist Development and Democracy*, 1992; Remmer, "Democracy and Crisis," and Remmer, "The Politics of Economic Stabilization," 1986; Kohli, "Democracy and Development"; and Centeno, "Between Rocky Democracies and Hard Markets."

22. Stephan Haggard and Robert Kaufman, "Economic Adjustments in New Democracies," in Nelson, ed., *The Politics of Economic Adjustment*.

23. Joel S. Migdal, *Strong Societies and Weak States: State-Society Relations and State Capabilities in the Third World*, 1988.

24. Samuel Huntington and Joan Nelson, *No Easy Choice: Political Participation in Developing Countries*, 1976.

25. Joan Nelson, "The Politics of Pro-Poor Adjustment," in Nelson, ed., *Fragile Coalitions*.

been institutionalized, or in which private and public elites cooperate;[26] that is, those states in which polyarchical arrangements have previously institutionalized the management and exclusion (or at least modification) of particular social voices. One recent study emphasizes the declining importance of the political left as critical to the success of democracies in implementing economic restructuring.[27] The absence of an organized left allows governments greater flexibility to impose social costs while also protecting them from the right, since this side of the political spectrum need no longer fear a populist backlash. Conversely, however, well-organized popular organizations provide the institutional control that may be required in order to strike bargains, moderate demands, and provide guarantees.[28]

Another possible resource that could assist democracies is a strong sense of political legitimacy that convinces the relevant groups to abandon their particular interests in favor of the greater good. Legitimacy, however, often depends on a state's ability to improve living standards, which is precisely what the new regimes cannot deliver in the short term.[29] Moreover, given that the states facing the "cruel choices" are often bereft of a single national identity, or have long-standing racial or class cleavages, the creation of such a patriotic fervor would most likely require an authoritarian regime. (These efforts also have a habit of degenerating into the pursuit of a minority blamed for the social and economic costs.) The one exception to this rule may be those cases where the downfall of an especially hated regime provides the new government with a prolonged honeymoon during which the population is willing to accept sacrifices. But such honeymoons do not provide guarantees. Argentina and Brazil in the 1980s and the ex-Soviet Union in the 1990s clearly demonstrate that more is required than a love of democracy.

The arguments for the link between authoritarian regimes and economic restructuring are essentially the mirror image of those presented against democracy. Authoritarian regimes are seen as capable of repress-

---

26. Peter Katzenstein, *Small States in World Markets: Industrial Policy in Europe*, 1985.

27. Karen Remmer, paper presented at Princeton University, April 1992.

28. David Cameron, "On the Limits of the Public Economy," 1982; Adam Przeworski and Michael Wallerstein, "The Structure of Class Conflict in Democratic Capitalist Societies," 1982.

29. On the fragility of legitimacy, see Juan J. Linz, ed., *The Breakdown of Democratic Regimes: Crisis, Breakdown, and Reequilibration*, 1978.

ing those social sectors that might oppose the costs of transition and are therefore better able to impose the resolution of an economic crisis on their population.[30] The state's central role is not necessarily representation but rather guiding the population toward "social optimality." Almost by definition this perspective assumes that the economic transition comes from above.[31] (Note that this argument is adaptable to a variety of economic models ranging from neoliberal to "socialism in one country.") If one of the problems with democracy is that participants must be willing to accept the rules and even consider them fair (difficult under the tension imposed by economic transition), authoritarian regimes provide a breathing spell during which the government need not justify its policies or defend its policy choices. Authoritarian regimes are able to define the new distribution of the public pie without having to necessarily consider the fragility of coalitions, prior understandings, or popular dissatisfaction.

The argument for the necessity of authoritarian control was supported by the experiences of the Asian "miracles" whose successes appeared to owe much to the ability of their governments to control social demands and impose the collective rationality required for development.[32] In Japan the long reign by the Liberal Democratic Party and the imposing power of such agencies as MITI (Ministry of International Trade and Industry) and the Ministry of Finance indicated that limits on popular participation were necessary in order to achieve sustainable economic growth. The brightest economic light in Latin America in the late 1980s, Chile, also supported such a conclusion, as much of the economic adjustment and restructuring had been accomplished prior to the plebescite of 1988.

30. This view is essentially an adaptation of the bureaucratic-authoritarian model. See Guillermo O'Donnell, *Modernization and Bureaucratic Authoritarianism*, 1979; James Malloy, ed., *Authoritarianism and Corporatism in Latin America*, 1977; and David Collier, ed., *The New Authoritarianism in Latin America*, 1979. Note that while much of the bureaucratic-authoritarian literature begins with radically different premises, it often comes to similar conclusions found in Huntington, *Political Order in Changing Societies*.

31. See Przeworski, *Democracy and the Market*, p. 183; Konrad Stenzel, "Markets against Politics in the Chilean Dictatorship: The Role of Professional Economists, 1973–1985," 1986; and Miguel Ángel Centeno, "The New Leviathan: The Dynamics and Limits of Technocracy," 1993. See also Ellen K. Trimberger, *Revolution from Above: Military Bureaucrats and Development in Japan, Turkey, Egypt, and Peru*, 1978.

32. Deyo, ed., *The Political Economy of the New Asian Industrialism;* Gereffi and Wyman, eds., *Manufacturing Miracles.*

Such arguments, however, tended to forget the often disastrous economic consequences of authoritarian rule. The model Chilean economy
certainly looked much worse in 1981 while its authoritarian counterparts in Argentina, Uruguay, and Brazil were unable to guarantee economic growth. Certainly, the command economies of Eastern Europe
did not provide supporting evidence in favor of authoritarian control,
nor did it necessarily appear that the PRC's economic success necessarily
owed much to the continuing presence of a police state. The empirical
correlation of the relationship between authoritarian control and economic efficiency was weak at best.[33]

Much of the argument in favor of authoritarian control is not based so
much on the weaknesses of democracy per se as on the problems associated with interest representation and negotiational politics; that is, any
situation in which political power would supersede economic rationality.
To a large extent such critiques of democracy or of politics favor a
Hegelian vision of a universal state above and beyond the clashes of
interests in civil society. But authoritarian regimes cannot escape these
concerns. The leadership of the PRC worries about urban residents'
resentment of rich farmers, the Soviet state maintained social contracts
with workers whom it could not afford to alienate while also supporting
a massive *nomenklatura* on whom it depended for its power. The petti-
ness and apparent inefficiency of patronage and pork barrels are not the
monopoly of democracies.[34]

How does the Mexican case contribute to our understanding of the
relationship between democracy and market reforms? The Mexican regime represents something of a hybrid that has always been difficult to
categorize within traditional notions of democracy and authoritarianism. In an earlier paper I have suggested that Mexico might best be
understood as an "electoral-bureaucratic" authoritarian regime.[35] The
practically monopolistic series of electoral victories by the PRI for nearly
sixty years clearly indicates that elections play a small role in determining the composition of the government. Nor is there much evidence to
indicate that the party has attempted to represent, much less succeeded

33. See notes 15, 16, and 21 for a list of sources.

34. See, for example, Barry Ames, *Political Survival: Politicians and Public Policy in Latin America*, 1987.

35. "Electoral-Bureaucratic Authoritarianism: The Mexican Case," in Arturo Valenzuela, ed., *Politics, Society, and Democracy: Latin America*, forthcoming.

in representing, the interests of the peasant and labor sectors that make up two-thirds of its coalition.[36]

Ultimate political control in Mexico is exercised within a civilian bureaucracy that uses electoral mechanisms to coopt opposition and legitimate its continuity. Unlike the majority of "reforms from above" guided by a technocratic elite, the military has been relatively removed from the process. While there is no need for *systematic* military repression, machine politics controlled from the center also negate the need for mass mobilization to assure compliance. Whatever its precise categorization, most analysts agreed with Mario Vargas Llosa's contention that the Mexican regime was the "perfect dictatorship," camouflaging its authoritarian nature with elections and elite circulation.[37]

There is little doubt that the policies of *salinastroika* would have been impossible without the prior existence of such a well-calibrated authoritarian machine. The economic policies of the past decade were directed by an elite of technocrats and with limited participation by popular social sectors. The success of the Cárdenas coalition in the 1988 elections demonstrates that, at the very least, a more democratic Mexico would have presented much more daunting obstacles to a technocratic revolution. But we cannot understand *salinastroika* as the victory of "competence over participation."[38] The argument for authoritarianism assumes that the state will function as an institutionalized "invisible hand" that will manage, precisely because of its distance from all the peripheries, to impose the general interest.[39] The process of institutionalizing such a state and how it helped shape the definition of the general interest are the keys to understanding the Mexican technocratic revolution.

36. There was some disagreement regarding the degree of "intraparty democracy" within the dominant PRI, with Needler (1971), Padgett (1966), and Scott (1964) contending that it did serve its original function as an arena for competing interests and Brandenburg (1964) arguing that the real power was outside the party. In *The Politics of Mexican Development* (1980), Roger Hansen also emphasizes that the PRI was always meant to control interests and not represent them.

37. Statement during an interview on TELEVISA, August 30, 1990. Even those who, at the time, sought to support Salinas limited their defense to claims that Mexico was a "dicta-blanda." Andrew Reding believes that precisely because such doubts are now openly expressed, the regime has lost some of its "perfection" (Mexico: The Crumbling of a Perfect Dictatorship," 1991).

38. Juan Carlos Torre, quoted in Przeworski, *Democracy and the Market*, p. 186.

39. Pierre Birnbaum, *States and Collective Action: The European Experience*, 1988, p. 186.

# The Technocratic State

A statist or institutional approach explains policy in terms of the prefer-ences and organizational power of elites and the relationship between state and society.[40] This approach seeks to explain differences in the reactions of states to the international and domestic pressures discussed above *and* their ability to act on these pressures. The issue here is no longer the degree of democracy but rather the analysis of which organiza-tional forms appear to be best able to manage the difficult challenges presented by transitions.

A state-led transformation in favor of the market represents what Miles Kahler has called the "orthodox paradox": the use of the state to reduce and diminish the economic influence of politics.[41] What is needed is an "embedded liberalism" in which market and political powers are balanced.[42] It has become increasingly evident that simple calls for the immediate removal of the state from the economy are unrealistic even if one is aiming for greater laissez-faire: "The final trend toward separa-tion of the economic realm from the political is, paradoxically, preceded by a temporary fusion of the political and economic spheres during which there is often an almost complete blurring of the boundary lines between political and economic decisions."[43] The transition to the mar-ket requires the "visible hand" of the state, just as managerial capitalism required the corporate firm.[44] But what kind of state? With what capaci-ties? Studies of adjustment policies indicate that for these to be success-ful, the relevant states must be "organizationally coherent collectives . . . relatively insulated from ties to currently dominant socio-economic inter-ests";[45] they must be autonomous and they must have the ability and power to exercise that independence.

The first criterion measures the state's ability to independently define policy preferences. If the state is controlled by a particular social group,

40. Haggard, *Pathways from the Periphery*, p. 43 and p. 264.

41. Miles Kahler, "International Financial Institutions and the Politics of Adjustment," in Nelson, ed., *Fragile Coalitions.*

42. Thomas Callaghy, "Towards State Capability and Embedded Liberalism," in Nelson, ibid.

43. Irma Adelman and C. Taft Morris, *Society, Politics, and Economic Development*, 1967.

44. Alfred D. Chandler, *The Visible Hand: The Managerial Revolution in American Busi-ness*, 1977.

45. Theda Skocpol, "Bringing the State Back In," in Peter Evans, Dietrich Rueschemeyer, and Theda Skocpol, *Bringing the State Back In*, 1985, p. 9.

then the decision to reform the economy merely reflects particular interests. The evidence of the Asian NICs seems to indicate that the most successful cases are those in which the state was able to supersede individual interests and impose a collective developmentalist rationality.[46] Insulation from political pressures, be they from those that advocate populist measures or from those that seek to maintain the control by a particular class, is especially critical in these cases because of the social costs previously discussed. Populist pressures make it difficult for a democracy to carry out the economic policies; elite constraints indicate why many authoritarian regimes fail to do any better. Whether one sees it as providing a Weberian corporate coherence or a Poulantzasian classwide rationality, the independence of the state is decisive. This is especially important for the effective operation of those state sectors in charge of economic policy.[47]

There is a critical difference, however, between insulation and isolation. Networks of relationships embed the state in the society, allowing it to receive information regarding popular preferences and reactions to policies and to coordinate its actions with other significant players.[48] These can include not only leading elements of domestic capital but also labor, peasant, and middle-class associations. The cooperation of at least some of these is critical not only for the initial stages of restructuring but for its institutionalization. The importance of these connections partly explains the failure of pure command economic structures, be they of the left or the right. Those authoritarian regimes that depend on pure repression are much less successful economically than those who have institutionalized mechanisms for co-opting opposition and maintaining social support. Even the most astute philosopher kings cannot afford to treat the society they wish to restructure as a passive object but must incorporate parts of the population into the process of social transformation.

An equally important consideration is the institutional structure of

---

46. Bruce Cumings, "The Origins and Development of the Northeast Asian Political Economy," and Chalmers Johnson, "Political Institutions and Economic Performance," in Deyo, ed., *The Political Economy of the New Asian Industrialism.*

47. See essays in Nelson, ed., *Fragile Coalitions,* and Nelson, ed., *Economic Crisis and Policy Choice.* Atul Kohli's analysis of Indian technocrats indicates that their influence was constrained by electoral pressures and the "rationality of democracy" ("The Politics of Economic Liberalization in India," 1989, p. 323).

48. Peter Evans, "The State as Problem and Solution," in Haggard and Kaufman, eds., *The Politics of Economic Adjustment.*

the state itself. In the nesting compartments of the theoretical analysis that includes international environments and domestic societies, the state remains the critical "black box." Insulation and autonomy will not be sufficient if the state lacks the instrumental capacity to impose its will. Centralization of resources inside the state can both help secure its autonomy and ensure that new measures will be implemented within a reasonable amount of time. If the state depends on external or domestic actors for its financial support, their votes will infringe on its ability to arrive at the *theoretically* optimal distribution of resources. Within the state, dispersal of financial authority will provide bases from which elite debates are transformed into political paralysis. The successful implementation of economic reforms appear to require a concentration of power not only inside the state but within a relatively small cadre and related agencies.[49] In this regard the new revolutions of the market appear to require the very same organizational qualities as the Leninist state. As Lenin recognized, a social transformation will produce conflict and opposition and only those with the appropriate amount of power will be able to accomplish the required tasks.

The cohesion of elites is also crucial. No reform program can proceed if there are divisions regarding appropriate policies within the ruling circles. The more radical the reforms, the more important such cohesion becomes. Precisely because of the often traumatic social costs involved, the state must speak with one voice and must remain committed to the program, especially during the initial and most difficult stages. The alternative to such a cohesion may be elite gridlock. This is especially problematic in democratic regimes where those who disagree with the policies may attempt to "bring society back in" and disrupt the relative isolation of the state. The difficulties encountered by the excommunist regimes in implementing reform programs may be partly explained by such elite disagreements.[50]

A final consideration is the mental and ideological predisposition of those making policy decisions. Related to the process of "social learning" discussed above, the leading elites must be intellectually prepared for the tasks ahead. Part of this involves the purely technical capacity

49. Note the critical importance of dominant agencies in Japan, South Korea, and Singapore.
50. In these cases the presence of external experts assuming control for the reform policies may overcome the problems by creating a "state within the state" and freeing local elites from responsibility for imposing costs.

required by the process of reform. Such training is not only important in order to understand the often complex interactions of policies but also provides a *lingua franca* for communication within the national elite and with international actors whose confidence may be required for capital infusion and political support. Obviously, the new elites must also accept the legitimacy of the rationales previously discussed. But this elective affinity may not be as important as a more general mentality committed to radical change and confident of the accuracy of the policy remedies. In addition to an ideological congruency, the leading elites in almost all cases of successful revolutions from above share a revolutionary fervor and what at times can appear to be a megalomaniacal assurance in their own abilities. In the end it is this confidence that allows them to wield the concentrated power of their autonomous agencies even in the face of horrifying social costs and daunting opposition.

Did the Mexican state satisfy these conditions? First, was the Mexican state the creature of those national and international interests whom its policies seemed to favor? Clearly, Mexico does not exist in an economic or political vacuum but is constrained by the order of the global capitalist system in which it functions. While the power and influence of the commanding heights of Mexican capital is extensive, however, the state does not merely defend the interests of this sector but has a considerable degree of autonomy. This is not to deny that state economic policies have benefited national capital and have done relatively little for the bottom two-thirds of the population, or that Mexico, given its position "so far from God and so close to the United States,"[51] has provided support and opportunities for MNCs. Aside from the oil nationalization of 1938, the Mexican state has never challenged their predominance in critical sectors. But even if the Mexican state only enjoys a limited autonomy, no analyst would deny the critical role it has played in the creation of *salinastroika*.

The "black box" of the state is not empty; something very important goes on inside it that plays a major role in defining present-day Mexico. If the last ten years have seen a greater willingness on the part of the

51. This is perhaps the only one of Porfirio Díaz's declarations that still enjoys support among a majority of Mexicans. Interestingly, Díaz is no longer such a hated figure, at least not among many in the middle class. Various persons with whom I spoke expressed considerable "nostalgia" for Díaz, saying that he at least "got things done." The Salinas administration has begun a revamping of primary and secondary school textbooks where Díaz, if not rehabilitated, is no longer portrayed as an ogre.

government to allow entry of MNCs into previously restricted areas and a general liberalization of trade policy, the origins of these policy changes may be found in the development of a new elite and dramatic changes in the institutional structure of the regime.

Because of its corporatist characteristics the Mexican state was able to strike the delicate balance between isolation and insulation. Contributing to the latter was its monopolistic control over the major peasant and labor organizations.[52] Although the extent of this monopoly has sometimes been exaggerated, it is widely accepted that the PRI was able to maintain its control over the leading corporatist sectors established in the 1930s and 1940s. These institutions, at least until the 1980s, could influence and even veto government policies, but they also assured that once decisions were made, organized protests would be kept to a minimum. Even many of the opposition political parties (until 1988) could be seen as extensions of the government. At the same time, the PRI "served to aggregate and represent a range of important elites (some of whom were linked to broader clienteles)."[53] By managing a corporatist machine that, through combinations of repression and coaptation, provided the government with an extraordinary level of political peace, the ruling party assured that the government did not become so isolated as to neglect the basis of that tranquility.

The election of 1988 and the rise of popular movements in the cities that climaxed with the campaign of Cuauhtémoc Cárdenas appeared to threaten this system.[54] But the challenge to the regime was weakened by two complementary trends. First, the attempt to institutionalize the coalition that had supported Cárdenas within the PRD led to the fragmenta-

52. See Kevin J. Middlebrook, "The Sounds of Silence: Organized Labor's Response to Economic Crisis in Mexico," 1989; Jonathan Fox and Gustavo Gordillo, "Between State and Market: The Campesinos' Quest for Autonomy," in Wayne Cornelius, Judith Gentleman, and Peter Smith, eds., *Mexico's Alternative Political Futures*, 1989; Susan Eckstein, *The Poverty of Revolution: The State and the Urban Poor in Mexico*, 1977; Judith Adler Hellman, *Mexico in Crisis*, 1983; Steven E. Sanderson, *Agrarian Populism and the Mexican State: The Struggle for Land in Sonora*, 1981; Nora Hamilton and Timothy F. Harding, eds., *Modern Mexico: State, Economy, and Social Conflict*, 1986; Gustavo Gordillo, "Estado y movimiento campesino en la coyuntura actual," in Pablo González Casanova and Héctor Aguilar Camín, eds., *México ante la crisis*, 1985.

53. Alan Knight, "Historical Continuities in Social Movements," in Joe Foweraker and Ann Craig, eds., *Popular Movements and Political Change in Mexico*, 1990, p. 96.

54. See Foweraker and Craig, *Popular Movements;* Cornelius et al., eds., *Mexico's Alternative Political Futures;* and Barry Carr and Ricardo Anzaldua Montoya, eds., *The Mexican Left, the Popular Movements, and the Politics of Austerity*, 1986.

tion of much of the left opposition.[55] Similarly, the ideological rapproche-
ment between the government and parts of the conservative National
Action Party led to less dramatic but equally debilitating divisions on the
right. Second, the new elite appeared successful in its attempts to restructure the political system while maintaining most of its critical functions.
Unlike Gorbachev, who was unable to reform without destroying the
CPSU, Salinas was able to simultaneously count on the still considerable
influence of the PRI while transforming its relationship to the corporatist
associations and the state. Most important, Salinas was able to reconstruct the patronage machine of the PRI within his National Solidarity
Program (Programa Nacional de Solidaridad, PRONASOL).[56] Thus,
while imposing severe social costs, the Salinas government was uniquely
able to both maintain its control over popular challenges while responding to strategic needs quickly enough to keep these manageable.

While all of the above conditions help to explain how the state could
impose its new policies, Mexico's technocratic revolution still required
that the regime accomplish three critical tasks: it had to maintain political stability without which economic fine-tuning would be impossible, it
had to legitimate the process of economic reform as the central responsibility of the state, and it had to generate enough financial and political
support to partly offset the costs of reform. In order to understand how
the regime was able to do so, we must analyze three developments *within
the organization of the Mexican state* during the past twenty years.

The first is the centralization of power within a group of state institutions espousing a technical-analytical model, that, through control of the
critical resources required by the regime, sought to impose the primacy
of their institutional perspective on the entire administrative apparatus.
Prior to the 1950s the federal government had successfully established
civilian control over the military, as well as the bureaucracy's ascendancy over the party. Within that dominant bureaucracy the next decades witnessed the increasing centralization of power within the presidency, the rise in importance of the planning and finance sectors, and the
creation of an alternative political machine and the subsequent transformation of the PRI. This centralization of power enabled the ruling elite

55. The strength of the popular protest movements, however, may represent a long-term
threat to the apparent success of the government project, especially given the intensification of
the inequality and poverty that afflicts the majority of the population.
56. Denise Dresser, *Neopopulist Solutions to Neoliberal Problems,* 1991.

to impose its policies on an often recalcitrant political apparatus. Yet the maintenance of the corporatist and electoral organs also assured that the elite would not isolate itself completely.

A second crucial development was the domination of the state by a cohesive elite with specialized training who claimed the ability to maximize collective welfare through the application of a set of instrumentally rational techniques and success criteria. The changes discussed above would have been impossible without the takeover of the bureaucracy by a group of technocrats who attained powerful posts in the government through bureaucratic, as opposed to electoral or corporatist, channels paralleling the rise of the *cientificos* during the Porfiriato and the decline in the fortunes of a more traditional elite of *politicos*.[57] The ascendancy of a leadership sharing a distinct profile contributed to the homogenization of the ruling elite and helped prevent internal divisions and disagreements that could have blocked the economic transformation. Unlike technical experts in other authoritarian regimes, this new elite established not just behind the scenes influence, or control within *limited* policy areas, but commanded the helm of the state as a whole. The rise of this new elite would have been impossible without the maintenance of a complex system of interlocking networks of patron-client relationships popularly known in Mexico as *camarillas*. These networks represent "the cement of the Mexican political system,"[58] and they assured the integration of the new elite, facilitated its rise to power, provided the channels through which they centralized control of resources, and contributed to the development of the political mentality that characterized the process of *salinastroika*.

The final development was the hegemony of a single, exclusive policy paradigm based on the theoretically optimal use of resources and the preservation of system stability. Obviously, part of this perspective consisted of the neoliberal model. But more than an explicit ideology, what

---

57. The *cientificos* were a closely knit clique of intellectuals, professionals, and businessmen who advised dictator Profirio Díaz. Their leader from 1895 on was Finance Minister José Limantour. Their name stems from their insistence on "scientific" administration of the state and espousal of positivism and the work of Comte and St. Simon. Their main policy focus was on economic development. They believed authoritarianism was necessary to guarantee the peace needed for economic advance. Most *cientificos* believed that the Indian and *mestizo* population was inherently inferior and that Mexico would have to rely on the leadership and capital of the native white elite and foreigners to guide their country to modernity.

58. Roderic Camp, "Camarillas in Mexican Politics: The Case of the Salinas Cabinet," 1990, p. 1.

characterized the new elite was an epistemological assumption that there was one truth and it was uniquely capable of interpreting it. In the final analysis these men and women were interested in "getting things done," in resolving Mexico's problems as quickly and thoroughly as possible.[59] What counted was accomplishing the task at hand while retaining control, and this, rather than a commitment to a specific set of strategies, dictated the policies of the new elite. This helps explain the relationship of the new elite to the legacy of the Revolution of 1910: they did not seek to displace it but rather to *reinterpret* it on their own terms. These included a partial commitment to democracy, which was always constrained by the more important needs of development. It was a democracy restrained by reason and by their interpretation of Mexican reality.

Unlike more traditional revolutions, the transition to the market is not accompanied by popular mobilization in favor of such policies; the masses will not congregate in the central square in order to assure that prices send the correct signals. The populace may express a desire to obtain the consumer goods that may be available through the market but will not agitate for the specific policies that can produce access to those goods. Nor do such policies originate in a process of consensus and compromise arrived through political negotiation. Economic adjustment programs are based on often abstract and technically complex frameworks that posit the existence of an optimal distribution of resources requiring the privileging of economic incentives over social and political considerations. According to the technocratic vision the role of the state "is not to express the unconsidered thoughts of the crowd, but rather to add to them more mature thoughts, which precisely because they are mature, cannot fail to be different. The essential function of the state is to think."[60] The next six chapters describe how the contemporary Mexican state came to think.

59. To an extent their commitment to a specific policy was an accident of historical timing. In the 1980s classical economics appeared to offer a solution. In a different time, or in a different international context, a command economy might have been adopted.

60. Bertrand Badie and Pierre Birnbaum, *The Sociology of the State*, 1983, p. 14.

# INSTITUTIONS

# 3

---

# The Autonomous Bureaucracy

The Mexican political system is often called unique or contradictory. The president is all powerful but only rules for six years. The principle of no reelection does not encourage interelite competition but promotes and sustains the domination by a single party and a small political class. The Congress has considerable constitutional powers but rarely challenges presidential authority. Indeed, the Mexican state seems to defy characterization as a regime type. During the 1950s and early 1960s some observers did express a limited hope for the democratization of the regime.[1] More pessimistic appraisals in the 1970s and 1980s debated the balance between the regime's authoritarian, corporatist, and populist characteristics.[2]

1. For a very optimistic view, see William P. Tucker, *The Mexican Government Today*, 1957, and Robert E. Scott, *Mexican Government in Transition*, 1964. Pablo González Casanova also expressed some hope for an opening of the regime in his *La democracia en México*, 1965. More typical perspectives were those of Frank Brandenburg, *The Making of Modern Mexico*, 1964; Frank Tannenbaum, *Mexico: The Struggle for Peace and Bread*, 1960; Raymond Vernon, *The Dilemma of Mexico's Development*, 1963; Vincent Padgett, *The Mexican Political System*, 1966; Martin Needler, *Politics and Society in Mexico*, 1971. For an interesting critique from the point of view of the Mexican right, see Kenneth F. Johnson, *Mexican Democracy: A Critical View*, 1971. For a discussion of these issues among Mexican intellectuals, see Carlos Pereyra, "Las vísperas de las urnas," *Nexos* 87 (March 1985), pp. 15–20. Also see Enrique Krauze, *Por una democracia sin adjetivos*, 1987.

2. See José Luis Reyna, "Redefining the Authoritarian Regime," in José Luis Reyna and Richard S. Weinert, eds., *Authoritarianism in Mexico*, 1977, p. 161, and John W. Sloan, "The Mexican Variant of Corporatism," 1985; Robert Kaufman, "Mexico and Latin American Authoritarianism," in Reyna and Weinert, *Authoritarianism in Mexico*, and Kaufman, "Industrial Change and Authoritarian Rule in Latin America: A Concrete Review of the Bureaucratic-

As I mentioned in the previous chapter, the authoritarian structure of the Mexican regime may be best characterized as electoral-bureaucratic.[3] While there have been few *institutional or legal* restrictions on the advocacy of political alternatives,[4] the historical record indicates the existence of stringent limits on the role of opposition parties. The practical monopoly of the PRI meant that elections served to legitimate the regime rather than present a real possibility of turnover. The party, however, was not a simple facade behind which a bureaucratic-military alliance conducted "real politics" but served as both an organizational arena for elite settlements and a means to organize the population into corporatist sectors and mobilize support for the government. The combination of political legitimacy, coaptation through the party, and the simultaneous ability of the bureaucracy to limit the development of a political institution that could represent a channel for populist sentiments allowed the regime the luxury of not relying on organized violence for control but on the disbursements of resources and economic incentives. The existence of this political machine allowed the predominance of civilian authority over the military.

How did these particular characteristics contribute to *salinastroika?* The origins of Mexico's technocratic revolution lie in the same economic and political crises that precipitated the rise of bureaucratic-authoritarian regimes in Latin America. Like its counterparts in the Southern Cone, the Mexican regime in 1970 faced both an accumulation crisis stemming from the exhaustion of Import-Substituting Industrialization and a legitimacy crisis brought to a head by the government's shooting of several hundred student demonstrators in 1968. But the institutional dominance of civilians allowed a political stability closer to the experience of Singapore and Taiwan than to that of the bureaucratic-authoritarian regimes of the Southern Cone. These conditions allowed the technocratic elite to

---

Authoritarian Model," in David Collier, ed., *The New Authoritarianism in Latin America*, 1979. Guillermo O'Donnell also discusses the applicability of the bureaucratic-authoritarian model to Mexico. Mexico shares many of the characteristics of 1960s and 1970s Argentina and Brazil, but there are critical differences largely stemming from the political stability provided by the PRI (*Modernization and Bureaucratic Authoritarianism*, 1979, p. 91).

3. I am following Juan Linz's definition of authoritarianism as discussed in "Totalitarian and Authoritarian Regimes," in Fred Greenstein and Nelson Polsby, eds., *Handbook of Political Science*, 1975.

4. Exceptions include the prohibition of the Communist party until 1976 as well as the actions against the Partidos del Pueblo in 1954 and the Frente Electoral del Pueblo in 1963.

dominate policy making without having to rely on military allies or drastically transform the organization of the state.

The Mexican regime was able to accomplish two of the tasks identified in the previous chapter as critical to the success of economic restructuring. First, it insulated itself from interest group pressure through its authoritarian political control. Second, it maintained a complex set of connections with social sectors through the corporatist arms of the party. The latter assured that it always could hear what society was saying, the former guaranteed that it did not have to listen.

The rest of this chapter will discuss the creation of this autonomous but embedded bureaucracy. The first section describes the establishment of civilian control over the military. The second analyzes the federal bureaucracy's ascendancy over the party. A third section discusses the rebellion against that control in the late 1980s and the regime's response. The concluding section of the chapter analyzes the relative autonomy of the state vis-à-vis domestic and international capital.[5] Chapter 4 will address the structure of power within the bureaucracy itself and the changes therein.

# The Rise of the Civilians

The historic predominance of the civilian bureaucracy has made postrevolutionary Mexico unique in Latin America.[6] Unlike its counterparts in the continent, the Mexican military played a minimal role in politics after the 1940s.[7] Moreover, while the Mexican military after 1960 did

---

5. Given that the basis for the government's relationship with the Church was formed in the mid-nineteenth century and contributed little to the policy decisions discussed in this book, I have not analyzed this aspect of Mexican politics. It is worth remembering, however, that after the Cristero Rebellion of the 1920s the government did not have to fear serious assaults on its legitimacy from the pulpit. The consequences of the regime's recent settlement with the Church may be important but should not significantly alter the political structures discussed below.

6. Robert Kaufman, "Industrial Change," pp. 221–222; and Kaufman, "Mexico and Latin American Authoritarianism."

7. The two other obvious exceptions (until the 1970s) were Chile and Uruguay. However, while the military in these countries had remained outside politics for most of this century prior to their return in the 1970s, they had retained the institutional capacity for intervention. That is, the military budgets of both countries allowed the maintenance of armed forces with the resources necessary to establish their total control of the society. Mexico's military, on the other hand, suffered severe and continued budget cuts from 1940 onward, and by 1970 its receipts

begin to receive training in U.S. institutions associated with "National Security" dogma, it never developed the same faith in its ability to run the country as its continental counterparts.[8] Certainly the data on education (see Chapter 5) would indicate a complete lack of interest in those subjects associated with the "modernizing" military of Brazil and the Southern Cone.

The transition to civilian power occurred during the period from 1929 to 1940 and was solidified in the following twenty years. After a decade of devastation and bloodshed during the Revolution and a decade of political instability during which various revolutionary warlords used their private armies and control over provincial centers to influence national politics, the Mexican state succeeded in centralizing control over the country and establishing its claim to a monopoly over the legitimate use of violence.

This demilitarization, however, did not lead to an electoral democracy but to an authoritarian regime in which power stemmed from control of the civilian bureaucracy and positions therein as opposed to democratic representation of some social group. President Plutarco Elías Calles (1924–1928, and unofficial "paramount leader" until 1934) designed a political system in which power struggles and interest conflicts were "civilianized" and institutionalized within the dominant party, the National Revolutionary Party, or PNR, the present-day PRI.

During the 1930s the military remained a potentially important political actor. President Lázaro Cárdenas (1934–1940), for example, had to replace regional commanders with those loyal to his administration, and he faced a military rebellion led by General Cedillo in 1938–1939. The election of 1940 was the last time the military was directly involved in the electoral process with large numbers of generals supporting the candidacy of General Almazán, but the central government's control of the electoral machinery and the loyalty of troops around the capital assured the victory of the party's candidate, Manuel Ávila Camacho.

---

accounted for 2.7 percent of federal expenditures as opposed to 11.6 percent and 13.1 percent in Chile and Uruguay respectively. While Chile and Uruguay had 6.2 and 7.2 soldiers per one thousand in population, the Mexican ratio was 1.6 (United States Arms Control and Disarmament Agency, *World Military Expenditures, 1967–1976*, 1978, pp. 55, 67, 42).

8. See David Ronfeldt, ed., *The Modern Mexican Military: A Reassessment*, 1984; and Edward J. Williams, "The Evolution of the Mexican Military and Its Implications for Civil-Military Relations," in Roderic Camp, ed., *Mexico's Political Stability: The Next Five Years*, 1987.

Ávila Camacho (1940–1946) was the last president with military experience, and he continued Cárdenas's efforts to reduce military expenditures, which shrank from 21 percent of the federal budget in 1940, to 10 percent in 1950, and to 7 percent in 1960.[9] The victory of the civilians was further assured by his choice of Miguel Alemán for the presidency in 1946 and the elimination of the special military "sectoral organization" within the party in 1943.[10] Since that date military background has been an automatic disqualification for presidential precandidates (for example, Miguel Henríquez Guzmán in 1951 and Alfonso Corona del Rosal in 1969). The representation of those with military experience in the upper levels of the elite drastically declined and was largely limited to the management of the defense establishment after the 1940s.

Unlike its equivalents in the Southern Cone, the Mexican military since that time has been unable to exploit moments of political crisis in order to expand its influence.[11] Even during the student demonstrations of 1968 and the guerilla activities of the early 1970s, the armed forces remained a closely controlled instrument of the president and were relatively marginal in decision making. The General Staff or "Estado Mayor" remained under the control of the president, who also chose all leading commanders.

Nor does it appear that the military as an institution was particularly interested in a more political role.[12] During the 1980s soldiers have

9. While the population of the country doubled between 1940 and 1965, the military personnel remained at fifty thousand. See Edwin Lieuwen, "Depoliticization of the Mexican Revolutionary Army, 1915–1940," in Ronfeldt, ed., *The Modern Mexican Military*, p. 61.

10. Alemán was also responsible for the creation of a presidential guard separated from the high command, and this probably also helped to limit the influence of the military. See David Ronfeldt, "The Mexican Army and Political Order since 1940," in Ronfeldt, ed., *The Modern Mexican Military*.

11. Pablo González Casanova emphasized the absence of a political role for the military in his classic *La democracia en México*. In the 1960s, however, other authors believed that the military still possessed veto power over some government policies. See Scott, *Mexican Government in Transition*, p. 134, and Howard Cline, *The United States and Mexico*, 1963, p. 415.

12. One expert with very close ties to the military indicated that the highest ranks of the military had no interest in expanding their political influence (interview, San Diego, November 1989). One possible (if symbolic) indication of the *voluntary* marginality of the Mexican military is the demeanor of its troops in charge of guarding the National Palace in Mexico City's *zocalo* or central plaza. Unlike their counterparts in those regimes where the military is the central political institution, the Mexican soldiers are *very* casual in the performance of their duties and have a great deal of difficulty in carrying out basic maneuvers such as changing the gigantic flag in the center of the plaza. I believe that this performance gives a good indication of the self-image of the Mexican military and that this, in turn, may provide an indication of its perceived role in Mexican society. If there is a correlation between political influence and

consistently resisted efforts to expand their role to include stricter policing of borders against Central American refugees and drugs.[13] The institutional incompetence of the military in what has been one of its traditional roles in Latin America, managing popular unrest and providing government control during times of crisis, was amply demonstrated during the earthquake of 1985. Its performance on that occasion further reduced what little status it had among the population.[14]

During the last few years there has been some evidence of the creation of a new alliance between the civilian administration and the military. The military budget increased during the 1980s from 1.7 percent to 2.4 percent of federal nondebt expenditures, and the military received significant salary increases during the de la Madrid *sexenio*.[15] Various observers noted that references to the armed forces were becoming more common in presidential addresses and that Salinas had established very close ties to the military.[16] On the other hand, there were some indications that the enlisted personnel had voted overwhelmingly for the opposition in the 1985 and 1988 elections.[17] Nevertheless, there was no evidence that the military was able or willing to begin acting as an independent political "wild card."[18]

It is possible that continued political instability will compel the armed forces to reenter the political arena.[19] Notwithstanding the possibilities

---

military pomposity, the Mexican armed forces would place at the very bottom of comparative importance.

13. During the 1980s the army was increasingly used as a police force against the drug mafia. One estimate is that 25 percent of military resources (50 percent during harvest season) were directed toward the "narco-war" (interview, San Diego, November 1989).

14. The military apparently resented the political leadership for placing it in a situation for which the armed forces were not prepared, and the generals made it very clear that they did not want to be responsible for political problems caused by the regime's incompetence and unpopularity (interviews, Mexico City, January 1988, and San Diego, November 1989). Despite Salinas's espoused commitment to "modernization," moreover, corruption remained endemic in the armed forces. The assassination of Mexican narcotics agents by soldiers in November 1991 demonstrated that the drug mafia had very powerful protectors in the army.

15. Presidencia de la República, *Primer informe de CSG*, Anexo, 1989; Roderic Camp, "The Military," in George Grayson, ed., *Prospects for Democracy in Mexico*, 1990.

16. David Ronfeldt, "Questions and Cautions about Mexico's Future," in Susan Kaufman Purcell, ed., *Mexico in Transition: Implications for U.S. Policy*, 1988; Camp, "The Military."

17. Camp, "The Military," p. 89. I heard unconfirmed rumors to this effect during visits to Mexico in 1988 and 1989.

18. Ronfeldt, "Questions and Cautions," p. 61; see also Luis Suárez, *Echeverría en el sexenio de López Portillo*, 1983, pp. 283–286.

19. They have been used to resolve some electoral disputes (for example, in Michoacán in April 1990) and against striking workers (for example, at Cananea in 1991).

that soldiers may need to rescue or even replace the new elite, however, the military did not place it in power. Unlike other potentially techno-cratic regimes in Latin America, the Mexican state has been completely in the hands of civilians for the past sixty years, and the latter have never had to respond to the dictates of armed superiors.

## The Institutionalized Party

The civilian bureaucracy was also free from the constraints placed by the demands of a political machine as it established its control over the PRI and its predecessors.[20] Even before the appearance of the new elite, the Mexican state had already become, in the words of Octavio Paz, "a government of functionaries."[21] While much attention has been paid to a division between a "political" wing in the PRI and a "bureaucratic" wing in the administration, the former does not have, nor did it ever have, anywhere near the amount of influence of the latter. The PRI and its precursors never functioned as a political party but rather as a "politi-cal control" secretariat within the governing bureaucracy. Despite its sixteen million members in 1986, it was "a party without militants" and subsequently without influence.[22]

It is important to remember that the PRI played no role in the Revolu-tion or the first ten years of regime consolidation. While it may claim to be the direct descendant of those forces that revolted against the Porfiriato and established the modern Mexican state, the party as an institution did not come to power through its own efforts but originated in the needs of those in control of the state.[23] Unlike the cases of the ex-

20. In order to facilitate the narrative below I will use the name PRI when discussing the government party even if there are some critical differences between it and its predecessors, the PNR and PMR.

21. "Burocracia y democracia en México," *Vuelta*, 1987, p. 62.

22. Luis Javier Garrido, "Un partido sin militantes," in Soledad Loaeza and Rafael Segovia, eds., *La vida política mexicana en crisis*, 1987. For an excellent history of the PRI, see Dale Story, *The Mexican Ruling Party: Stability and Authority*, 1986. On the lack of PRI autonomy and the control by the president, see Manuel Moreno Sánchez, *Crisis política en México*, n.d., pp. 160–162. On the centrality of the bureaucracy and the powerlessness of the traditional *políticos*, see Marcela Bravo Aluija and Carlos Sirvent, "La elite política de México," in Germán Pérez and Samuel León, *Diecisiete ángulos de un sexenio*, 1987, pp. 373–374.

23. The efforts by the PRI to claim Revolutionary heroes and symbols as its unique prop-erty have been a critical part of its success but have encountered some resistance in recent years. In 1988 the opposition PAN sued the party in order to stop it from using the national tricolor in

USSR, the PRC (People's Republic of China), or postcolonial regimes in Algeria, Kenya, and Zimbabwe, the leadership of the party, as a political or revolutionary organization, did not establish control over the state apparatus but just the opposite. Power never flowed from the party but toward it.[24]

The government party was intended to control and coordinate the political ambitions of various military and regional *caciques;* to institutionalize power so that conflicts could be resolved, compromises reached, and spoils divided without recourse to the open conflict that had dominated Mexico for twenty years. In the words of ex-President Luis Echeverría, the party was meant to serve as the national *caudillo.*[25] The formation of the party allowed "the transference of the fight for power between factional and regional groups to the interior of the party, where mechanisms were created to resolve these and to substitute negotiation, discussion, and commitment to shared national interest for armed struggle."[26]

The party was also meant to assure the predominance of its founder, Plutarco Calles, and it did so during his *maximato,* which lasted until 1934. The subservience of the party to the government was further strengthened during the 1930s when Lázaro Cárdenas, in his battle with Calles, worked to establish the dominance of the president's office and government, which he controlled, over the party apparatus still led by men loyal to the ex-president. In order to solidify his position Cárdenas sought to replace the territorial organization of the party, which guaranteed the political autonomy of the *caciques,* with a corporatist structure controlled from the center.[27] The victory of the new president was

---

its symbols. In turn, the PRI forced the Cárdenas forces to be more circumspect and indirect in its use of his father's name.

24. One indication of the relative weakness of the PRI is that it was never able to establish a parallel hierarchy of commissars to watch over the activities of government bureaucrats. To a large extent the latter made the decisions, while party functionaries were limited to legitimating these in any way possible. Another good indicator of the domination by bureaucratic as opposed to elected/political leaders is the almost total absence of references to members of Congress or party officials in the press *prior to 1988.* Yet the speeches of ministers and even those two or three rungs down the ladder were given exhaustive coverage.

25. Suárez, *Echeverría en el sexenio de López Portillo,* p. 220.

26. Alejandro Carrillo Castro, *La reforma administrativa en México,* 1982, 2:25.

27. Daniel Casío Villegas, *El sistema político mexicano,* 1975, p. 49; Susan Kaufman Purcell, "Mexico: Clientalism, Corporatism, and Political Stability," in S. N. Eisenstadt and René Lemarchand, eds., *Political Clientalism, Patronage, and Development,* 1981, p. 198.

clearly assured by the late 1930s when the party underwent its first name change to become the Partido Revolucionario Mexicano (PRM) in 1938 and established the two organizations on which its power would depend: the Workers Confederation of Mexico (Confederación de Trabajadores de México, CTM) in 1936 and the National Peasant Confederation (Confederación Nacional Campesina, CNC) in 1938.

Even if one treats the 1934–1940 period as potentially leading to a more corporatist-democratic rule through the various branches of the party, Cárdenas's inability to guarantee the continuation of his social and economic policies after his term in office, combined with the monopolistic control of the party, assured that those whose power rested on some form of constituency representation would give way to those for whom access to government positions, patronage, and resources were critical.[28] The government's efforts to establish central control through the PRI were successful in providing Mexico with a political stability unique in Latin America. But this centralization gave power not to those who could get votes but to those who controlled the bureaucratic apparatus in charge of government expenditures. On the one hand, this partly freed the population from the arbitrary control of local bosses, but it also led to an increasing monopolization of power in the hands of a relatively small political elite.

Another potentially crucial factor in the weakening of the party was the constitutional prohibition of reelection. Again, this freed the population from the dominion by a self-perpetuating local elite. However, it also made the development of independent politicians impossible. Since they could not be reelected, politicians had little interest in responding to the needs of their constituencies. Since they did not enjoy independent sources of power based on electoral support, they could not challenge the dictates of the central government, in which lay their only promise for future employment.[29] The no-reelection clause did prevent the return of *caudillismo*, but it may have also discouraged the development of a more competitive party system.

28. See Ruth Berrins Collier and David Collier, *Shaping the Political Arena: Critical Junctures, the Labor Movement, and Regime Dynamics in Latin America*, 1991.

29. See Miguel Ángel Centeno, "Electoral-Bureaucratic Authoritarianism: The Mexican Case," in Arturo Valenzuela, ed., *Politics, Society, and Democracy: Latin America*, forthcoming. According to PAN activist Jaime González Schmall, the no-reelection clause made it especially difficult for the opposition to recruit candidates as, even if they were successful, their careers would be very short. See Carlos B. Gil, *Hope and Frustration: Interviews with Leaders of Mexico's Political Opposition*, 1992, p. 101.

The decline in influence of the party (never high to begin with) contin-ued during the 1940s, culminating in the government's successful efforts to curtail the autonomy of the most important sector of the PRI, the labor unions. This involved the replacement of the increasingly indepen-dent Vincente Lombardo Toledano by Fidel Velázquez as the leader of organized labor. By the 1950s, with few exceptions,[30] the labor move-ment had been purged of any potentially independent leaders or organi-zations, particularly those with the remotest left-wing leanings. During the Ávila Camacho *sexenio* the labor and peasant organizations were also joined by the National Confederation of Popular Organizations (Confederación Nacional de Organizaciones Populares, CNOP), which sought to balance the influence of the first two with greater appeal to the middle classes and the petite bourgeoisie.

After 1946 the corporatist sectors, and particularly the CNC, no longer played a major role in policy making but were reduced to support-ing the legitimacy of decisions made above them. The sectors had ex-changed resources and organization for independence and mobilization, and found that their bargaining power with the government was very constrained.[31] Increasingly, the organizations' functions were reduced to the management of a patronage machine that compensated some groups for their support of an essentially nondemocratic system. In the words of a leading member of the Salinas elite, "the basic function of the syndical organizations . . . is to *regulate* labor participation and mobilization."[32]

Miguel Alemán (1946–1952) was not only the first civilian president but he was also the first representative of a group that I have called the *burocratas políticos* (Chapter 5). What distinguished Alemán from other potential candidates was his experience as chief of political control dur-ing the Ávila Camacho administration. While he had served as a gover-nor and senator of his home state of Veracruz, Alemán's career and influence were not based on support from a key sector or constituency

30. These included the railroad workers in 1958 and the electricians during the early 1960s.
31. Purcell, "Mexico," p. 199.
32. Manuel Camacho, "Los nudos históricos del sistema político mexicano," in Centro de Estudios Internacionales, *La crisis en el sistema político mexicano, 1928–1977,* 1977, p. 188 (my emphasis). The CTM is, of course, the possible exception to this pattern of dependence. I would argue, however, that it was never designed to represent a social interest institutionally and politically divorced from the government but rather was in charge of maintaining labor acquiescence to government policy. For an analysis of the condition of the corporatist sectors in the late 1980s, see Wayne Cornelius, Judith Gentleman, and Peter H. Smith, eds., *Mexico's Alternative Political Futures,* 1989.

but on his loyal service to the president as Secretary of Government from 1940 to 1945. Alemán was the first president to establish complete control by the federal bureaucracy over the other members of the "Revolutionary Family," and he began the homogenization of the leadership that characterizes it to this day.[33]

The selection of Alemán and the political "reforms" of 1946 (which changed the PRM into the PRI) established a pyramidical hierarchy that severely limited the autonomy of local and grass-roots organizations in favor of the Executive Committee of the party. For example, Alemán was able to impose governors on thirteen states whose provincial political machines had previously enjoyed a measure of independence. In 1950 the party also eliminated primaries for the selection of candidates.[34] After 1946 the PRI was no longer a mass party (and it is questionable to what extent it was ever such) but became a specialized arm of the bureaucracy. The party's function increasingly focused on providing a veneer of democracy and managing the patronage machine on which political stability depended rather than on the representation of its constituent sectors. It lost any ideological autonomy and became what some have called a "vote-sucking machine."[35]

Unlike Cárdenas, Alemán was able to assure that those who followed him to the presidency continued with his government project. The defeat of the dissident movement led by Miguel Henríquez Guzmán in the election of 1952 marked the final victory of the right wing of the political elite over the "Cardenistas" as well as the consolidation of political control by the central apparatus of the party. Although López Mateos (1958–1964) is generally seen as moving the regime somewhat to the left, his terms as Minister of Labor and President were characterized by the violent suppression of dissident labor movements. He and his successor Gustavo Díaz Ordaz (1964–1970) continued the institutionalization of the party into a political control bureaucracy, or into what one leading Mexican politician has called a subsecretariat within Gobernación

---

33. According to one PRI militant, Alemán created the generation that was to remain in power until 1970 (Tomás Brito Lara, *La sucesión presidencial de 1910 en 1988*, 1988, p. 39). Alemán's three immediate successors had either been in the cabinet or in the Senate during his administration. It was during the Alemán *sexenio* that we first detect the rise of a group of professionals to political prominence, and it was during these years that the National University (UNAM) began to play its role as the institutional producer of the future elite.

34. Arturo Sánchez Gutiérrez, "México 1950–1954: The Political Consolidation during the Transition towards Stabilizing Development," 1986.

35. Cosío Villegas, *El sistema político mexicano*, p. 81.

(Ministry of Government).[36] In 1965 PRI President Carlos Madrazo attempted to rejuvenate the party by limiting the power of the central organs and expanding grass-roots participation and influence, but his efforts were frustrated by the apparat of the Central Committee (Comité Ejecutivo Nacional, CEN) and the *charros* who were in charge of the sectoral organizations.

In the late 1960s, therefore, the PRI had become "not a political party in the traditional sense, but a governmental organization responsible for coordinating the electoral process, mobilizing and desciplining the members of its organizations, and defending government policy in whose formulation it has no effective influence."[37] The party, never meant to dispute an opposition for the right to govern, now merely served to impose decisions taken by the bureaucrats.[38]

By increasing government commitment to social services and establishing a network of federal agencies to manage it during the 1970s, the bureaucracy also assumed many of the functions that had been previously handled by the party. Much as in the United States during the New Deal, the expansion of the welfare functions of the state helped destroy the traditional political machine. Patronage did not disappear, but the institutions in charge of this largess and their relationships with the recipients changed: "[T]he executive organizations formed the focus of [a] new form of political domination in Mexico . . . to the decline of representative organizations, more typically or traditionally political."[39]

The loss of direct control over government patronage made the fulfillment of the party's basic function, maintaining the legitimacy of the regime, increasingly difficult. The decline in support for the PRI even in Mexico's managed contests reflects the deteriorating ability of the party to serve as the legitimating arm of the regime. Prior to 1988 elections served as a form of plebiscite for the government's legitimacy. The point was not to allow electoral opposition but to regularly demonstrate that the majority of the population supported the regime's policies. After 1970 the PRI had much greater difficulty in obtaining the vote of a majority of the registered electorate. While abstentions cannot be auto-

36. Interview, Mexico City, March 1988.
37. Lorenzo Meyer, "El estado mexicano contemporaneo," in Colegio de México, *Lecturas de política mexicana*, 1977, p. 33.
38. Lorenzo Meyer, "La democracia política: Esperando a Godot," in *Nexos, México mañana*, 1988, p. 194.
39. Héctor Aguilar Camín, *Nexos* 100 (April 1986), p. 10.

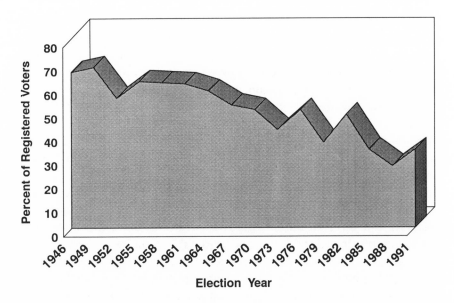

Fig. 3-1.   PRI performance, 1946–1991. (Source: Juan Molinar Horcasitas, *El tiempo de la legitimidad*, 1991.)

matically classified as antisystem votes, the dramatic increase in the number of citizens unwilling to play their part in electoral charades marked a critical point for the regime. Rather than supporting the PRI, the majority of the voting population chose to either abstain or voted for the opposition.

The increasing degree of abstentionism led President López Portillo (1976–1982) to attempt a partial reform in the system in order to encourage competition.[40] The political reforms of the Ley Federal de Organizaciones Políticas y Procesos Electorales (LFOPPE) of December 1977 did open the political possibilities for opposition and succeeded in establishing a slightly freer press, but they were never meant to remotely challenge the PRI's hegemony.[41] Moreover, while the LFOPPE was de-

40. Edgar W. Butler and Jorge Bustamante, "Introduction," in Butler and Bustamante, eds., *Sucesión Presidencial: The 1988 Mexican Presidential Election,* 1991, p. 5; and Rafael Segovia, "Modernization and Political Restoration," in Butler and Bustamante, eds., *Sucesión Presidencial,* p. 66.

41. On this issue see Kevin J. Middlebrook, *Political Liberalization in an Authoritarian Regime,* 1985. Juan Molinar Horcasitas believes that the LFOPPE represented a much more

signed to broaden the representation of political parties, these, with the possible exception of the National Action Party in some northern states, had never served as the critical organs of opposition. Certainly after 1968 smaller and less institutionally concrete popular movements had played the central role in voicing and organizing communities.[42]

Whatever the original intent of the electoral laws and subsequent reforms in 1982, however, they did give the opposition a chance to call into question the political legitimacy of the regime. The PAN victories in municipal and provincial elections throughout the 1980s and the federal elections of 1985 further demonstrated that the PRI could no longer even guarantee the professional stage management of Mexican electoral farces.[43] These shifts led to further changes in the relative influence of the PRI and the distribution of power within it. Since this institution could no longer deliver a claim of legitimacy to the regime, its already limited influence within the government declined further. Since sustaining popular support was no longer an effective strategy for the state, those better able to control opposition gained more influence within it. These same changes further increased the importance of those in the government who managed the repression apparatus, which was required whenever coaptation failed. Simply put, those whose function was to co-opt the population into saying yes were replaced by those who could impose a no.

With the selections of Miguel de la Madrid and Carlos Salinas the marginalization of the party was complete. As the data in Chapter 5 will demonstrate, careers in the electoral and corporatist arms of the party had become irrelevant (if not actually counterproductive) for achieving power in Mexico. This led one pro-PRI journalist to ask: "If party activity counts for nothing, who is going to accomplish the political tasks needed by the regime? If someone doesn't do it, what of the PRI?

dramatic break with the traditional system. See "Vicisitudes de una reforma electoral," in Soledad Loaeza and Rafael Segovia, eds., *La vida política mexicana en crisis,* 1987.

42. Joe Foweraker and Ann Craig, eds., *Popular Movements and Political Change in Mexico,* 1990; Susan Eckstein, ed., *Power and Popular Protest: Latin American Social Movements,* 1989.

43. Soledad Loaeza claims that the results of these elections shocked and frightened the government. See "The Impact of Economic Crisis on the Mexican Political System," in Purcell, ed., *Mexico in Transition,* pp. 46–47. See also Juan Molinar Horcasitas, *El tiempo de la legitimidad,* 1991.

And without the PRI, what?"[44] Given that the PRI had played such a critical role in maintaining legitimacy, organizing support, and controlling popular demands, the answer to this question would determine the fate of the Mexican regime.

## Rebellion and Response

The economic crisis of the 1980s and the government's policies created a new threat to the political order. This challenge, and the subsequent response by the Salinas administration, resulted in a transformation of the political system perhaps as radical as that managed by Cárdenas in his battle with Calles.

Those sectors of the political class that had been increasingly excluded during the past decade openly objected to the rule by the new leadership after 1982.[45] On October 1, 1986, a group of PRI dissidents announced the formation of the Movement for Democratic Renovation (Movimiento de Renovación Democrática), which was later to be known as the Democratic Current (Corriente Democrática, CD). This revolt, which climaxed with the political cataclysm of July 1988, could be interpreted as the response of the traditional elements of the ruling elite, or at least the more liberal or populist wing of this group, to the complete imposition of the bureaucracy's hegemony over the PRI. The CD rejected the imposition of a single dogma and the exclusion from power of the various sectors of the PRI and their allies in what had always been a relatively heterogenous and pragmatic organization.[46]

The political battle inside the PRI became increasingly public after the party's XIIIth Assembly in March 1987. The leaders of the CD made it clear that they were not challenging the legality or political hegemony of the PRI over the government but rather the absence of democracy *within* the party, which was now dominated by the *arribismo* (the imposition of all decisions from above).[47] While the discourse of the CD emphasized the

---

44. Mario Ezcurdia, *De la política*, 1983, p. 125.
45. See, for example, the declaration by Alfonso Corona del Rosal in *Excelsior* (Mexico City), July 30, 1986.
46. See the interviews in Gil, *Hope and Frustration*.
47. *Proceso*, no. 569, September 28, 1987, p. 13.

lack of democracy within the party, many of its leaders had participated in and benefited from the same exclusionary policies for several years. If for no other reason, their protests seemed somewhat disingenuous. The revolt of the CD did not arise because the PRI had suddenly become less democratic but because the bargaining position and influence of a particular sector had been drastically reduced during the past ten years. The rise of the CD thus marked the end of the PRI as an institution able to encompass the entire spectrum of political ideologies and interests.[48]

The regime made some concessions to the changing political circumstances by staging a pseudoprimary for the presidential nomination.[49] In August 1987 PRI chief Jorge de la Vega Domínguez announced the names of the leading precandidates for the party's presidential nomination. While the "short list" had been common knowledge in previous elections, this was the first time in over three decades that the party had attempted to organize some form of official nomination process with the public participation of PRI activists. But the members of the CD were consistently excluded from this process.

One week after the announcement of Salinas's nomination for the presidency, Cuauhtémoc Cárdenas formally accepted the presidential nomination of what had been a marginal party widely considered a satellite of the PRI, the Partido Auténtico de la Revolución Mexicana (PARM). He refused to renounce his membership in the PRI, claiming that he was the authentic representative of the traditions of that party. The PRI, on the other hand, formally advised Cárdenas that his acceptance of a rival candidacy would lead to his expulsion. Given that the PARM had never been a major political actor outside of selected states such as Tamaulipas, few in the leadership took this challenge seriously. During late 1987 and early 1988, however, the strength of the Cárdenas campaign grew dramatically. The National Democratic Front succeeded in linking together the various parties of the Mexican left, including the relatively large Mexican Socialist Party (PMS) in April 1988.

48. Not only did the CD claim significant parts of the party leadership but it could obtain a major part of the PRI vote. It could even be said that the CD was the more authentic representative of the traditional party and that it was Salinas who led a "dissident" wing (Juan Molinar, comments in conference presented by PRD, Center for U.S.-Mexican Studies, February 28, 1990).

49. I qualify the term *primary* because while this process was supposed to allow more popular participation in the decision, no elections were held. In any case, it was widely assumed that the president would still select his successor.

There were several reasons for the success of the campaign. First, many of those in the FDN had served in the electoral arm of the PRI and possessed a sophisticated knowledge of how a campaign was run in Mexico. These were not, as had normally been the case with the Mexican left, idealistic intellectuals who rarely left the ivory tower of Coyoacán, but experienced *políticos*. Second, while he was not personally charismatic, Cárdenas could count on the symbolic appeal of both his first and his family name and the links these provided to Mexican history and the traditional ideals of the Revolution.

Third, and most important, the opposition developed at precisely the moment when dissatisfaction with the PRI and the regime was at its height, and the FDN succeeded in replacing the PAN as the leading antisystem choice. As the PRI apparently never learned, each attempt to use the resources of the regime to intimidate the opposition (for example, trying to prevent Cárdenas from speaking at the National University, UNAM) only added to the appeal of the FDN. The opposition's platform focused not on specific recommendations for the political economy (other than a repudiation of the debt), which might have alienated potential supporters, but on the respect for the vote and support for democracy in Mexico. That is, the FDN based its appeal on the call to "throw the rascals out," precisely when this was probably the majority sentiment in the population. The Cárdenas coalition was also able to draw upon what some have called the mobilization of civil society following the earthquake of 1985.[50] The rise of popular movements and grassroots activity provided the organizational and motivational resources that both left and right utilized in their campaign against the PRI.[51]

The resulting protest vote, whether favoring the left or the right, produced the smallest *official* majority for a PRI candidate in the history of the party. Aside from the loss of political legitimacy this entailed, the election also had a significant, concrete effect as it created a possible challenge to the executive branch's domination of the legislature. The Mexican Congress did have substantial constitutional powers, but as long as the same party controlled both branches of government, the executive would predominate. The election of 1988, however, left the PRI with a thin majority and without the required margin to pass the constitutional amendments and presidential decrees that had been com-

---

50. Gil, *Hope and Frustration*, p. 47.
51. See Foweraker and Craig, eds., *Popular Movements and Political Change in Mexico*.

mon during the past twenty years. If the president could no longer depend on the legislature rubber-stamping his decisions, the overwhelming power of the bureaucracy would be radically constrained. Because of the election results, Salinas was the first postrevolutionary president who had to genuinely negotiate with opposition forces in Congress.[52]

In order to meet this challenge the Salinas administration established an alliance with the conservative PAN, which appeared to agree with many of its economic policies. In the first three years of the Salinas *sexenio,* it became clear that the PAN was much more interested in collaborating with the ruling PRI than with the left opposition.[53] The PAN votes, as well as those of parties who had deserted the Cárdenas coalition after the election, provided the required legislative majority to approve the constitutional changes proposed by the president. The Cárdenas forces were therefore marginalized by a center-right coalition.

The left was also hampered by its inability to convert the coalition that united behind Cárdenas into a strong political party. In the fall of 1988 Cárdenas announced the creation of the Party of the Democratic Revolution. This was to include the militants from those parties (PARM, PPS, PFCRN, PMS, and PCM) that had supported his candidacy. Despite the fact that their insistence on running as separate parties (even while sharing candidates) had cost them several congressional seats in 1988, these institutions resisted a formal union. From the beginning it was clear that both the PARM and the PFCRN were unwilling to lose their institutional autonomy and that even among those willing to join the PRD, ideological and strategic disagreements were rife.[54] After the Congress passed a new electoral law that prohibited political parties from supporting the same candidate, these divisions made it unlikely that the left could re-create a version of the FDN in 1994.[55]

---

52. Cornelius et al., eds., *Mexico's Alternative Political Futures,* p. 25.

53. See Miguel Ángel Centeno, *Mexico in the 1990s: Government and Opposition Speak Out,* 1991. One of the few exceptions was the joint effort supporting the candidacy of Salvador Nava for the governorship of San Luis Potosí in 1991, but even here the PAN appeared to have the upper hand.

54. Part of the weakness of the PRD was that the alliance was based not so much on shared organization or ideology but on a strategic choice as how best to challenge the government. There were, for example, clear disagreements concerning the new clerical laws, privatization, agrarian reform, and the degree to which the PRD should establish alliances with the PAN or accommodate the government. Perhaps most important, the PRD was divided on the question of Cárdenas's role in the national leadership.

55. Secretaría de Gobernación, *Código federal de instituciones y procedimientos electorales,* 1990.

The PRD also suffered from the fact that much of its support had been a protest vote against the PRI rather than a commitment to the values represented by the leadership. The shift from PRD support to the PAN in Baja California (Norte), for example, indicated that a significant percentage of the population would vote for whichever opposition sent the best message to Mexico City. Grass-roots organizations, the organizational backbone of the FDN, were also more concerned with negotiating a solution to their particular problems (for example, housing in Mexico City) with *whomever* was in a position to help rather than in maintaining the organizational unity required by an opposition party.

Salinas also sought to minimize the need for negotiation by constitutionally guaranteeing that the PRI's now-limited ability to produce a plurality would still assure it majority control of the Congress. In 1990, thanks to an alliance between the PRI and the PAN, the Congress passed constitutional reforms that could radically alter the manner in which elections were managed. The new electoral law established the "principle of governability" that, in the absence of an electoral majority, would grant whichever party won 35 percent of the vote a majority of the seats in the lower house of the legislature.[56] At least in the legislature the PRI could remain hegemonic without being monopolistic. The electoral victory of August 1991 once again allowed the executive branch to ignore the legislative.[57] Changes in Article 107 of the Constitution also made it impossible for the Supreme Court to challenge the constitutionality of proposals approved by the dormant Congress.[58]

# A New PRI?

Despite the alliance with the PAN and the new constitutional arrangements, the events of July 1988 did demonstrate that the PRI was no longer

56. Article 54 IVc of the Constitution (later rescinded) stipulated that in the absence of a clear majority, the party that won the plurality of single member seats (three hundred of the total five hundred) in the House of Representatives and 35 percent of the national vote would receive an automatic majority of 50 percent plus one taken from the two hundred proportional allocation seats. The text of the changes are in Fernando Franco, "La reforma electoral," in Diego Valadés and Mario Ruiz Massieu, eds., *La transformación del estado mexicano, 1989.*

57. Out of the twenty-seven legislative initiatives in the Congress elected in August 1991, twenty-six came directly from the executive (*El Financiero* [Mexico City], May 15, 1992).

58. See Andrew Reding, "Mexico: The Crumbling of a Perfect Dictatorship," 1991, p. 4.

an adequate political mechanism and that the traditional system of representation was exhausted. Carlos Salinas recognized this weakness, as well as the permanent disruption of the noncompetitive party system, by declaring on July 7, 1988, that the single-party system was dead. But this did not necessarily imply the development of a competitive democracy. The bureaucratic elite chose to maintain its control over the government through a reconstruction of the PRI rather than an attempt to save the political system as a whole. In other words, they sought to democratize in a controlled fashion so that they could remain in power.[59]

The first indication of the new nature of the party came in the spring of 1989. The fall of La Quina and Carlos Jongitud Barrios signalled an open assault on the traditional *político* structure. Salinas appeared to feel that he no longer needed these men to manage the votes of the oil workers and teachers. Yet the appointment of their successors indicated that Salinas's idea of change had serious limitations and that the labor sector could not yet claim its independence from the government. The response to the strike at the Modelo Brewery, including the removal of strikers by security forces, further demonstrated the limits of *salinastroika*.[60] Salinas continued his assault on the autonomy of the unions by taking over the port facilities in Veracruz from the previously untouchable longshoremen's syndicate.[61] The influence of Fidel Velázquez and the CTM, already declining in the 1980s, was also further undercut by changes in the control of retirement funds.[62]

The corporatist structure of the party was replaced by a territorial organization similar to that originally envisioned by Calles.[63] (But Salinas was careful not to create potential regional rivals. The president dismissed several governors and placed loyalists in one-third of the state capitals thereby strengthening central control.)[64] The corporatist sectors appeared to accept the new political order after the "Abrazo de Merida" in July

---

59. Molinar Horcasitas, *El tiempo de la legitimidad*, p. 234.

60. The government also wished to maintain the unity of the labor movement under its control. In 1991, for example, Labor Secretary Farrell Cubillas assisted the CTM in defeating a dissident organization in the Ford auto plants.

61. *Excelsior* (Mexico City), June 3, 1991, p. 1. Salinas was also seen as trying to organize the takeover of the CTM by his ally, Arturo Romo Gutiérrez.

62. *El Universal* (Mexico City), February 11, 1992, p. 1.

63. See comments by PRI chief Luis Donaldo Colosio in Centeno, *Mexico in the 1990s*.

64. By 1993 this number should increase to one-half.

1990 when labor leaders and the new party leadership finally agreed to live with each other. The new elite (or *filósofos* as they were called by the old guard) realized that they needed the corporatist organizations. The traditionalists or *dinosaurios* realized that there was no possibility of a return to the previous situation. The actual change was minor, however, as many of the labor and rural organizations dominated regions and could control a territorial delegation as easily as one officially defined by corporatist membership. The PAN successfully lobbied for the end of automatic enrollment in the PRI of all union members. However, given the reality of politics inside these organizations, the vast majority of their members would "voluntarily" join the PRI anyway.

By the early 1990s one could argue that the PRI was becoming irrelevant to the government's political strategy. The new "party of citizens" (as opposed to corporatist sectors) was increasingly perceived as a lame-duck anachronism waiting for the president to finally declare it officially dead and replace it with an institution more to his liking.[65] There was considerable speculation that the PRI would soon be replaced by a new entity based on the government's Solidarity Program (Programa Nacional de Solidaridad, PRONASOL).[66] Founded on the first day of Salinas's presidency, PRONASOL was "an umbrella organization aimed at developing health, education, nutrition, housing, employment, infrastructure, and other productive projects to benefit 17 million Mexicans living in extreme poverty."[67] Perhaps more important, it was the core element of the Salinas administration's formula for maintaining political control.

PRONASOL served to provide the government with the political space needed to marginalize the opposition while the regime underwent its restructuring. In many ways PRONASOL was the key to the success of the technocratic revolution. Salinas began to build a new political structure at the same time that he dismantled the old. With an official budget of $1.7 billion (U.S.) in 1991 and control over an unquantifiable

65. Interviews, Mexico 1991 and Princeton, N.J., 1990–1991. See also columns by Carlos Ramírez in *El Financiero* (Mexico City) in March 1992 and analysis by *Excelsior* (Mexico City), February 21, 1992.

66. See *El Financiero* (Mexico City), March 9, 1992, p. 44, and *Excelsior* (Mexico City), March 9, 1992.

67. Denise Dresser, *Neopopulist Solutions to Neoliberal Problems,* 1991, p. 1. Unless otherwise noted, the information on PRONASOL comes from this source.

percentage of other agencies' budgets, PRONASOL became the most visible representative of the government in the urban shantytowns and rural communities.[68] The flow of funds and subsequent political influence were so great that the provincial chiefs of the program were known as "vice-governors."

PRONASOL was a perfect example of classic PRI tactics, whereby opposition and discontent could be co-opted through patronage. Yet while it could be seen as a continuation of previous populist measures, there were critical differences. Perhaps most important was that the president controlled PRONASOL directly. There were no mediating institutions between recipients and the president such as the party or the government health bureaucracy. Second, PRONASOL, encouraged local participation in the design and management of the projects, which not only increased efficiency but, proving the thesis of the president's Ph.D. dissertation, also appeared to generate much more political support than other welfare programs.[69] Finally, PRONASOL avoided blanket coverage through subsidies and emphasized the "truly needy." While this partly reflected the ideological perspectives of many in the cabinet, it was also politically profitable. The distribution of PRONASOL projects appeared to follow political logic as they were usually concentrated in those districts where the opposition posed the greatest threat. Moreover, the funds were not distributed to assist PRI candidates as a whole but only those closely associated with the president's clique.

If it could have little impact as a social program (annual per capita expenditure was fifteen cents), and while it largely ignored the real roots of poverty in Mexico, PRONASOL appeared to diffuse much of the grass-roots opposition faced by the government in 1988. If Cardenismo had succeeded in temporarily uniting all the isolated local movements into a national opposition, then PRONASOL was successful in once again atomizing these into individual bodies that could be "bought off and conquered."[70]

The results of the election of August 1991 seemed to support the

---

68. These are Dresser's figures. *El Financiero Internacional* (Mexico City) calculated PRONASOL's budget at $3 billion (U.S.) for 1991 (September 23, 1991).

69. Carlos Salinas de Gortari, *Political Participation, Public Investment, and Support for the System*, 1982. Salinas's ability to use his government to verify his social scientific hypotheses was the ultimate symbol of the degree of technocratic domination in Mexico.

70. Dresser, *Neopopulist Solutions to Neoliberal Problems*, p. 19.

Salinas strategy.[71] By all accounts the "new" PRI staged a remarkable comeback. The new Congress would include 321 PRI representatives as well as 48 more from satellite parties, providing a comfortable margin for the president and possibly signaling the return of the legislature to its traditional passivity. The official results of 61.5 percent for the PRI, while reflecting some of its vote-rigging habits, did indicate real support for the president's policies. According to surveys reported in a widely respected Mexican magazine, the PRI had the support of 49 percent of the voters while 62 percent approved of Salinas's performance.[72]

The victory of 1991, however, did not belong to the PRI, or at least the PRI as it existed before the 1980s. The true winners of 1991 were Salinas and PRONASOL. With its over seventy thousand local offices, portfolio of favors, and inescapable propaganda, PRONASOL could match the PRI's organizational resources. But this organization owed its existence, and each member owed his or her influence and/or livelihood, to one man, Carlos Salinas. Through PRONASOL the president assured that the bureaucracy managing the technocratic revolution would be both insulated from popular pressures and protected from the consequences of its own actions.

## The Limits of Autonomy

To what extent was this insulated bureaucracy independent from the private sector? This has been the subject of considerable debate. We can distinguish three positions regarding the autonomy of the Mexican state. For those in the first category, Mexican public policy since the Revolution, and especially since 1940, has largely reflected the interests of international and national capital, and the state has lost most of its capacity to control the activities of either. The second group of authors see a partnership between two different factions of a dominating elite, one based on the control of the governing institutions and the means of repression, the other based on control of national capital. The interests of the two groups often conflict, and neither one can dominate, but each

71. See *El Cotidiano*, no. 44, November–December, 1991.
72. *Este País,* August 1991.

exercises a limited veto on the policies followed by the other. While recognizing the critical importance of capital, this perspective does assign the state some form of "relative" autonomy. The final perspective defines a more autonomous state that does not necessarily require the approval of the private sector for its activities. The state and private capital operate in different spheres, interacting much less than in the second model, but the state is clearly dominant. This view also holds that the state, as an institution, can be treated as an independent social actor which supports policies beneficial to itself and to a distinct class of government personnel.[73]

Autonomy, unfortunately, is often in the eyes of the beholder. It is probably impossible to convince any one school's adherent of the need to accept a different position. For example, the same economic policy may be interpreted as either following the dictates of a dominant social group or as the product of rational analysis by an autonomous, developmentalist state. In the case of Mexico we can clearly rule out deterministic or instrumental perspectives in which the state serves as some "executive committee" for either international or domestic capital.[74] Obviously, since much of this book analyzes the state, I consider what goes on within it decisive. As Nora Hamilton demonstrates, however, even the Mexican state's most determined attempts at autonomy were limited.[75] Since 1940 the Mexican state's relations with capital may be seen as a continual process of negotiation in which the state attempted to exercise as much control as possible but was constrained by the reactions and expectations of capital. These provided structural limits on how far the state could go in challenging dominant class or international interests. While capital could not necessarily tell the state what to do, its disapproval had disastrous consequences for economic policy and could therefore not be ignored. Thus, the Mexi-

73. Representative works include Nora Hamilton, *The Limits of State Autonomy: Post-Revolutionary Mexico*, 1982; Gary Gereffi, *The Pharmaceutical Industry and Dependency in the Third World*, 1983; Juan Felipe Leal, *La burgesía y el estado mexicano*, 1980; Alonso Aguilar, *La burgesía, la oligarqía, y el estado*, 1983; Jorge Alonso, *La dialectica clases-elites en México*, 1976; Roger Hansen, *The Politics of Mexican Development*, 1980; Susan Kaufman Purcell, *The Mexican Profit-Sharing Decision: Politics and Economic Change in an Authoritarian Regime*, 1975; Douglas C. Bennett and Kenneth E. Sharpe, *Transnational Corporations versus the State: The Political Economy of the Mexican Auto Industry*, 1985; Judith Teichman, *Policymaking in Mexico: From Boom to Crisis*, 1988; James M. Cypher, *State and Capital in Mexico*, 1990.

74. Peter H. Smith, *Labyrinths of Power: Political Recruitment in Twentieth-Century Mexico*, 1979.

75. *The Limits of State Autonomy.*

can state is autonomous in the sense that it is not reducible to social or economic struggles, but it is not autonomous in that it is continuously penetrated by these same struggles.[76]

During the "Mexican Miracle" business and government established a mutually beneficial partnership in which the first fueled and managed growth while the latter provided monetary and political stability and protection. The private sector exercised considerable influence through its ties to the economic ministries and the threat of capital flight. The government, in turn, provided a considerable share of the investment capital available and could manipulate monetary and trade policy to reward or punish individual economic groups.

In a radical break with the pattern that had predominated during the previous two decades, the government lost the support of significant sectors of national capital during the administration of Luis Echeverría in the early 1970s. Partly because of the real growth in state intervention in the economy, partly because of Echeverría's increasingly anti–private sector rhetoric, the alliance that had existed between state and national capital was severely strained during this period. When the oil crisis of 1973 began to affect Mexico's economic performance, the private sector became much more vocal in its opposition. With the founding of the Consejo Coordinador Empreserial in 1975, the private sector for the first time proposed an economic policy in opposition to that of the government.

The new oil revenues and the subsequent opening of the international credit markets did free the government from some of the constraints imposed by private capital, and it used the new monies to buy the support of even those who might object to the expanded role of the state by assuring that they could participate in the bonanza. But the collapse of oil prices and the debt crisis of the early 1980s once again constrained the government's policy autonomy. By late 1982 the Mexican government found itself in a position analogous to that of 1975–1976: unable to procure significant resources to maintain its expansionary policies, it could no longer challenge domestic or international capital but had to seek the approval of these sectors in order to remain financially viable.

The collapse of private sector confidence supported the selection of Miguel de la Madrid as the PRI's presidential candidate. That is, López

---

76. Charles C. Bright and Susan F. Harding, eds., *Statemaking and Social Movements: Essays in History and Theory*, 1984, p. 4.

Portillo chose someone who would inspire confidence and assure the private sector that the government would follow a more conservative path in the future partly because the government needed to reestablish some form of cooperation with domestic capital.

From the point of view of the government it became increasingly important to at least reflect some of the concerns and preferences of the private sector. During the 1980s conservative forces were able to express their opposition to government policies in a manner that, at least until the creation of the Cardenista opposition, was not available to the left wing.[77] As the conservative PAN's vote increased both in the north and in middle-class neighborhoods throughout the country, the most significant electoral threat to the regime appeared on the right. While the government was able to practice its traditional alchemy in various local and provincial elections, it was clear that the PAN was becoming a major threat to the legitimacy of the regime.

More important, during the first years of the de la Madrid administration, domestic capital continued its flight out of the country (begun in the 1970s) with an estimated $17.7 billion (U.S.) leaving between 1983–1984.[78] With an accumulated capital flight of over $50 billion (U.S.) during a single decade, representing nearly one-third of GNP, it is not surprising that the government in the 1980s took the opinions of domestic capital into account when making its decisions. No country could afford to lose such a large part of its investment base. Yet largely because of the proximity of the United States, the government could not hope to establish a secure control over capital transfers. Throughout the 1980s and into the 1990s the government offered extremely high interest rates and attractive privatization schemes in order to entice both the private resources that remained in the country and the massive amounts in foreign banks.

So even in the absence of instrumental links between the public and private sectors of the ruling class, the government would be structurally conditioned to respond to the perceived needs of one set of political and economic actors. As I emphasize in Chapter 7, however, the government never completely surrendered its autonomy to domestic capital and was

77. See Sylvia Maxfield and Ricardo Anzaldua Montoya, eds., *Government and Private Sector in Contemporary Mexico*, 1987.
78. Stephen A. Quick, "Mexico's Macroeconomic Gamble," 1989, p. 4. For an analysis of the private sector's disagreements with the state, see Benito Rey Romay, *La ofensiva empresarial contra la intervención del estado*, 1984.

willing to use its still considerable power to take on the private sector. If the government appeared to be saving the Mexican bourgeoisie from itself, it was nevertheless doing so independently.[79]

The autonomy of the state was also constrained by the international economic environment. As their support for the regime became increasingly important after 1981, international monetary and financial institutions insisted on the type of planning and policy rationales in which the technocrats excelled. As relations with the banks became more and more critical to the economic survival of the regime, it had to increasingly rely on the talents of those who could speak the same language as the bankers. The new elite, therefore, partly owes its rise to the fact that they were the candidates of what had become the most important external actor for the Mexican state.

After an initial confrontation in August 1982 Mexico never again challenged the bankers and soon became the model debtor for the international financial community. Such efforts were rewarded by periodic rollovers or infusions of new capital and the renegotiations of the Brady plan. The good behavior also brought other significant economic benefits, including continued acceptance of massive migration to the United States and the promise of access to the North American market. The United States also rewarded the new elite's efforts by not challenging the regime's electoral legitimacy. The Mexican government could dismiss suggestions that it allow international observers a role in elections without facing the type of pressures imposed on Chile or Nicaragua. Unlike Gorbachev, who confronted an internationally recognized nationalist and democratic opposition, the Mexican regime enjoyed a surprising degree of sovereignty in dealing with its internal challenges.

The acquiescence to the needs of foreign capital of the regime and the subsequent support enjoyed by the government led the opposition to accuse the elite of being nothing but the clones of the IMF or the tools of the United States.[80] This type of conspiracy theory simplifies a much

---

79. However, even publications that supported *salinastroika* recognized that the interlocking links between the political and economic elite would protect Mexican capital from too much loss: "[Salinas's] goal is to use free-trade to encourage Mexico's power brokers to recast the structure of Mexican business, . . . [but he] knows better than to put his powerful friends out of business" (*Business Week*, July 22, 1991, pp. 40–42).

80. Porfirio Muñoz Ledo claimed that the elite was reluctant to challenge banks that knew the location of their secret bank accounts (conference at Center for U.S.-Mexican Studies, University of California, San Diego, February 28, 1990). The disinclination of the Mexican government to confront the creditors after August 1982 is difficult to understand. It appears

more complex phenomenon. That the policies followed by the government, at least in the short term, benefited shareholders of major banks more than they did the majority of the Mexican population is unarguable. But the origins of these policies are not to be found in instrumental links between the international capital and the elite but in the manner in which the latter perceived the economic conditions of Mexico, the logic with which it analyzed the situation, and the priorities it assigned to the various steps of its programs. The Mexican case is a perfect illustration of what O'Donnell and Frankel call a "convergence of determination," where even without the need for the blessings of international bodies, governments design orthodox stabilization programs.[81] In the words of one of the decision makers in 1982: "The [economic] program was by no means imposed by anyone. The weight of circumstance, the deficit, the increase in prices, and the external disequilibria, had reached such levels that we would have done the same thing with or without the IMF."[82]

In an interesting twist Salinas also appeared to be using external constraints on the future autonomy of the state in order to assure the survival of his program. The GATT agreements of 1986 and the NAFTA negotiations of 1990–1992 committed the Mexican state to the neoliberal policies of *salinastroika* even after the end of the president's term.[83] In conjunction with the increasingly close relationship that the regime had established with domestic capital and creditor banks, this meant that in the future the Mexican state would not be as free to shape the destinies of the country as it had been during the past sixty years. Much as he used the call to modernization to challenge the political order that brought him to power, Salinas utilized his definition of a new

---

that Mexico had little choice at the beginning of the crisis. As a leading player in these negotiations pointed out, Mexico had roughly one month of grain supplies available in August 1982 and could not have borne the costs of a confrontation with the United States for any extended period of time (interview, Providence, November 1988). But by 1984 pressure was increasing in Latin America to create a "debtors' cartel" that would force the banks to either provide new financing or reduce the service requirements. The bargaining position of such an association would have been considerable as a declaration of default by the major creditors would have created a financial catastrophe in the United States and Europe.

81. Roberto Frankel and Guillermo O'Donnell, "The Stabilization Programs of the IMF," in Richard R. Fagen, ed., *Capitalism and the State in U.S.-Latin American Relations*, 1979.

82. Jesús Silva Herzog, comments in conference on planning quoted in Secretaría de Programación y Presupuesto, *Planeación en tiempos de crisis*, 1986, p. 338.

83. Katrina Burgess, "Fencing in the State," Princeton University, 1992, mimeographed.

nationalism to prescribe the considerable powers he had used in constructing *salinastroika*. International resources had provided the margin that the regime required to provide immediate benefits from its policies. They would also serve to protect their legacy. It appeared that Salinas wished to use the very same forces that had constrained the Cardenista revolution of the 1930s in order to assure the continuation of his technocratic revolution.

The Mexican technocratic revolution owes much to the political machine it sought to dismantle. Thanks to the combination of repression and coaptation for which the PRI was justly famous, the bureaucracy could remain isolated from political pressures that so often stymie economic restructuring. With the consolidation of bureaucratic power the new elite was also able to act without deferring to either the military or the party. This provided a much more stable arena in which to impose the new economic policies than other nations enjoy. When that traditional order threatened to break down, the elite responded quickly enough to assure its political security. The creation of a new patronage machine demonstrated that in order for the economic project to succeed, the regime was willing to use very traditional methods. It once again established a vertical link to the society to augment its technocratic isolation. The technocratic revolution would clearly have been impossible without the support of domestic, and more importantly, international capital. While this may constrain the autonomy of the state, *salinastroika* was not the product of some boardroom. The Mexican regime did accept limits on its independence, but that decision was made inside the "black box" of the bureaucracy. The next chapter will analyze how this operated.

# 4

## Inside the Machine

The autonomy of the bureaucracy, its insulation from political pressures, and its control over corporatist organizations were obviously crucial in providing the political environment required by economic restructuring. In such a massive organization, however, debates as to which policy would be best, divisions regarding acceptable means to achieve these ends, and simple struggles for bureaucratic power could have led to the squandering of such an opportunity. Moreover, the problems of coordination and management of such an enterprise could have also frustrated the technocratic revolution.[1] *Salinastroika* would have been impossible without the centralization of power within a small nucleus inside the bureaucracy able to establish internal ideological homogeneity and to impose that vision on the rest of the regime.

After the bureaucracy assumed control over the party and the military in the years 1940–1970, the next decade saw critical changes in that institution. These included the increasing centralization of power within the presidency, the imposition of global planning in policy making, the rise to institutional predominance of the Ministry of Programming and Budget (Secretaría de Programación y Presupuesto, SPP), and the return

---

1. We still know relatively little about how bureaucratic organizations work in developing countries. See, for example, Fred Riggs, *Thailand: The Modernization of a Bureaucratic Polity,* 1966; Martin Greenberg, *Bureaucracy and Development,* 1970; Peter Cleaves, *Bureaucratic Politics and Administration in Chile,* 1974; Peter Cleaves and Martin Scurrah, *Agriculture, Bureaucracy, and Military Government in Peru,* 1980; Vivianne Márquez and Rainer Godau, "Burocracia y políticas públicas: Una perspectiva desde America Latina," 1983; Rainer Godau, "Mexico: A Bureaucratic Polity," 1976; Ben Ross Schneider, *Politics within the State: Elite Bureaucrats and Industrial Policy in Authoritarian Brazil,* 1992.

to ministerial balance with Salinas. Each of these will be discussed in turn, but first it is essential to analyze the structure of the bureaucracy prior to the administration of Luis Echeverría.


# The Bureaucratic Triumvirate

Before discussing the transformations that took place in the bureaucracy, it is important to keep in mind that the autonomy of the provincial governments was always extremely limited and that the central government has been the key actor in public administration since the 1940s. The efforts by Calles to centralize political control within the PRI also had their equivalents on the level of the bureaucracy. Not only did the states lack an independent source of income but the majority of the expenditures were directed through the capital. In the 1970s, for example, 77 percent of government income was controlled by the federal government, 19 percent by the states, and 4 percent by municipalities. A decade later, despite the supposed decentralization of the system, the federal share had climbed to 85 percent while states depended on the center for 80 percent of their budgets.[2] The centralization of the federal civil service is highlighted by the relatively small number of leading politicians and bureaucrats who began their careers in local or state governments. Certainly after the 1960s experience outside of the capital was increasingly considered irrelevant. By 1983 less than 6 percent of those at the top levels of the bureaucracy even had any experience with nonfederal institutions.[3] As I will discuss in later chapters this contributed to the insulation of the regime and the homogeneity of policy perspectives within it.

The office of the president was the apex of this powerful federal bureaucracy. The president calibrated the needs of the assorted parts of the government and the demands of the various members of the ruling class. In many ways his power was absolute. Miguel de la Madrid, for one, described the political system as "pure presidentialism."[4] The presi-

---

2. Early figures are from Miguel Basáñez, *El pulso de los sexenios: Veinte años de crisis en México*, 1990, p. 115. Numbers for the 1980s are from Wayne Cornelius and Ann Craig, *Politics in Mexico: An Introduction and Overview*, 1988, pp. 16–17.

3. For details on sources for this data see Chapter 5.

4. *Estudios de derecho constitucional*, 1980, p. 239.

dent was the head of the political class, the main arbitrator between forces, the focus of the transition of power, the ultimate manager of the distribution of resources, as well as being in possession of extensive constitutional powers.[5] While the practically supreme powers of the president have long been noted in analyses of Mexican politics, I contend that there existed some limits before 1970 and that the elimination of these constraints created the circumstances that permitted the technocratic revolution.[6]

Prior to the 1970s the president institutionally delegated a great deal of administrative control. Below his unquestionable authority, Mexico had a powerful "double vice presidency." The Ministry of Government (Gobernación) was in charge of politics, and the Ministry of the Treasury (Hacienda) managed the economy.[7] The first was responsible for the preservation of the political system. Along with its satellites, which included the PRI, the Ministry of Labor, and the state governments, it managed the delicate balance of carrot and stick, coaptation and repression, that was the hallmark of the Mexican system. The Ministry of the Treasury and its associated institutions, such as Banco de México and Nafinsa, sought to promote enough investment and economic growth to assure a continued improvement in the living standards of the population, thereby strengthening the government's legitimacy as a provider.

Each "parallel government" was staffed by two separate elite wings: *burocratas políticos* in Gobernación and *técnicos* in Hacienda (see Chapter 5).[8] The divisions were not unlike those between marketing and finance in a private corporation. Just as salesmen have a different relation to product and customer than accountants, the *burocratas políticos* had closer ties to the electoral/clientelistic side of the regime, while the *técnicos* took care of those functions associated with corporate headquarters. Each elite group and representative institution tended to respect the professional prerogatives and domains of the other. The *burocratas po-*

5. For a summary of these powers, see Luis Javier Garrido, "The Crisis of *Presidencialismo*," in Wayne Cornelius, Judith Gentleman, and Peter H. Smith, eds., *Mexico's Alternative Political Futures*, 1989, pp. 422–426.

6. See Jorge Carpizo, *El presidencialismo mexicano*, 1983. For a different view on the development of the presidency after 1970, see Samuel Schmidt, *The Deterioration of the Mexican Presidency: The Years of Luis Echeverría*, 1991.

7. The concept of co-vice presidency was first suggested by a mid-level PRI politician interviewed in Mexico City, February 1988. See also Gabriel Zaid, *La economía presidencial*, 1987.

8. Mario Ezcurdia, *Hubo alguna vez un gobierno paralelo?* 1982.

*líticos* allowed the *técnicos* to make many of the financial and economic decisions, while the latter did not challenge the central control of the *burocratas políticos*.

Gobernación and associated agencies dominated the government because they were in charge of what was considered the most important function of the regime: guaranteeing political stability. They also had access to what was still considered the regime's dominant resource: an elaborate mechanism for maintaining political legitimacy and control. The Minister of Gobernación controlled not only the security apparatus (in collaboration with the military) but perhaps more important, managed the patronage system through the appointment of governors, municipal authorities, and, more indirectly, the leadership of the corporatist sector organizations.

Because of this power the incumbent minister was able to create the strongest network of supporters within the "Revolutionary Family" whose collaboration was required for the implementation of government policy, and presidents normally came from Gobernación.[9] Naturally, the expectation that the Minister of Gobernación would also be the next president further strengthened his position within the system.[10]

The *técnicos* of Hacienda and other economic agencies were also extremely powerful. This personnel had already established their control over the Banco de México in the 1930s, but during the years of Stabilizing Development they became increasingly important in other segments of the bureaucracy.[11] The power of the Minister of the Treasury during these years was matched only by that of the president and the Minister of Gobernación. For all intents and purposes he had absolute control over the budget and the general economic policy of the government. More-

9. Four of the five presidents from 1946 through 1976 served as Ministers of Gobernación during the preceding administration and could be classified as *burocratas políticos*. The fifth, Adolfo López Mateos, had served as Minister of Labor.

10. It is not very clear to what extent the head of Gobernación independently exercised authority. For example, there is some debate in Mexico regarding who actually ordered the troops to fire on the students in 1968. Some say that Echeverría, Minister of Gobernación at the time, made this decision, while others claim that it came from President Díaz Ordaz.

11. In various ministries such as Commerce and National Properties (Sepanal, the precursor of today's SEMIP), the *técnicos* occupied only midmanagement positions and were often accountable to political appointees on the cabinet and subcabinet levels. In the two agencies in charge of financial policy (Treasury and the Bank of Mexico), however, *técnicos* had established clear control. See Fernando Zamora Millán, *México: Ahora hacia donde?* 1987; and Jaquelina Peschard et al., "De Avila Camacho a Miguel Alemán," in Germán Pérez Fernández del Castillo, ed., *Evolución del estado mexicano, 1940–1983, 1986*.

over, Treasury also controlled fiscal policy and its implementation, as well as the public debt. This institution had enormous influence as it was not only the collector of income but also the dispenser of these resources within the bureaucracy. As such it was able to determine not only the size of the government but its investment priorities.[12]

Treasury could even resist presidential efforts to curtail its autonomy. This precedent is worth analyzing in detail since it helped shape the direction of administrative reform in the 1970s. In the 1950s President López Mateos wanted to limit the power of Treasury, and particularly its new leader, Antonio Ortiz Mena, who had competed with him for the presidential nomination.[13] According to an exmember of the elite, there were three major institutional motivations for López Mateos's attempts to constrain the influence of Treasury.[14] First he wanted to establish a more equilibrated balance of power within the bureaucracy's economic sector, which he felt was far too dominated by the Treasury clique. Second, he wanted to end the limits that Treasury's budgetary constraints placed on government spending. Third, he wanted to reduce the direct power that Treasury exercised through its control of the various investment banks and trust funds (*fideicomisos*), which were often more influential in particular sectors than were the relevant ministries.

In order to accomplish these goals López Mateos sought to divide control of the economy between three ministries. The new Ministry of National Resources (Sepanal) would oversee the parastatal sector, the

---

12. See Leopoldo Solís, *La realidad económica mexicana: Retrovisión y panorama*, 1970; Alejandro Carrillo Castro, *La reforma administrativa en México*, 1982; and José Bustani Hid, "El presupuesto federal: Elaboración, aprobación y ejecución," in José Bustani Hid et al., *La administración pública federal*, 1973. The Sub-Secretariat for Expenditures managed these investment priorities. Based on previous budgets, it would assign each ministry the money it could spend during the next year. Each September Treasury would produce a preliminary budget for approval by the president. The budget limits would be sent to the other ministries which would then return a "wish list" to Treasury for its approval. Once the budget had been defined, the rubber-stamp Congress would approve it. (Arturo Cantu describes how Ortiz Mena would walk around his offices with a small card in his pocket in which he would jot down his estimates for the budgets of the main governmental sectors. Only after he had made up his mind regarding these totals would he inform the directors, who would then have to draw up budgets for these same sectors. "El estado programador," *Nexos* 51 [March 1982], pp. 15–22.)

13. The fact that Ortiz Mena could remain in the cabinet after openly seeking and losing the presidential nomination indicates both the solidarity of the "Revolutionary Family" at that time *and* the ability of Treasury to protect its personnel from political fallout.

14. Interview, Mexico City, November 1989. See also Alejandro Carrillo Castro, "El sistema nacional de planeación," in Secretaría de Programación y Presupuesto, *Aspectos jurídicos de la planeación en México*, 1981.

capital goods of the federal institutions, contracts for public works, and all general acquisitions, while the Ministry of the Presidency would serve to coordinate all economic programs, particularly those having to do with investment and programming. Treasury, however, would retain control over federal income and expenditures. (Miguel Alemán had attempted a similar strategy with the creation of the Ministry of National Goods and Administrative Inspection in 1946.) Despite his efforts, however, López Mateos failed to control the power of Treasury, and Hacienda was able to circumvent the new controls and largely disempower the new Ministry of the Presidency. It was, however, forced to share some power with Sepanal, as the latter agency had been given exclusive control over the parastatals and, perhaps more important, was, during this period, led by bureaucrats with considerable political clout and connections of their own.

The key to the president's failure was his unwillingness or inability (it is not clear which) to remove Treasury's hold on the budget. López Mateos appeared incapable of challenging the powerful financier-*técnico* wing in Treasury. Because it kept control over expenditures, Treasury had a very well-developed network of supporters, including much of private capital.[15] Moreover, there were no other economic institutions with resources capable of temporarily replacing Treasury as the main channel for state income. Equally important, there was a considerable myth regarding Treasury's functions and expertise that surrounded and empowered the ministry. Treasury was the "owner of all the intimate secrets of an exclusive area, which no one, not even the presidents, dared enter."[16] Finally, and perhaps most important, while López Mateos wanted to restrict the influence of Treasury, he was in basic agreement with its economic policy. The success of his sexenial project did *not* depend on the outcome of this institutional struggle, and he was therefore more willing to accept a continuation of Treasury's dominance than was Luis Echeverría when he faced the same dilemma.

Despite the impressive influence of Ortiz Mena as minister and Trea-

15. On this relationship see Sylvia Maxfield, *Governing Capital: International Finance and Mexican Politics,* 1990.

16. José López Portillo, *Mis tiempos,* 1988, p. 316. López Portillo described his first encounter with the power of Treasury in the 1960s as follows: "Presidents resolved not to interfere with Treasury, full as it was of esoteric complications and led by a sage and remote wisdom. . . . it was dangerous to disturb what could be broken. Treasury was a funnel with many openings and complicated valves. I imagined Treasury as a very old countess, heiress of various subterranean mother goddesses, full of wisdom and wrinkles, omnipresent and invisible" (p. 286).

sury as an institution, however, the *técnicos* as a group were never able to establish control over the entire bureaucratic apparatus during this period.[17] The *técnicos* were very influential, but they remained bounded by other power relationships in which they played a limited role. The Ministry of Gobernación, and the elite group that staffed it, served as a counterweight to the power of Treasury. The latter institution would decide how much money a particular state would have in the next year's budget, but Gobernación would determine who would be in charge of actually doling out this money in that state. As long as neither agency could usurp the other, a balance of power was maintained. Their combined influence, in turn, also helped check the power of the president.

## Bureaucratic Growth and the Rise of Planning

This delicate equilibrium between the various wings of the bureaucracy was disrupted when power became even more concentrated in the presidency and the national planning system further limited the autonomy of federal agencies. The technocratic revolution of the 1980s can be traced to the breakdown of the traditional power-sharing arrangements as it created the opening for the domination by the new elite and their representative institutions. As the functions of the various groups inside the "Revolutionary Family" were taken over by the new circle around the president, the organizations to which they were linked lost autonomy and influence.

President Luis Echeverría began the process through which the Mexican presidential office came to completely dominate the bureaucracy without checks and balances from other powerful institutions. He disrupted the organizational structure on which the traditional corporatism had been built, weakened the institutional autonomy of the bureaucracy, and centralized power in the already dominant presidency. If in the past the president was first among equals in the "Revolutionary Family," after Echeverría he was the only one that counted.[18]

17. Ortiz Mena did campaign internally for the PRI presidential candidacy in 1957 and 1963 but lost to representatives of the still dominant *burocratas políticos*.

18. See Manuel Villa Aguilera, *La institución presidencial*, 1987; Soledad Loaeza and Rafael Segovia, eds., *La vida política mexicana en crisis*, 1987; and Schmidt, *The Deterioration of the Mexican Presidency*.

These changes are partly explained by the spectacular expansion of the state that Echeverría hoped would help him reestablish the legitimacy of the regime following the 1968 student revolt. While GNP increased by 51 percent from 1970 to 1976, the entire public sector budget (including parastatals) increased by over 116 percent.[19] Between 1970 and 1976 the number of parastatal organizations also increased from 84 to 845. By the late 1970s there were over 1,000.[20] This expansion of the state naturally meant an explosion in the number of positions available. There were 616,000 public servants in 1970, 2.1 million in 1976, and 3.3 million in 1983.[21] The expansion allowed Echeverría to bring in more loyalists and allies than would have previously been the case, and this gave him much greater personal control over the bureaucracy.

As we saw previously, the budgeting of public expenditures had been largely in the hands of Treasury. Since both revenue and expenditures were managed by Treasury, and a group of fiscal conservatives were in charge of this body, deficit budgets were a practical institutional impossibility prior to the 1970s. Treasury had traditionally placed fiscal balance above any other considerations. This went against both Echeverría's and his successor's visions of the role of the state. In López Portillo's words: "[I] conceive of planning and not the capture of resources as the origin and goal of development. To tie fundamental decisions to the plan and not to income constitutes the key secret of our administrative reform."[22]

Echeverría's attempts to dramatically increase the scope of government action ran into considerable opposition from the orthodox economists at Treasury and Banco de México. Echeverría's policies could not succeed with Hacienda in charge of financial policy. He therefore refused to share power with this institution and declared that "economic policy

---

19. Secretaría de Programación y Presupuesto, *Información sobre el gasto público, 1970–1980,* 1982. One should be careful with all budget figures, however, as the accounting labyrinth erected by the technicians in charge of reporting can make comparisons across years—or even across tables in the same year—almost impossible. For the best guide on how to read the budgets (unfortunately now a bit dated), see James Wilkie, *The Mexican Revolution,* 1970.

20. Carrillo Castro, *La reforma administrativa en México,* 2:221.

21. Secretaría de Programación y Presupuesto, INEGI, *Participación del sector público en el producto interno de México, 1975–1983,* cited in Zaid, *La economía presidencial,* p. 20; John Bailey, "The Bureaucracy," in George Grayson, ed., *Prospects for Democracy in Mexico,* 1990, p. 18. Luis Pazos contends that the trend continued into the 1980s with a 40 percent increase in the inscriptions at ISSSTE during the de la Madrid *sexenio (Hacia donde va Salinas,* 1989, p. 43).

22. López Portillo, quoted in Secretaría de Programación y Presupuesto, *Memoria institucional de la SPP, 1977,* 1981, p. 57.

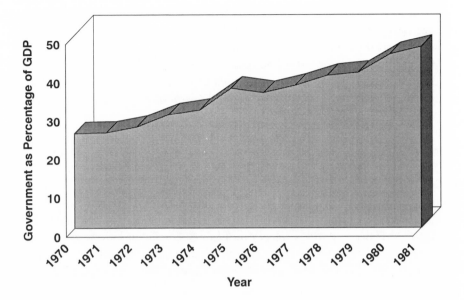

Fig. 4-1.   The growing state, 1970–1981. (Source: Secretaría de Programación y
Presupuesto, *Diez años de indicadores económicos y sociales en México,* 1982.
Includes debt service and parastatals.)

is made at Los Pinos" (the presidential mansion). Early in his *sexenio*
Echeverría began to turn the office of the presidency into a shadow
economic cabinet that persistently and often successfully fought with the
older institutions.

A critical factor in Echeverría's circumvention of the power of Treasury and the formulation of his own economic policy was his ability to
obtain financial resources through nonfiscal means. The expansion of
the government was partly financed by massive new public borrowing.
By 1975 new loans accounted for 25 percent of the federal budget.
López Portillo continued this trend to which were added the revenues
from oil (over 25 percent of the state budget by 1982). While the dependence on these new resources would later limit the autonomy of the
government, during the 1970s they dramatically increased the ability of
the president to reshape the bureaucracy and the policies it implemented.

During the Echeverría *sexenio* the government also began to pay
much more attention to the potential design of "global plans" of politi-

cal and economic development. In 1971 the Secretariat of the Presidency was charged with elaborating administrative reforms that would permit more central planning of public policy. This accompanied the creation of planning units inside each line ministry; these would serve to report to the president regarding its institution's programs. The 1975 budget was the first that replaced the institutional division of resources with a more programmatic orientation.[23]

The focus on planning was particularly obvious during the presidential campaign of López Portillo in 1976. For the first time the party's think tank (Instituto de Estudios Políticos, Económicos y Sociales, IEPES) began to play a leading political role, managing the elaboration of a government plan that would dictate actions. Perhaps as part of Echeverría's strategy of establishing a *maximato* or as an attempt to quiet the resistance to his selection of López Portillo as his successor, the campaign hinted that no matter who the candidate was, the plan would be there; in the famous words of Jesús Reyes Heroles, then head of the PRI, "First the plan, then the man."

President López Portillo shared Echeverría's desire to maintain control over government policy making and to disallow the return of institutional fiefs such as Treasury's, as he sought to remake the entire bureaucratic apparatus of the government.[24] As the head of the Commission for Administrative Reform during the Díaz Ordaz *sexenio*, López Portillo had noted the need for a revamping of the organizational structure of the bureaucracy. López Portillo did not consider that the administrative reform would be a panacea, but he felt that the government had to make an effort to eliminate "the arbitrary employment of policies, which while healthy in and of themselves, are lost in the chaos of the bureaucracy and breed disorder."[25]

Many agreed that a new instrument was needed to manage the increas-

23. For a summary of the history of planning before 1970, see Pedro Aspe and Javier Beristain, "The Evolution of Distribution Policies during the Post-Revolutionary Period in Mexico," in Pedro Aspe and Paul Sigmund, *The Political Economy of Income Distribution in Mexico*, 1984, pp. 19–28; Leopoldo Solís, *Planes de desarollo económico y social en México*, 1975; Horacio Flores de la Peña et al., *Bases para la planeación económica y social de México*, 1966; and Carrillo Castro, "El sistema nacional de planeación."

24. López Portillo's reform program affected 95 percent of the public sector departments and in the first month alone shifted or eliminated sixty administrative units and seventy-nine thousand staff positions (Alejandro Carrillo Castro, *La política y la administración pública en México*, 1982, p. 22).

25. Speech to CEPES conference in Chihuahua, November 16, 1975.

ing demands placed on the government. Prior to 1976 there existed very limited coordination between the various public institutions. López Mateos's failed attempt to reduce the power of Treasury had created a complex labyrinth of regulations that required a myriad of signatures before any initiative could be approved.[26] The so-called "triangle of efficiency" consisting of Treasury, Sepanal, and Presidency was not working: "[N]othing got done and the workings of the public sector were deformed and crushed by a web of relations determined by laws, regulations, accords, uses, vices and abuses."[27] Each line ministry received a share of that year's expenditures and proceeded to spend it without much consideration of how its investments fit into an overall scheme.

This system functioned relatively well as long as the government's agenda was essentially limited to providing infrastructure development and constructing a minimal welfare system. The bureaucracy, however, did not have the organizational resources with which to manage the new emphasis on economic growth fueled by government expenditures. The great expansion in the size and functions of the public sector required a radical change in the way the state was managed and a more complex and sophisticated planning machinery: "The political decisions which barely two *sexenios* previously would have been considered something routine, came to be enveloped in an enormous technical and administrative complexity which made it necessary to create a larger and more efficient bureaucracy."[28]

López Portillo sought to remedy this situation by imposing the supremacy of a new form of economic rationale over the corporatist negotiating of the past. Instead of interest representation through social sectors and negotiation within the "family," planning would resolve problems and provide administrative efficiency. The National Planning System would be the "instrument to define objectives, proposals, means, resources, and actions with the goal of reaching the national objectives of economic and social development."[29]

Planning represented a new manner of formulating government policy. If the traditional budgeting technique was "expressed as a list of

26. Interview, Mexico City, November 1989.
27. López Portillo, *Mis tiempos*, p. 313.
28. Cantu, "El estado programador," p. 19.
29. Carlos Salinas de Gortari, "La inducción en el sistema nacional de planeación en México," in Secretaría de Programación y Presupuesto, *Aspectos jurídicos de la planeación*, 1981, p. 167.

administrative units, . . . the modern technique is expressed in programs and subprograms."[30] Instead of basing each ministry's budget on previous requirements and the availability of funds, the new budgeting procedures would allow the government to become an "instrument in a radical social change."[31] Rather than receiving a percentage of public funds that it then could manage with some autonomy, each ministry's activities would be coordinated through sectoral committees, particularly the Inter-Secretarial Committee on Public Expenditures and Finance.[32] The new Organic Law of the Public Administration and the Law of Budgeting, Accountability, and Public Expenditures of December 1976 required that all new budget items be assigned on the basis of global goals and objectives.[33] These decrees were formalized with the constitutional reforms of 1983, which completed the institutionalization of planning as the central focus of public policy making.[34]

The Basic Plan of the Government (Proyecto de Plan Básico de Gobierno, 1976–1982) was the first example of programming documents that began to circulate following López Portillo's designation as presidential heir in 1975. As the administration progressed, plans became more common. In May 1978 the National Plan for Agri-Fisheries Development was announced, followed by ones for urban development and tourism. But the culmination of these efforts were the National Plan for Industrial Development (Plan Nacional de Desarollo Industrial, PNDI) of 1978 and the Global Development Plan (Plan Global de Desarollo, PGD) announced in April 1980. Not only were these documents much more explicit in their directives, they were also much more detailed than any previous ones, and included quantitative targets.

As the man responsible for the most significant planning effort during the López Portillo *sexenio,* it was no surprise that de la Madrid also emphasized the central role that such methods would play in his administration. In his inaugural address he indicated that the new National

30. Ignacio Pichardo Pagaza, *Introducción a la administración pública de México,* 1984, 2:59.

31. López Portillo quoted in Secretaría de Programación y Presupuesto, *Aspectos jurídicos de la planeación en México,* 1981, p. 489.

32. For a summary of these new procedures see Pichardo Pagaza, *Introducción a la administración pública en México,* pp. 63–73.

33. *Diario Oficial* (Mexico City), December 29 and 31, 1976.

34. See Articles 26–29 in Enrique Calvo Nicolau and Enrique Vargas Aguilar, *Constitución política,* 1989. For a schematic formal description of the planning system in the 1980s, see Secretaría de Programación y Presupuesto, *Sistema nacional de planeación democratica,* 1984.

Development Plan (Plan Nacional de Desarollo, PND) would serve as the basic guideline for his policies. Even more than his predecessor, "Miguel de la Madrid established economic and social planning as the central element of government action."[35] In turn, Carlos Salinas, whom one observer described as a "compulsive planner," helped create the National System of Planning that served to further centralize power in the president's office.[36]

The new emphasis on planning did not simply lead to a generic rationalization, however, but also had political consequences. While partly motivated by considerations of administrative efficiency, planning was also meant to assure the president's control over the government and curtail the institutional autonomy of the individual ministries.[37] Program budgeting would make "policy decisions obligatory for all the centralized and parastatal organs of the Federation."[38] Instead of a myriad of institutions that each had a distinct set of interests, ideologies, and modes of behavior, planning would institute a more centralized control structure.[39] The new institutional order significantly increased the power of the executive and the agencies directly linked to the president vis-à-vis other government organizations on the federal, state, and local levels.

The administrative reforms of 1976 and the accompanying plans allowed an elite to centralize control over policy making and the general agenda of the government while apparently attempting to decentralize the bureaucracy. "The administrative reforms were part of a political process in which the modernization and decentralization become a factional strategy."[40] Some observers believe that the increasing importance of planning is precisely what gave the new elite the opportunity to come to power,[41] but one could also view the causal order running in the opposite direction, with the new elite establishing a set of political and

35. Zamora Millán, *México: ¿Ahora hacia dónde?* p. 79.

36. Remberto H. Padilla, *Historia de la política mexicana*, 1988, p. 226. For the "Salinista" view of planning, see Diego Valades and Mario Ruiz Massieu, *La transformación del estado mexicano*, 1989.

37. For an analysis of the resistance to these changes in the Ministry of Agrarian Reform, see Tatiana Elena Beltran y Puga and José Miguel de la Torre Yarza, *El predominio de las presiones políticas sobre un ensayo de racionalidad en las decisiones gubernamentales*, 1980.

38. López Portillo, inaugural speech, December 1, 1976.

39. Manuel Camacho, "Los nudos históricos del sistema político mexicano," 1977, p. 186.

40. Susan Street, "Burocracia y educación: Hacia un analisis político de la desconcertación administrativa en la SEP," 1983, p. 251.

41. Rosa María Mirón and Germán Pérez, *López Portillo: Auge y crisis de un sexenio*, 1988, p. 11.

professional criteria that would naturally favor their careers. Planning allowed the technocratic elite to circumscribe the power of various sectors of the bureaucracy and the ruling coalition. Therefore, "specific political-bureaucratic interests, along with general state interest in maintaining the continuity of the political system, were instrumental in patterning the direction of policy from the Spring of 1981."[42]

In sum, the 1970s witnessed the rupture of a delicate balance of power by the domination of the presidential office. The creation of the planning apparatus allowed the elite around the president to dramatically increase the already established power of the central administration. With this new mechanism the president and those around him could exercise much more direct control over the activities of the federal government. Whichever institution or group of persons dominated this planning structure would be able to exercise unprecedented control over the government.

# The Ministry of Programming and Budget

In order to consolidate presidential power over economic decision making, Echeverría and López Portillo sought to create a new "superagency" that would be free of the old institutional ties.[43] Their efforts were supported by various experts who believed that the increasing complexity of the state made it impossible for a single ministry to manage both income and expenditures as well as coordinate the new planning efforts that were being developed.[44]

The process of taking economic policy making away from Treasury

42. Judith Teichman, *Policymaking in Mexico: From Boom to Crisis*, 1988, p. 127.

43. For the best description of the rise of SPP, see John Bailey, "Presidency, Bureaucracy, and Administrative Reform in Mexico: The Secretariat of Programming and Budget," 1980. There is some debate regarding whether SPP was meant to assume such a complete hold on the state apparatus. According to one of the men responsible for the design of SPP, it was originally conceived as a consulting office or, at most, as an equivalent to the OMB in the United States. Only in the later stages of its organizational design did SPP become a fully fledged ministry (interview, Mexico City, March 1988).

44. Leaders of this group included the head of IEPES, Julio Rodolfo Moctezuma Cid, who apparently thought he would be given its leadership and who reportedly was not pleased to find that he had been given the now truncated Treasury. Another prominent supporter was Fernando Solana, then head of planning at CONASUPO and later a member of Salinas's cabinet. The leading "academic" supporter was Alejandro Carrillo Castro (interviews, Mexico City, April 1988).

and the classic *técnicos* culminated in the creation of the SPP in December 1976. The new agency combined all the planning functions that had been distributed between the old Secretariat of the Presidency, Sepanal, and Treasury, as well as the statistical office from the Ministry of Commerce. The most radical change, however, and the key to the success of López Portillo's restructuring, was the removal of expenditure control from Treasury. In order to avoid the problems that had plagued López Mateos and to consolidate the changes that Echeverría and López Portillo advocated, it was imperative that those in charge of programming also have control over the budget.[45] This would not only give the new institution the power with which to enforce the new planning system but it would also liberate government expenditures from the limits placed by fiscal policy. With one administrative move López Portillo destroyed the traditional power of Treasury. This institution, "which used to be involved in a very large way in the economy, was now reduced in scope to a tax-collecting and fund-raising entity."[46]

The Ministry of Programming and Budget was given the central role in the new planning and budgeting scheme. While the new planning system was designed to theoretically permit more discussion and popular participation, the budgeting scheme required SPP's approval at every stage. The ministry's responsibilities included the design and supervision of basic economic development plans, the budgeting and authorizing of federal and parastatal expenditures, oversight of plan implementation including the establishment of norms for all purchases by the government, the design of regulations for recruitment, administration, renumeration, training, and development of public personnel, and the coordination and development of all information services including statistical offices throughout the administration, as well as providing guidelines for the elaboration of government reports. Thus, SPP was responsible for planning the future of the country, assigning the distribution of funds necessary to achieve that future, designing the procedures by which the administration would achieve these goals, and measuring the relative success of these policies.[47]

45. Carillo Castro, *La reforma administrativa en México*, 2:174.
46. Mark O. Rorem, "Mexico's Organic Law of Federal Public Administration," 1978, p. 368.
47. If we were to translate SPP into an equivalent U.S. institution, we would have to include the OMB, the Congressional Budget Office, the Treasury, the House Ways and Means Committee, and significant parts of GSA. Considering the nature of the Mexican system, one would

The new ministry utilized each of these responsibilities to practically create a mini state inside the bureaucracy. Each of these attributes parallels the key resources defined by scholars who have analyzed the relative power of organizations.[48] First, with its supervision of the budget and personnel, SPP established direct control over the two most important resources in the bureaucracy. Second, SPP also controlled all the major sources of information regarding the status of plans and projects. Since these were then used to determine future funding, SPP could assure that only those projects of which it approved would "look successful." Third, as we will see in the next chapter, the agency's personnel was also characterized after 1979 by a social, educational, and professional homogeneity that fostered a unitary perspective on the problems facing Mexico. This allowed it to avoid the internal battles that weakened other contenders for power. Fourth, since after 1982 the budget cuts were the most important source of uncertainty for both bureaucratic institutions and personnel, SPP also served as the manager of contingency. Finally, its obvious importance and power led other institutions both to adopt procedures and stances that would win SPP's approval and to emulate the SPP style in general. It is not surprising that the ministry came to dominate the bureaucracy so thoroughly, a condition recognized by all the sources with whom I discussed this issue.[49]

The administrative reforms of 1983 and 1985 sought to reestablish some balance in the relative influence of the different ministries in charge of economic policy.[50] The Secretariat of Commerce was expanded and was given greater authority over industrial policy. The renamed National Patrimony Secretariat (now the Energy, Mines, and Parastatal

---

also have to include the major funding organizations of the two political parties. Finally, since its head served as the closest assistant to the president, one would also have to include much of the White House staff. In this way the SPP was very similar to the equally powerful Ministry of Finance in Japan.

48. See Jeffrey Pfeffer, *Power in Organizations*, 1981; James D. Thompson, *Organizations in Action*, 1967; J. Meyer and R. W. Scott, *Organizational Environments: Ritual and Rationality*, 1983; Paul DiMaggio and Walter Powell, "The Iron Cage Revisited: Institutional Isomorphism and Collective Rationality in Organizational Fields," 1983; Charles Perrow, *Complex Organizations*, 1986.

49. By 1986, for example, party workers began to refer to SPP as the "fourth sector" of the PRI, able to control the more traditional peasant, worker, and middle-class groups (Bailey, "The Bureaucracy").

50. See David Ibarra and José Luis Alberro, "Mexico," in Joseph Pechman, ed., *The Role of the Economist in Government*, 1989.

Industry, SEMIP) was granted greater control over the parastatals and energy policy. Treasury continued to manage revenues and the debt, while the Banco de México dictated monetary policy. These four agencies were supposed to coordinate policy with SPP through the Council of Economic Advisers and the Economic Cabinet, managed in turn by the Secretariat of the Presidency. But SPP's control over expenditures was never challenged, and this allowed it to maintain overall command of economic policy.

Given this concentration of resources, whoever was in command of SPP would be able to dictate policy to the entire bureaucracy. During the first year of its existence SPP was led by Carlos Tello, and the ministry was largely dominated by what could be called the "technocratic left." The selection of Miguel de la Madrid as head of SPP in 1979 marked a critical juncture in the development of this organization. Certainly an SPP led by Carlos Tello would have used its influence to impose a very different path in Mexican economic policy. While de la Madrid did not belong to the old generation of *técnicos* who had managed Treasury prior to 1970, he did have strong institutional ties to that ministry and staffed SPP with those with whom he previously worked. Ironically, by late 1979 the agency that López Portillo hoped would finally free the government from the control by financiers was dominated by a new generation with strong ties to these very same men.

Yet the new elite had a very different vision for the bureaucracy and for the government than its Treasury colleagues. According to participants in this early part of the agency's history, the individuals who staffed SPP were different from those who remained in Treasury.[51] They were younger, had much more training in the quantitative techniques required for econometric planning, and were more willing to accept a powerful public role in economic development. As we will see in the next chapter, these were critical attributes of the new elite who would dominate the state after 1982.

The bureaucrats inside SPP used the resources available to challenge the three most powerful institutional rivals they faced on their way to assuming control: Gobernación, SEMIP, and Treasury. First, SPP defeated Gobernación by using the new planning mechanisms to establish a network of offices throughout the country. These coordinated regional pro-

---

51. Interviews, Mexico City, February–June 1988 and November 1989; San Diego, September–December 1989.

grams and maintained much tighter control over local expenditure than had Treasury. Although the administrative reforms of 1983 did assign formal authority to local governments over some budget items, the federal government maintained complete control over fiscal administration thereby keeping provincial and municipal authorities dependant on the cash flow from the capital.[52] Since decentralization favored municipal over provincial governments, it did more to redistribute what little power there existed outside the capital than to challenge the dominance of Mexico City. Moreover, because of confusion surrounding the planning system, control over the budget became *the* central political tool.[53] Because of their access to the budget, the area representatives of SPP came to hold much more power in the governors' offices than did their Gobernación counterparts. Governors soon learned that their most important ally in the capital was not the Minister of Gobernación but the head of SPP.[54] Moreover, partly through its official management of these posts, partly because of the personal influence of its chief with the president, SPP was even able to challenge Gobernación's control over patronage. For example, while Minister of SPP and prior to his designation as de la Madrid's heir, Salinas was able to place several of his allies in governorships over the objections of the Secretary of Government, Manuel Bartlett.[55]

A parallel process also reduced the already limited independence of the state governments. As a result, the governors stopped being political bosses in their regions and became just another hierarchical step within the functional bureaucracy.[56] The power of SPP was such that it allowed its chief after 1982, Carlos Salinas, to challenge the authority of perhaps the most powerful of the traditional *políticos,* the leader of the Oil Workers Union. Up to 1984 the Pemex union had automatically been awarded 50 percent of the firm's local contracts. Salinas was able to reduce that to an insulting 2 percent.

52. Centro de Investigación para el Desarollo, AC (CIDAC), *Reforma del sistema político mexicano,* 1990, pp. 92–93.

53. See Bailey, "The Bureaucracy."

54. Interviews, Mexico City, May 1988 and November 1989.

55. Interview, Mexico City, May 1988. See also Tomás Brito Lara, *La sucesión presidencial de 1910 en 1988,* 1988, pp. 12–13. These appointments included Enrique González Pedrero, Fernando Gutiérrez Barrios, Heladio Ramírez López, Genaro Borrego Estrada, Luis Martínez Villicana, and José Francisco Ruiz Massieu. While the first two clearly belonged to the *político burocrata* wing, they appeared to support Salinas at a relatively early stage of his 1987 campaign for the PRI nomination.

56. José María Calderón, "Perspectivas de la democracia," *Excelsior* (Mexico City), June 9, 1988, p. 4-A.

The institutions in charge of the industrial apparatus of the state, particularly those that oversaw oil production, presented another potential challenge to the domination by SPP. After 1978 petroleum exports became an important part of government revenues. Simultaneously, institutions such as Pemex accounted for an increasingly large portion of public sector expenditures. This gave them the opportunity to create a network of allies whose support could be purchased by contracts and patronage while also strengthening their position as the providers of government financial resources. The collapse of the oil prices and the drastic decline in industrial investment (54 percent from 1982 to 1988) weakened the bargaining position of these institutions. In a time when expenditure cuts were a daily occurrence and new resources were a thing of the past, the institution with the "budget scissors" would naturally exert much more influence than one that had previously provided a funnel of funds.[57]

The enormous loans obtained by Mexico during both the Echeverría and López Portillo *sexenios* also complemented the financial training of a group of *técnicos* and *tecnócratas* and reduced the influence of specialists with more expertise in engineering and management. As long as those in the developmentalist wing were providing or controlling a large part of the government's revenues and expenditures, they could not easily be phased out of the administration. However, as loans became both the lifeline and the greatest challenge to the regime, those who manipulated financial equations and negotiated with the banks naturally rose to prominence.[58] As the debt service absorbed a large slice of the federal pie, and public works and welfare expenditures were reduced in response, those whose expertise was in the financial areas naturally came to command and control a larger percentage of government resources, while the industrial specialists were relegated to a more maintenance role.

Finally, aside from any ideological differences, SPP and Treasury would almost naturally have institutional rivalries. The institutional logic of the two ministries was diametrically opposed: while Treasury gained power through its control over fiscal policy, SPP did so by spending money. Treasury was the one who always placed fiscal limits on

57. Mirón and Pérez, *López Portillo,* p. 119.
58. A parallel process would occur in private corporations in the United States when the management of investment portfolios came to play a much larger role in the final bottom line than the production and marketing of a product.

actions and projects while SPP could use control of the purse strings to enhance its influence. Treasury did possess an extremely important resource: management of debt negotiations. After 1982 this not only made it the key agency in the relations between Mexico and the critical institutions in the country's external environment, the international banks, it also provided an opportunity to demonstrate that it could fulfill a critical function for the state. The continued failure to permanently resolve the debt crisis, however, meant that Treasury could not capitalize on these critical resources. Without a victory in the debt negotiations, Treasury could not provide new resources or claim a special institutional legitimacy. Minister of the Treasury Silva Herzog was apparently not willing to make what he considered a dangerous move such as declaring a moratorium in order to win the 1988 presidential sweepstakes.[59] In a purely functional world of technocratic domination, the orthodoxy of Silva Herzog's move would have been rewarded (whatever its merits), but as we will see in Chapter 6, politics in technocratic Mexico had retained many of the traditional rules.

The critical characteristic of SPP was that it combined the previously divided powers of Hacienda and Gobernación. On the one hand, it involved the resolution of highly complex technical issues; on the other, it served as the president's organizational representative, and through its control of the budget process, could expand its control to more general or political questions. Because of the combination of powers granted to it, the influence of SPP was not limited by the balance that had previously existed between the political and technical arms of the government. Much more so than either Treasury or Gobernación during their glory years, SPP was able to establish practically absolute control over the entire bureaucratic apparatus. Thus, if the period after 1940 assured the victory of the bureaucracy over the PRI and its associated *políticos*, the period after 1976 saw the empowerment of SPP over that bureaucracy.

# The Zenith of Presidential Power

While de la Madrid used the resources of SPP to climb to the presidency, he found that the power of this agency could also limit his personal

59. Interview, Mexico City, April 1988.

influence once in that office. Observers, both inside and outside the bureaucracy, considered de la Madrid a relatively weak president who merely oversaw the decisions made within his inner circle.[60] Partly because of the institutional structures, partly because of his own personality, de la Madrid did not continue the domination exercised by his predecessors. The de la Madrid *sexenio* in some ways represented a return to a balance of power between the president and his ministers. The policies followed by the government in the 1980s described in later chapters were largely the product of that "collective leadership."

Six years later, facing an even worse crisis than had confronted Echeverría, Salinas decided that he had to construct an even more powerful presidency than had existed in the 1970s. By 1992 he had reestablished the predominance of the presidency in practically every political sphere. As we saw in the previous chapter, the new president had practically created a new party in his image. Salinas also redesigned the federal bureaucracy to feature a powerful presidency at its center.

In retrospect, Salinas's initial appointments could be seen as an indication of the changes to come. Mexican incumbents soon became obsessed by their succession and the potential betrayal by those closest to them. The new president wanted to control his *sexenio* without the creation of bureaucratic fiefs that could serve to dilute or challenge his policies by strategies oriented to the political futures of the individual ministers.

Salinas was masterful in balancing institutional powers with personal influence in his distribution of the cabinet seats. By placing someone who had no chance for the nomination in 1994 in Gobernación, he effectively marginalized this ministry's influence. His closest friend and collaborator was given the unenviable task of managing the federal district. While Manuel Camacho could achieve considerable prestige by resolving the problems of the world's largest city, he could not use it to build a national network with which to challenge presidential authority.

Salinas was also careful to divide responsibility for economic policy making between four men, Jaime Serra Puche in Commerce, Pedro Aspe at Treasury, Ernesto Zedillo in SPP, and José Córdoba in Presidency. Serra Puche was responsible for the North American Free Trade Agreement.

---

60. There were several jokes in Mexico regarding the ineffectiveness of de la Madrid and the control exercised by others in the elite. Many of those in the elite with whom I discussed this topic agreed that Salinas was the effective president after 1986 (interviews, Mexico City and San Diego, 1988–1990).

This gave him considerable influence, particularly among those in the private sector, but he had little power inside the bureaucracy. Moreover, because his parents were not born in Mexico, he was constitutionally prohibited from the presidency, and this further reduced his influence in the political class. Aspe and Zedillo repeated the pattern observed for the past fifteen years, as each fought to establish his predominance in financial affairs.[61] Aspe's success in renegotiating the debt did not provide much leverage, as he was not in control of the savings generated by it. The president was also careful not to allow Zedillo to use SPP's control over the budget to establish the minister's dominance over the economy.[62] This made it easier for Córdoba to establish his predominance and become known as the second most powerful man in Mexico.[63] Since Córdoba, a naturalized citizen, was also constitutionally prohibited from running for president, Salinas was assured that his aide would not follow a personal political agenda. With such a balance of powers between the different cabinet members, Salinas was thus able to direct his project with little concern for internal complications.

The administrative changes announced in early 1992 institutionalized this internal balance of power. The merger of SPP and Hacienda under Aspe in January once again created a single economic "czar" in the tradition of Ortiz Mena. To balance this new "superagency," Salinas also created the new Ministry of Social Development (Secretaría de Desarollo Social, Sedesol) in April 1992. The new ministry combined the old Ecology and Urban Development Secretariat (SEDUE) with the government's housing arm (Infonavit) and the development bank in charge of infrastructural investment (Banobras). Most important, Sedeso contained the office of PRONASOL, over which the president retained some direct control.[64] The president named the ex-PRI chief, Luis Donaldo Colosio, as the first minister of this agency. Combined with his considerable influence in the PRI he had led for three years, the massive reservoir of patronage available in Sedesol made Colosio the equal of any of the heads of Gobernación in the years of that agency's glory.

61. *El Universal* (Mexico City), January 8, 1992, p. 1.

62. One source told me that since Salinas had followed this strategy to overshadow de la Madrid, especially after 1986, he was well aware of the potential of Zedillo's power. He was committed to preventing a "salinazo" during *his* presidency (interview, Mexico City, November 1989).

63. Various persons with whom I spoke about Córdoba in 1990 to 1991 agreed with this assessment.

64. *La Jornada* (Mexico City), April 13, 1992.

Salinas thus appeared to have re-created the parallel government that existed prior to 1970. The economic power of Hacienda would balance the political clout of the new Sedesol. There were also rumors that the president would create yet a third superministry around Gobernación for his good friend Manuel Camacho. The president could thus dominate the entire government using this new political triangle as his base. What is particularly interesting is that Salinas had constructed this system after he had already established his supremacy, thereby assuring that no single minister or alliance would challenge his authority. The centralization of authority within the state and inside the bureaucracy had reached its apex.

The institutional structure of the Mexican state satisfied two of the conditions identified in Chapter 2 as critical to the success of economic restructuring: autonomy and centralization. Prior to 1970 a balance of power inside the historically dominant bureaucracy prevented any single group from controlling policy. After this date a core within this institution was able to amass resources and further increase the already significant centralization of the Mexican regime. In responding to the crises of the 1980s, this central power was able to impose its particular view of Mexico's future. Political machines do not move by themselves, however, but require someone to guide them. In the next chapter I will describe the men and women who occupied the labyrinths of power I have defined.

# ELITES

# 5

## The Technocratic Vanguard

Nearly thirty years ago Frank Brandenburg defined the Mexican state as being ruled by an elite or "Revolutionary Family" consisting of the president, members of the cabinet, the heads of the major decentralized agencies and the large parastatals, the executive committee of the party, and prominent governors, senators, and deputies.[1] Few families have been analyzed in so much detail in the three decades since Brandenburg's definition, and certainly no other Latin American state personnel has undergone the scholarly scrutiny to which the Mexican political and administrative elite has been subjected.[2]

1. *The Making of Modern Mexico*, 1964, pp. 158–159. See also Carolyn Needleman and Martin Needleman, "Who Rules Mexico? A Critique of Some Current Views on the Mexican Political Process," 1969. Robert E. Scott, *Mexican Government in Transition* (1964), and Frank Tannenbaum, *Mexico: The Struggle for Peace and Bread* (1960), agreed that the Mexican chief executive was one of the most powerful in the world but believed that this power was shared by the political bureaucracy of the PRI and some of the state agencies.

2. See Peter H. Smith, *Labyrinths of Power: Political Recruitment in Twentieth-Century Mexico*, 1979. The work of Camp on Mexican elites may only be described as encyclopedic, and the reader is referred to the bibliography for a list of relevant works. Other sources include: Raymond Vernon, *The Dilemma of Mexico's Development*, 1963; James Cochrane, "Mexico's New Científicos," 1967; Wilfred Gruber, "Career Patterns in Mexico's Political Elite," 1971; Merilee Grindle, "Policy Change in an Authoritarian Regime: Mexico under Echeverría," 1977; Grindle, *Bureaucrats, Politicians, and Peasants in Mexico*, 1977; Grindle, "Power, Expertise, and the *Técnico*," 1977; C. E. Grimes and Charles Simmons, "Bureaucracy and Political Control in Mexico: Towards an Assessment," 1969; Christopher Mitchell, "The Role of Technocrats in Latin American Integration," 1967; John Nagle, *System and Succession: The Social Bases of Elite Recruitment*, 1977; Guillermo Kelley, "Politics and Administration in Mexico: Recruitment and Promotion of the Político-Administrative Class," 1981; and Claude Gilbert, "Le Mexique: Les hauts fonctionnaires introuvables?" in Daniele Lochak et al., eds., *La haute*

What makes the current Mexican elite particularly interesting is that in analyzing recent trends in its composition, one may find evidence supporting practically every theoretical proposition regarding elites.[3] Some refer to the increasing representation of those bureaucrats with links to private capital (through family, education, or career) as evidence of a class-based domination of the state.[4] Others emphasize changes in the type of expertise required by the regime and analyze the rise of technocrats with scientific and managerial training and the subsequent decline of the more traditional political elite.[5] A third approach focuses on the relative power of political institutions and the definition of a dominant elite by career patterns.[6] Finally, a great deal of attention has been paid to the role of networks and bureaucratic cliques known as *camarillas*.[7]

More significant than the relative importance of specific elite attributes is the manner in which each of these characteristics contributes to a specific elite profile and outlook on the world. Through education, ideology, functional position, and network membership technocrats

*administration et la politique*, 1986. For Mexican views see Pablo González Casanova, *El estado y los partidos políticos en México*, 1982, pp. 114–122; Carlos Sirvent, *Las clases dirigentes en México*, 1973; Jorge Alonso, *La dialéctica clases-elites en México*, 1976, pp. 140–142; Héctor Aguilar Camín, *Transición política: El monstruo que vendra en el desafío mexicano*, 1982, pp. 91–95; Gilberto Ramírez and Emilio Salim Cabrera, *La clase política mexicana*, 1987. For an excellent summary of the personnel trends, see "El sistema político mexicano," 1980, pp. 37–60. For a summary of the literature on Latin American technocratic elites, see Miguel Ángel Centeno, "The New Científicos: Technocratic Politics in Mexico, 1970–1990," 1990, Chapter 3.

   3. For an analysis of the inevitability of political control by a technocratic elite, see Alfred Frisch, "Les previsions a l'épreuve de la réalité: L'exemple de la technocratie," 1973, pp. 267–291; and Juan Ferrando, "Las elites," 1976, pp. 7–26. For a parallel discussion regarding the role of managers and owners within private firms, see Adolph Berle and Gardner Means, *The Modern Corporation and Private Property*, 1932. On elite theory see the work of Gaetano Mosca, Vilfredo Pareto, Robert Michels, C. Wright Mills, Michel Crozier, Alain Touraine, Floyd Hunter, G. William Domhoff, Robert Putnam, Ezra Suleiman, Mattei Dogan, and Serge Mallet.

   4. Bertha Lerner de Sheinbaum, "La technocracia en México: Ni embrión, ni garantia de profesionalismo," 1983.

   5. Raymond Vernon used this argument to explain the rise of an earlier generation of experts in the economic ministries (*The Dilemma of Mexico's Development*). See also Peter H. Smith, "Leadership and Change, Intellectuals and Technocrats in Mexico," in Roderic Camp, ed., *Mexico's Political Stability: The Next Ten Years*, 1986.

   6. Miguel Ángel Centeno and Sylvia Maxfield, "The Marriage of Finance and Order: Changes in the Mexican Political Elite," 1992.

   7. Roderic Camp, "Camarillas in Mexican Politics: The Case of the Salinas Cabinet," 1990; Rogelio Hernández Rodríguez, "Los hombres de Presidente de la Madrid," 1987; Miguel Ángel Centeno and Jeffrey Weldon, "Small Circle of Friends," 1991.

bring to policy making a distinctive perspective centered on the application of theoretical knowledge. That perspective helps determine the political and economic development of the state on whose commanding heights they sit. If we are to understand the new elite's prevailing biases for perceiving, assessing, and acting upon social problems and how these helped shape the technocratic revolution, then we must understand their social origins, education, and professional training. In short, who they were helped determine what they did.

The changes in elite composition and the resulting personnel profile analyzed in the following pages parallel the institutional transformations described in the previous two chapters. The Mexican technocrats utilized their organizational strength, ideological cohesion, and institutional autonomy to seize power and lead Mexico through a restructuring of its political and economic systems. The success of the technocratic revolution required not only the autonomy of the bureaucracy and the centralization of power within it but the willingness and inclination to use this opportunity. Revolutions require a vanguard, if not necessarily to inspire at least to organize and define some of its directions. Technocratic revolutions are no different. The leadership may not be dynamic and may operate in bureaucratic labyrinths rather than in the barricades, but its influence can be as important to the shape of the revolution as the that of the most romantic leader on horseback. The new elite's willingness and readiness to use all power available to enforce its view of the political and economic future of Mexico played a significant role in shaping the new state.

## Técnicos and Políticos

In recent years a great deal of attention has been devoted to the development within the Mexican elite of a new group of *técnicos* and the decline in the fortunes of a more traditional elite of *políticos*. In Mexican popular usage the two terms are used to distinguish differences in career patterns (bureaucratic versus electoral experience), qualifications for entry (expertise versus loyal service to the party), basis for legitimacy (professional administration versus continuation of Revolutionary heritage), and ideological guidelines (technical versus political rationales). They may also reflect geographical (Federal District versus provinces), generational (post–1940 versus pre–1940), and possibly racial and class differences.

While the selection of Miguel de la Madrid and Carlos Salinas de Gortari as the PRI candidates of 1982 and 1988, and their subsequent personnel appointments, confirmed that a new generation had taken over as the leading elite group, there was some debate as to whether these changes implied a significant break with the past. A prominent journalist, Elías Chavez, claimed that Miguel de la Madrid's cabinet marked a break with the previous regimes as important as that which occurred between military and civilian control in the 1940s and that their empowerment would bring on a "new government project."[8] Various Mexican experts, however, while accepting the rise of the *técnicos* as a given, questioned their capacity or willingness to change government policies in any significant manner.[9] While noting the important differences between *políticos* and *técnicos,* many observers also have suggested that, in practice, the two were hard to tell apart. "*Técnicos* often bear a close resemblance to *políticos,*" Peter Smith notes, and both get their jobs through direct or indirect personal ties.[10]

A major obstacle to the systematic analysis of the different subtypes within the governing elite has been the generally vague criteria used to label individuals and the failure to establish the comparative significance of each factor.[11] I am proposing a more complex analytical definition of the elite that will clarify the particular combination of attributes that both supported the rise of those currently in power and helped shape their policies. The Mexican elite consists of four different groups, *políticos, burocratas políticos, técnicos,* and *tecnócratas.* Each has a distinct background, professional profile, and political function.

The *políticos* are the true "dinosaurs"[12] of the regime, managing the nominally representative sections of the PRI and the communications

8. "Primero los militares; luego los civiles; ahora, a salvar la nave, los financieros," *Proceso,* no. 321 (December 31, 1982), pp. 7–9.

9. Lerner de Sheinbaum, "La tecnocracia en México"; Arnoldo Cordova interview with Oscar Hinojosa, *Proceso,* no. 229 (March 16, 1981). Interviews, Mexico City, June 1986, January–June 1988, November 1989.

10. Smith, *Labyrinths of Power,* pp. 248, 252.

11. But see the work of Miguel Basáñez (1982), who divided the bureaucratic elite into three components—*políticos, técnicos,* and *especialistas*—each with a set of representative organizations (for example, the PRI, and the Treasury and Agriculture Ministries, respectively) that both shaped and supported the policy perspectives of each group. Camp (1985) also distinguished between three career paths: the electoral, which dominated until the 1930s; the electoral-administrative, which lasted through the 1960s; and the purely administrative, which has dominated since the 1970s. These are similar to those defined by Smith (1979).

12. This is the name by which these persons are widely known in Mexico.

between these sectors and the national executive. The *políticos* serve as the ward bosses of the system, managing the distribution of patronage and arranging for attendance at political rallies and the subsequent electoral support for PRI candidates. Their power has been steadily declining for years due to cuts in government revenues, the urbanization of the population, the development of independent organizations, and their gradual disappearance from the bureaucracy. Among them one will find the highest relative representation of worker and peasant backgrounds, the lowest percentage born in the capital, the lowest average educational attainment, and the highest degrees of party militancy. One might also expect, at least among the younger members, a stronger commitment to the ideals of the Revolution than that found in the other groups, but much of this militant generation has moved to the opposition PRD.

The *burocratas políticos* differ from the *políticos* in that they do not directly represent any constituency but make their careers inside the national office of the party and *were* responsible for deciding how the federal pie would be distributed among the various sectors. One would expect to find lower representation of upper-class backgrounds than among the *técnicos* and *tecnócratas* but much fewer with working-class or peasant origins than among the *políticos*. *Burocratas políticos* will have attended UNAM and other state universities, and, if they have studied abroad, they will have done so in Europe or Latin America and *not* in the United States. The majority will have studied law. They have worked for the PRI in relatively high posts but have little experience with mass-level militancy. Career experience does not make them electoral politicians but rather political managers. They have developed little functional or substantive specialization. Traditionally, this was the most powerful wing of the governing elite concerned with the maintenance of political stability with a minimum of change in the system. Presidents prior to 1970 could be classified as such, but the power of this elite group has been declining since the *sexenio* of Luis Echeverría.

*Técnicos* originate in the professional and managerial middle class. They attend state schools and U.S. universities where they obtain Licenciaturas in a variety of fields, but especially technical areas such as economics, engineering, agriculture, and the natural sciences. This wing really consists of two groups: the economists in Treasury and the banking sector and the engineers in the ministries of Ecology and Urban Development (SEDUE) (before 1992), Agriculture, Energy (SEMIP), parts of Communications (SCT), Commerce, and the parastatals. It also includes doctors and scientists in the Ministry of Health and in the Social Security Administration (IMSS) as well as the diplomats in the Foreign Service.

The *técnicos'* commitment to their area of expertise and their refusal to play the "dirty games" of politics strengthened their positions but also limited their influence. The professional and civil service tradition that supported the autonomy of the *técnicos* depended on maintaining limits on the role of the state in Mexican society. As the scope of government action became more politically sensitive, the *técnicos'* orthodoxy and unwillingness or inability to play politics became both a liability and an obstacle to their maintaining their influence.[13] The traditional *técnico* who did not normally belong to the party, much less participate in it, who quietly rose through the professional ranks and only attained cabinet-level positions after a long career, and who kept a disdainful distance from "politics," has largely disappeared, at least within the economic/financial ministries, if not the more technical services such as Agriculture, Health, and Communications and Transport.

The authority of these technicians has been consistently eroded by the rise of the new group, what Grindle and Camp have called "political technocrats" and I am calling *tecnócratas*. The new political generation cannot be squeezed into either a *político* or a *técnico* box. Rather, these persons represent a new hybrid with characteristics of its own, as well as several borrowed from both groups. They combine the educational credentials of one and the political access and acumen of the other. If they have taken over the top of the political pyramid from the *burócratas políticos,* they have also challenged the control of *técnicos* over economic decision making. Unlike the *técnicos, tecnócratas* were able to transfer their control over technical areas to overall command of the state through access to dominant positions in the hierarchy. Where previously the cabinets were political mosaics in which various groups were represented and formed a synthesis of interests, styles, ambitions, and

---

13. A classic example of this behavior was the tenure of Jesús Silva Herzog as director of the Infonavit, the government's main agency for providing low-cost housing. Upon arriving at Infonavit, Silva Herzog established a computer system that would assign housing priorities and distribute units in a "just, efficient and noncorruptible" manner. This, of course, met opposition from the labor unions who wished to utilize the sources of Infonavit to support its patronage machine. When in 1976 López Portillo needed the support of labor in passing the IMF austerity program, the labor leadership demanded control of Infonavit. In these circumstances the "just" and "efficient" system was no longer convenient and Silva Herzog was forced out. See José Antonio Aldrete, "Hacia un nuevo enfoque para el estudio de la acción burocrática estatal: La política de vivienda del INFONAVIT," 1983, p. 347.

talents, the technocrats established a practical monopoly over large parts of the state administration and used this organizational base to launch their revolution.[14]

This group is much more homogenous in terms of educational and social background than the others and possesses much stronger intragroup network linkages than the other types. The *tecnócratas* are the most likely to have fathers in the political and economic elite. They study economics in UNAM or private universities (especially ITAM and Colegio de México) and obtain graduate degrees from elite schools in the United States. They are politically active in the national level of the PRI, but mostly in the "technical" branch (IEPES) or shadow cabinet around the president-elect. They are not party militants but have used the PRI to encroach on the territory of the *burocratas políticos*. Career patterns are characterized by entry into the bureaucracy at relatively high levels, which allows them to skip long institutional apprenticeships. They are concentrated in those organizations in charge of planning, particularly SPP (before 1992). Despite the smaller number of professional years (the result of their relative youth), they exhibit more institutional mobility and are less bound to specific bureaucratic territories.

As we will see in the following pages, the attributes associated with this last group have come to largely dominate the Mexican elite. The first section below analyzes demographics and social origins. The second discusses educational patterns. The next section focuses on political activity. The fourth and fifth sections analyze career patterns in the private and public sectors.[15] Chapter 6 will analyze the structure of their professional and personal networks.

14. Saul Álvarez Mosqueda, quoted in Alejandro Ramos, José Martínez, and Carlos Ramírez, *Salinas de Gortari: Candidato de la crisis,* 1987, p. 331.

15. The following information is partly based on a data bank created using the *Diccionario biográfico del gobierno mexicano,* published by the Unidad de la Crónica Presidencial in the Ministry of the Presidency. Unless otherwise noted figures cited are from this data bank. The three editions (1984, 1987, 1989) were based on surveys taken in 1983, 1986, and 1989 of all persons in the bureaucracy at the level of director general or above as well as all members of Congress and officers in the judicial system. The response rate for the bureaucracy was over 95 percent. I obtained a copy of these studies and proceeded to code the biographical entries for computer analysis. The details on categories and criteria used will be given for each set of variables as they are analyzed. When entries were missing data for critical variables, I decided not to eliminate them from the entire sample as these gaps were relatively sparse and well distributed. Some parts of the 1989 data bank are taken from preliminary research by Maria Isabel Reuter on contemporary networks. I have also utilized the statistical summaries provided in each edition and Roderic Camp's *Mexican Political Biographies 1935–1981,* 1982.

# Cohorts and Social Origins

Age cohort effects are an important factor in determining the perspective of any group. First, the historical environment in which one grows up helps shape political and social attitudes.[16] Second, future elites may also be shaped by the particular moment during which they entered government. The crises faced in their professionally formative years, the solutions offered, and the success and failures of these, will, no doubt, provide an important reference with which to appraise current situations.

One of the most distinguishing characteristics of the Mexican bureaucratic elite is its relative youth. Half of those in the middle to upper levels of the bureaucracy in 1983 were born after 1939, and over a quarter were in their thirties.[17] This generation remained the largest block in 1989, representing nearly 40 percent of those in the upper reaches of the bureaucracy. In 1983 the cabinet and subcabinet were dominated by personnel born before 1940 (81.5 percent and 58.3 percent respectively) and by those who entered the government service before 1970. By 1989, however, over 50 percent of the subcabinet (including roughly one hundred positions below the ministers) was born after 1942. While the median age of the first Salinas cabinet was fifty-two, it was really composed of two cohorts: the relatively young, in their late thirties and early forties, who occupied the majority of the most powerful positions and were closest to the president (born in 1948), and those in their middle to late fifties who occupied second-rank positions or who were without consistent access to Salinas.

Most of the bureaucratic personnel were recruited during the *sexenio* in which they reached their mid-twenties (median age in 1983: 27). The median year for entry into the civil service among the bureaucratic elite of Miguel de la Madrid was 1968. By the late 1980s the majority had entered

16. In the United States, for example, there are many references to the different views of generations who came of age during the Great Depression, during World War II, Vietnam, et cetera.

17. Unless otherwise specified the terms bureaucracy, upper level, or elite refer to the over one thousand functionaries with a position of director general or above. The director general is the third highest hierarchical level in the bureaucracy and probably the lowest level at which policy decisions are made. When discussing more specific grades (for example, the subcabinet), I will make explicit references to the definition of the group.

**Table 5-1.**  Social Origins of Political Elite

|  | Executive | | | Legislative | | Provincial |
|---|---|---|---|---|---|---|
|  | 1983(a) (%) | 1986(b) (%) | 1989(c) (%) | 1983(d) (%) | 1989(e) (%) | 1989(f) (%) |
| Age at survey(g) | | | | | | |
| Below 30 | 1.1 | 0.3 | 0.0 | 2.7 | 2.7 | 2.9 |
| 30–39 | 27.7 | 18.8 | 10.3 | 21.7 | 24.8 | 21.5 |
| 40–49 | 38.9 | 46.0 | 45.0 | 35.0 | 32.7 | 45.0 |
| 50–59 | 21.4 | 23.0 | 28.3 | 25.3 | 19.6 | 22.5 |
| 60 and over | 10.9 | 11.8 | 16.4 | 15.3 | 11.1 | 8.0 |
| DK | 0.0 | 0.0 | 0.0 | 0.0 | 9.1 | 0.0 |
| Total(j) | 100.0 | 100.0 | 100.0 | 100.0 | 100.0 | 100.0 |
| Place of birth(h) | | | | | | |
| Federal district | 52.2 | 55.2 | 55.8 | 10.0 | 13.0 | 10.4 |
| Other urban | 14.1 | 14.0 | 12.2 | n.a. | n.a. | n.a. |
| Rural | 34.1 | 30.9 | 31.9 | n.a. | n.a. | n.a. |
| Total(j) | 100.0 | 100.0 | 100.0 | | | |
| Father's occupation(i) | | | | | | |
| Professional | 38.2 | 39.4 | 40.9 | n.a. | 13.5 | 28.6 |
| Business | 34.8 | 34.2 | 31.5 | n.a. | 24.8 | 30.0 |
| Government | 14.2 | 13.5 | 13.7 | n.a. | 4.1 | 7.1 |
| Peasant/labor | 6.7 | 6.3 | 6.3 | n.a. | 5.6 | 1.0 |
| Other/DK | 6.0 | 6.6 | 7.6 | n.a. | 52.0 | 33.3 |
| Total(j) | 100.0 | 100.0 | 100.0 | n.a. | 100.0 | 100.0 |

(a) Data bank of bureaucratic personnel (Director Generals or above) based on 1984 edition of *Diccionario biográfico* with N=1278.

(b) Data bank of 1983(a) list also appearing in 1987 edition of *Diccionario biográfico* with N=606.

(c) Data bank of 1983(a) list also appearing in 1989 edition of *Diccionario biográfico* with N=381.

(d) Statistical Summary of Legislative Branch (Senate and House of Representatives), *Diccionario biográfico* (3rd ed.). N=451.

(e) Statistical Summary of Legislative Branch (Senate and House of Representatives), *Diccionario biográfico* (3rd ed.). N=560.

(f) Statistical Summary of State Governments (Governors and Staffs), *Diccionario biográfico* (3rd ed.). N=311.

(g) I have used age at time of survey instead of YOB in order to compare with information from the statistical summaries. Note that the age-increases in the executive branch from 1983 to 1989 reflect the aging of a single cohort who remained in power.

(h) "Other urban" includes cities with population over 50,000 in 1960 and provincial capitals. Note that data for rural areas are higher than in previously published versions of the data because of different category definitions.

(i) Professions includes lawyers, doctors, technicians, teachers. Business includes *comerciantes*, businessmen, private-sector employees. Also includes *agricultor/ganadero*, as this implies larger property size than *campesino*.

(j) Might not equal 100% due to rounding.

after 1970.[18] The post-1982 elite thus entered the government in the period during which the central bureaucracy, and particularly the agencies around the president, began to distance themselves from the party and the traditional political class, and government policies began to emphasize complex plans and technical sophistication in policy making.

The leading elite group also grew up during the years of Mexico's economic miracle and stable political rule. This was the generation that witnessed the rupture of that model in 1968 and the changes of the 1970s. They not only saw that growth was possible under certain circumstances but also witnessed how fragile this economic model could be if not supported by adequate policies. In the absence of systematic interview data and without access to detailed intellectual biographies, it is difficult to judge how much these experiences helped mold the new elite's attitudes toward state policies. The socialization by both the success and failure of the "Miracle" and the problems experienced thereafter must have helped shape generational attitudes toward the relative roles of public and private investment, democracy, and political legitimacy. Even if we cannot define exactly what these may be, it is likely that the common experiences contributed to a shared perspective that would further strengthen the social, educational, and professional homogeneity of the elite.

The social origins of the elite can also provide useful insights into the mechanisms that determine access to political power in Mexico. The extent to which the upper reaches of the bureaucracy represent a very select socioeconomic sector has implications for the supposed meritocracy of the administrative system. Social background may also contribute to the creation of a shared elite mind-set that in turn helps determine public policy.

Place of birth is an important indicator of social position as there remain significant differences in income and access to social services between the various regions in Mexico. Moreover, each region is associated with diverse cultural and political attitudes.[19] The wide gulf that

18. Rogelio Hernández Rodríguez identified the *sexenio* of Luis Echeverría (1970–1976) as the turning point leading to the domination by a new elite ("Los hombres del Presidente de la Madrid").

19. The north has traditionally been the stronghold of the conservative opposition party, the PAN. Monterrey, which serves as the urban center for this area and is the home of many of Mexico's most powerful private firms, has traditionally served as a counterpoint to Mexico City. Opposition to the Revolutionary government in the 1920s was concentrated in the central

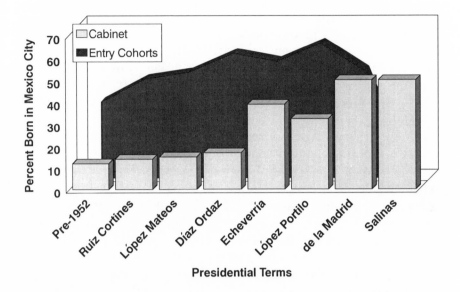

Fig. 5-1.    Representation of Mexico City. (Source: Roderic Camp, *Mexican Political Biographies, 1935–1981*, 1982; Presidencia de la República, *Diccionario biográfico del gobierno mexicano*, eds. 1st, 2nd, 3rd. Cohorts are based on elite's date of entry into government.)

exists between the major cities and the countryside may be even more significant than regional differences. As in most of Latin America the population in the small towns and villages lives in practically a different country from those with access to the financial and cultural resources of the towns. Even within classes these differences can be substantial, not only in terms of opportunities for education and professional success but also in helping to shape general attitudes.

During the twenty years following the fall of Díaz in 1911, the leadership was dominated by northerners who had served in the victorious

region, particularly during the Cristero Rebellion. Like Monterrey, Guadalajara is considered a more conservative city than the capital, but it is less linked to private sector manufacturing and more associated with a "traditional" opposition led by the Church. The Cardenista opposition in 1988 received its greatest support in the state of Michoacán (home of the candidate) and in the Federal District. The south has historically been and remains the poorest area of the country and the one with the stongest indigenous presence. The massive deposits of oil found in Tabasco and off the Gulf Coast have not directly benefited its population, but it is widely considered the safest region for the PRI.

Revolutionary armies, but since the 1930s those from the central region, and especially from Mexico City, have predominated.[20] While the countryside never produced many cabinet members (usually around one-fourth depending on the *sexenio*), other urban centers were important. While the capital accounted for less than 10 percent of the Cárdenas cabinet, its representation increased with Luis Echeverría, and by the 1980s more than half of the cabinet had been born in Mexico City and an even larger percentage had been raised there. This pattern persists if we look at the different entry cohorts of the elites in 1983 and 1989. If we compare these figures with those for the distribution of the population as a whole, the overrepresentation of the capital is clear. Even using the highest population estimates, Mexico City accounts for less than one-quarter of the total population. Given the wide discrepancies between regions and cities, this indicates that the elite represents a very favored sector of the Mexican population.

The exclusive and selective character of the elite becomes more obvious if we analyze its class origins. The racial/ethnic makeup is perhaps an even more dramatic example, but I do not have systematic data on this issue. While father's occupation can only serve as a rough approximation of socioeconomic position, much less class, it can provide an indication of the social representation within the bureaucratic elite. Combining information from Peter Smith's study (1979) with the 1983 data divided by entry cohorts, we find that the representation of bureaucrats from working-class and peasant families has declined steadily, accounting for 3.8 percent of those who entered during the de la Madrid *sexenio* and 7.0 percent of the total of those in the upper levels of the bureaucracy at the beginning of his administration, as opposed to 24 percent during 1946–1971. By 1989, out of a total of 1,113, 8 bureaucrats said their fathers were peasants while 10 listed them as workers. Even if we include the more *político* positions where one would expect a greater representation of working-class and peasant backgrounds, we find that in 1989 only 8.3 percent of all governors, senators, cabinet, and subcabinet members emerge from peasant or working-class origins. The membership of the legislature was somewhat more representative (the figures for state government are even worse), but even there peasant or laborer fathers account for less than 6 percent of the sample in 1989.

---

20. The only exceptions are those cases where a president has established a regional political machine and brings some of these allies with him into the cabinet (for example, the overrepresentation of natives from Veracruz during the *sexenio* of Miguel Alemán).

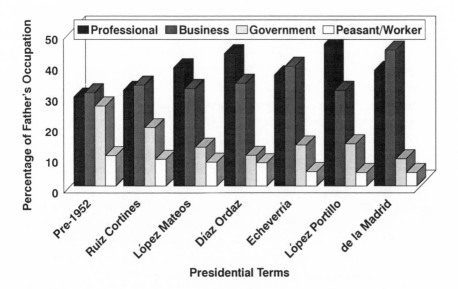

**Presidential Terms**

Fig. 5-2.   Social origins by entry cohorts. (Source: Presidencia de la República, *Diccionario biográfico del gobierno mexicano,* eds. 1st, 2nd, 3rd. Cohorts are based on bureaucratic elite's date of entry into government service.)

Studies by Miguel Basáñez indicate that the representativeness of the elite has declined since the 1970s. According to his figures (which include nonbureaucratic political elites), the number with "popular" origins has declined steadily since Echeverría and plummeted during the de la Madrid *sexenio*.[21] Overall, the bureaucratic elite has very few representatives of the classes for which the Revolution was supposedly fought. The elite in control of the state administration is perhaps even less representative than the Porfiriato that it replaced.[22] This is even clearer if we compare these figures to the information available for the Mexican population as a whole. In 1960, for example, only 17.6 percent of the population was categorized as belonging to the upper or middle

21. *El pulso de los sexenios: Veinte años de crisis en México,* 1990, pp. 123–127.
22. All the sources attest that a circulation of elites did occur after 1910 and that those in commanding positions today do not represent the same families that were in power seventy years ago. However, there are some indications that the families to which some of these persons belong had been in positions of privilege before the Revolution. For example, while not as significant as the German "von," the use of "de" in the family name or "y" linking two family names indicates aristocratic origins, and these are fairly common in the elite.

classes, as compared to over 90 percent of the bureaucratic personnel for whom we have adequate information.[23]

Few bureaucrats' fathers had served in the government, while a significant percentage (34 percent in 1983 and 27 percent in 1989) had fathers in private business.[24] This would refute Smith's contention regarding the split between public and private elites and would indicate that, at least in recent years, the progeny of these two groups have come to share some career patterns.[25] The relatively small representation of bureaucrats' children indicates that we cannot speak of a government *nomenklatura*. If the bureaucracy belongs to any class, it is to the professional and business sectors from the major cities.[26]

Social origins are relatively poor predictors of a bureaucrat's relative position and were insignificant predictors of survival once in the elite.[27] The pattern suggested by the data would seem to indicate that social origins do affect one's chances of entering the elite, but once inside the "inner circle," these factors become less significant.

The only possible exception to this rule may be at the very top of the hierarchy, and it is difficult to determine how much of a systematic effect exists. On the one hand, among members of the cabinet and subcabinet, and governors and senators in 1989, only 10.4 percent could be classified as the progeny of civil servants. On the other hand, the families of the three presidents since 1970 had been prominent in state politics and

23. Quoted in Smith, *Labyrinths of Power*, p. 43. The 1960 figures are useful because they reflect the social structure of the country when the new elite was growing up and when their father's occupation was most relevant.

24. The actual percentage of civil servants' children, however, is probably much higher but is obscured by the number of respondents who list their father's original profession as opposed to that role for which he is best known. The representation of those whose fathers worked in the government declines through entry cohorts since 1952 but this may reflect the concentration of diplomats and military men in the older cohorts, since these groups include the largest percentage of second generation civil servants.

25. *Labyrinths of Power*, pp. 214–216. I do not have similar data on private sector employees, but it *appears* that the children of government workers are much less likely to cross this career line.

26. While there did not appear to be a strong relationship between father's occupation and place of birth, it does seem that the sons of professionals are associated with the capital and business origins are more closely correlated with the provinces (particularly the cities of Monterrey and Guadalajara). This finding might be of particular importance given that the business sector of the latter cities is closely associated with a conservative market-oriented approach. Moreover, the large representation of these persons also contradicts the idea of the northern bourgeoisie being reluctant to participate in government.

27. Centeno and Weldon, "Small Circle of Friends."

in local affairs for several generations, and the fathers of the three leading candidates for the 1988 PRI presidential nomination had all served
as governors, senators, ministers, or a combination of the three.

I would propose that this phenomenon has less to do with the direct
inheritance of a position than with the cultural capital obtained by those
from prominent political families. That is, those from such backgrounds
can access an already established network of potential supporters and
are familiar with intraelite negotiations and alliances, the structure of the
various factions, and the history of these relationships. This informal
knowledge of the rules of the game would be invaluable in establishing
their domination. As I describe in the next chapter, the skill with which
members of the elite played the organizational politics inside the bureaucracy made a significant contribution to their success. Such expertise is
not usually acquired in the classroom but through an intensive exposure
to elite politics. The children of a lawyer or businessman share with that
of a prominent public figure clear advantages over the progeny of poorer
parents. In the competition for leadership posts, however, the politician's
child has an apparent advantage.

The gender makeup of the elite also contributes to its relative homogeneity and exclusivity. In 1983 there were only 65 women in the entire
sample of 1,278, and in 1989 there were 58 out of 1,113, most of whom
were relegated to either marginal positions (personal assistants) or "ghet-
toized" in ministries such as Education. The legislature was slightly more
representative with 10.9 percent women in 1983 and 12 percent in 1989.
The only ministry with a significant number of women in high-level
positions in 1983 was the Secretariat of Programming and Budget. While
this might indicate Salinas de Gortari's commitment to less sexist recruitment, he did not significantly increase representation of women in his
bureaucracy. He did, however, name two women to his cabinet, both of
whom were considered quite influential despite the relatively marginal
position of their posts (Fisheries and Auditing).

The unequal access to bureaucratic positions reflects the rampant
inequality that still dominates Mexican society. Such inequality in access
helped shape the technocratic revolution in two ways. First, it is important to recognize that much of the new elite grew up in the rarefied
atmosphere of upper-class Mexican society. Such economic segregation
means that these persons' perspective on Mexican reality inevitably reflected their social background. This is not to say that their policies
should be understood as originating in an instrumentalist class strategy.

Rather, I wish to emphasize the role played by early socialization in defining what possibilities existed for Mexico, what costs were acceptable, and who would have to bear these burdens. This specific construction of reality and of political and economic potential was reinforced by the personal networks built during the elite's youth which later served as channels of information. While some members of the elite later spent considerable amounts of time outside of Polanco and Las Lomas, a limited exposure to the misery of large parts of the population could not possibly overcome decades of socialization.

Second, the most significant lesson to be found in this data is not only the general exclusivity of the bureaucratic elite or its potential identification with the interests of a particular class but its geographic and social homogeneity. This, in turn, contributed to the cohesion of the elite and facilitated the implementation of its program. While there were significant disagreements regarding the best policies for Mexico, the elite shared a set of assumptions and outlooks that mitigated divisions and allowed it to speak with a single voice.

# Education

Since the *sexenio* of Luis Echeverría educational credentials have become increasingly important both for access to the very top of the bureaucratic pyramid and for recruitment at all levels.[28] Moreover, a very specific type of training has come to dominate, as the representation of those who studied economics, who attended Mexican private universities and foreign institutions (especially in the United States), and who obtained a graduate degree increased after 1970.

Throughout the 1980s the bureaucratic elite represented a highly educated sector of the Mexican society with over 97 percent of the sample having obtained at least a college degree, compared to a national percent-

---

28. The sources used to compile the information in this section do not include data on education prior to college. However, it is possible that secondary schools may serve a critical function in the establishment of elite networks even prior to university. While the National Preparatory School (associated with UNAM) had previously served this function, it appears that the new elite received their preuniversity education at private—and most significantly, given the history of state-Church battles over education—at religiously affiliated schools. See Roderic Camp, *Mexico's Leaders: Their Education and Recruitment*, 1980.

**Table 5-2.**   Education of Political Elite

| | Executive | | | Legislative | | Provincial |
|---|---|---|---|---|---|---|
| | 1983(a) (%) | 1986(b) (%) | 1989(c) (%) | 1983(d) (%) | 1989(e) (%) | 1989(f) (%) |
| Level of education(g) | | | | | | |
| B.A. or less | 41.7 | 37.0 | 35.4 | 86.0 | 75.4 | 67.8 |
| Some grad | 24.9 | 26.2 | 25.2 | 14.0 | n.a. | n.a. |
| Master's | 20.2 | 22.0 | 22.8 | n.a. | 10.7 | 26.4 |
| Ph.D. | 13.1 | 14.9 | 16.5 | n.a. | 4.1 | 5.8 |
| DK | 0.0 | 0.0 | 0.0 | 0.0 | 9.8 | 0.0 |
| Total(j) | 100.0 | 100.0 | 100.0 | 100.0 | 100.0 | 100.0 |
| Place of education(h) | | | | | | |
| UNAM B.A. | 57.9 | 62.3 | 62.8 | 30.8 | 23.4 | 31.2 |
| Mexican private B.A. | 13.6 | 14.0 | 15.6 | 4.0 | 5.0 | 5.1 |
| U.S. | 22.1 | 23.8 | 25.5 | 2.9 | 3.0 | 5.0 |
| Subject(i) | | | | | | |
| Law | 25.0 | 24.6 | 26.5 | 32.7 | 29.1 | 40.5 |
| Engineer/science | 30.0 | 25.7 | 26.2 | 12.0 | 19.0 | 26.0 |
| Econ/administration | 42.0 | 45.6 | 45.7 | 13.0 | 14.0 | 23.0 |

(a) Data bank of bureaucratic personnel (Director Generals or above) based on 1984 edition of *Diccionario biográfico* with N=1278.
(b) Data bank of 1983(a) list also appearing in 1987 edition of *Diccionario biográfico* with N=606.
(c) Data bank of 1983(a) list also appearing in 1989 edition of *Diccionario biográfico* with N=381.
(d) Statistical Summary of Legislative Branch, *Diccionario biográfico* (1st ed.).
(e) Statistical Summary of Legislative Branch, *Diccionario biográfico* (3rd ed.).
(f) Statistical Summary of State Governments, *Diccionario biográfico* (3rd ed.).
(g) Because of different reporting procedures, the figures in the last three columns may not be comparable to those in the first three. The category "Some grad" includes those who attended graduate school but for whom I have no record of completion.
(h) Categories are not exclusive. Note that the last three columns may overestimate number.
(i) Categories are not exclusive. Note that the last three columns are approximations based on imperfect information.
(j) May not equal 100% due to rounding.

age of university attendance (without necessarily obtaining a degree) of 4.9 percent.[29] While one-third of the ministers under Cárdenas had not

29. If one looks at the entire bureaucratic apparatus, the figures are of course lower. The latest figures available are for 1975 and at that time 12.8 percent of *all* government employees had a Licenciatura (Censo de recursos humanos del sector público, 1975, pp. 45–47 and 140–143). Note should also be made of the apparently common habit of embellishing one's résumé with false educational credentials. For example, in early 1990 there was something of a

graduated from college, such credentials were practically required for entry into the de la Madrid and Salinas cabinets. This trend is even more striking if we look at postgraduate education. The percentage of those who obtained at least a master's degree increases across the entry cohorts of the de la Madrid bureaucracy for a total of 33.1 percent. In 1989 this figure had risen to 48 percent. We also find a similar trend within the *político* wing of the regime as nearly one-third of the senators and governors in 1989 had attended graduate school. At least with regards to education, therefore, the division between *técnico* and *político* career paths may be declining. These high educational requirements further reenforced the unequal access to elite positions by social origins described above.[30]

The National Autonomous University of Mexico (UNAM) has always played a critical role in the formation of the elite, and it remains the most important educational institution with over 50 percent of the 1980s bureaucratic population having obtained their undergraduate degrees there. This supports previous analyses of the elite that have emphasized the central role played by UNAM in establishing lifelong personal and professional relationships.[31]

Notwithstanding the importance of UNAM and other public universities, their influence or centrality appears to be declining.[32] Breaking down

---

miniscandal in Mexico regarding whether Salinas's assistant José Córdoba had received his Ph.D. from Stanford. Unfortunately, there is no way of systematically confirming the educational background of the entire elite population. For my analysis I have assumed that the proclivity to lie regarding one's education is randomly distributed across the relevant series of variables and that comparisons across them are therefore still significant. Moreover, even in those cases where respondents have lied, this demonstrates a preceived need for such credentials that indirectly attests to their importance in determining professional entry and success.

30. In the 1983 sample those from rural areas are much less likely to have continued their education past college, while those from the south (the most impoverished region) are also relatively unlikely to have done so. Those from Mexico City are more likely to obtain a postgraduate education than those from other urban centers. Regarding the importance of fathers' professions, the relationship is not so clear. What is interesting is that those whose fathers were in business are less likely to have advanced degrees than those whose fathers were professionals. This would support sociological analyses of the transference of cultural as opposed to financial capital. Supporting the work of Bourdieu, it appears that those from professional families place greater weight on educational credentials as a way of attaining and maintaining career success.

31. See Smith, *Labyrinths of Power*, 1979, pp. 84–86; and Camp, *Mexico's Leaders*. Other public schools such as the Instituto Politécnico Nacional, the Agricultural University, the Normal University, military acadamies, and the state universities are also important sources of elite recruitment accounting for a quarter of Licenciaturas.

32. The disciplinary trends discussed later in this chapter also have an effect on the relative influence of educational institutions. The National Autonomous University of Mexico

the 1983 sample into age and entry cohorts, the percentage of UNAM and other public school graduates declines for those born after 1944. While private universities remain relatively unimportant as sources of under-graduate education for the elite as a whole, and are barely represented in the cabinet, they played a major role in the recruitment of the youngest quartile in 1983. During the 1980s the percentage of the upper level of the elite who had obtained their undergraduate degree in a private university increased from 13.4 percent to 17.2 percent.

The distinctions between public and private are especially important in Mexico.[33] Not only does attendance in the latter automatically indi-cate membership in the upper class but the economic orthodoxy taught is significantly different. In UNAM, for example, Marxist analysis and a political-economy approach remain dominant, while most private univer-sities (with the possible exception of El Colegio de México) emphasize orthodox economics. Of special importance is the network development associated with each set of institutions detailed in Chapter 6.[34] This increase in the recruitment of personnel from private universities has accompanied an increase in the number of bureaucrats teaching in them, particularly the Autonomous Technological Institute of Mexico (ITAM) and Colegio de México. This further augments recruitment from such schools as the first contact between bureaucratic "fathers" and their "godchildren" often occurs in the classroom.[35]

Perhaps the most significant educational trend is the increasing impor-tance of graduate training outside of Mexico, which reinforces the process of international intellectual isomorphism described in Chapter 2.[36] By

---

(UNAM) is clearly dominant in most fields of undergraduate study, but its percentage of graduate students in economics and administration declines dramatically. So, while UNAM remains an important center of bureaucratic recruitment, it is particularly weak in that category which is becoming more and more important for a successful career, graduate training in economics and administration.

33. Daniel Levy, "The Political Consequences of Changing Socialization Patterns," in Roderic Camp, ed., *Mexico's Political Stability*, 1986.

34. My personal contacts in Mexico indicated that there is little social interaction between graduates of the different schools. For example, my closest contact graduated from Monterrey's ITESM and most of his personal acquaintances came from this school or Mexico City's private Anahuac.

35. One indication of the importance assigned to teaching is that 64 percent of the 1983 sample had taught either before or during their bureaucratic careers. Ninety percent of the original Salinas cabinet taught in a university. Prominent bureaucrats who have taught in the *private* schools include Salinas, Pedro Aspe, Ernesto Zedillo, José Córdoba, and Jaime Serra.

36. Licenciados from UNAM are more likely to remain within the university or study in countries other than the United States. Given the "American bias" of the Mexican upper class,

1983 nearly 40 percent of the bureaucratic elite had studied in at least one foreign locale, and one-third of the de la Madrid and Salinas cabinets had done so. There is also a clear trend across the age groups, with the youngest quartile in 1983 almost twice as likely to have studied abroad as the oldest generation. The most popular destination seems to be the United States, particularly the Ivy Leagues, the University of Chicago, and Stanford. Even senators and governors studied abroad (11 percent and 22 percent respectively in 1989), but in general those in the *político* or *burócrata político* wing were much less likely to have left Mexico.

Turning to what the elite learned while in school, law has retained its importance, with a quarter of the various samples throughout the 1980s having studied that subject. However, the distributions by both sexenial and age cohorts indicate that its popularity is waning and that this discipline can no longer claim the monopolistic status it once enjoyed. The field remains important for some posts, however, as over half of governors and senators in 1989 had studied law at some point in their careers. A third of the bureaucratic elite throughout the 1980s studied science and engineering, but neither field appeared to play an important role in the historical composition of the cabinet.[37] Economics and administration, on the other hand, have dramatically increased in importance both on the cabinet and more general bureaucratic levels and have become the most popular subjects for the youngest cohorts. These two were the most popular *graduate* subjects in 1983 and the only ones that attracted a large number of Licenciados from other disciplines. Over 50 percent of the de la Madrid and Salinas cabinets had studied economics or administration. This indicates that the two subjects are becoming increasingly important for professional success and that those with other specializations are required to possess some form of economic literacy.[38]

---

it is not surprising to find that private school graduates are the most likely to attend graduate school in the United States (again, however, field specialization, that is, economics and administration, plays a role here).

37. Concentration in these fields shows a dramatic decline across generations. An important factor here is that those in scientific fields have much longer tenure within the government. Precisely because their power and influence is limited and because they largely remain outside of politics, these *técnicos* possess greater job security. This would tend to skew the age distribution as not only is the personnel older but opportunities for recent graduates to enter the government are more limited.

38. This last phenomenon is apparent among lawyers and engineers who have sought to "modernize" their educational credentials with some sort of business or administrative train-

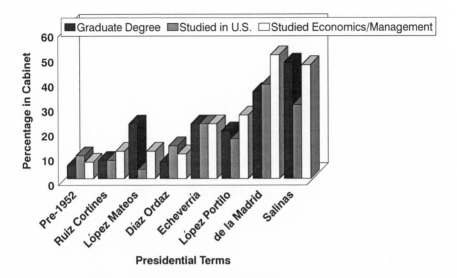

**Presidential Terms**

Fig. 5-3.    Cabinet education. (Source: Roderic Camp, *Mexican Political Biographies, 1935–1981*, 1982; Presidencia de la República, *Diccionario biográfico del gobierno mexicano*, eds. 1st, 2nd, 3rd.)

Over half of those who do graduate work in economics do so in the United States.

In sum, the bureaucratic elite has become much more educated, with increasing reliance on training in private and non-Mexican institutions and concentrating much more on those subjects associated with technocratic policy making. It would be incorrect to assume a functional relationship between such expertise and empowerment. The government did not necessarily need economists to make policy. Rather, a cohesive group inside the state first established their dominance and *then* utilized supposedly meritocratic criteria to benefit those with whom they shared key

---

ing. The one exception in this trend is the continued functional specialization of the military personnel. Unlike their counterparts in Brazil, Chile, and Peru, Mexico's military have not yet attempted to obtain expertise in areas other than their very specific institutional domain. This supports the widely stated assertion that Mexico's military plays a very restricted role in determining economic or social policy and, at least for now, appears to accept these limits. One characteristic that the Mexican soldiers share with their continental counterparts is the significant role of U.S.-sponsored training. Over 44 percent of the 1983 sample who did pursue postgraduate military training did so in the United States.

attributes. The education of the elite helped shape the perspectives used by the state. The elite's faith in the rationality of economics not only helped determine the kinds of policies adopted by it but also served to exclude rival claims to knowledge. These educational qualifications further increase the social exclusivity and homogeneity of the ruling elite by requiring financial and professional commitments to education that only a select few can make. The relationship between background variables and educational attainment could suggest that the imposition of technocratic qualifications for entry may serve as a means of legitimating unequal access to positions of power. That is, the bureaucracy may be technocratic, but before anything else it remains elitist.

## Political Activity

Before discussing the relationship between the elite and the PRI, I wish to distinguish between four different types of political activity. The first we may call "grass roots," involving the representation of constituency demands. Even in a system such as Mexico's, experience in an election campaign or within the corporatist arms at least familiarized elite members with popular aspirations and needs. These may not have been satisfied, or they may have been embedded in patronage, but no one involved in this part of the regime could afford to ignore these or rely purely on repression. A second class of political activity could be called "control" or "stability maintenance." This involves both the management of the stick that goes with the patronage carrot and negotiation between different factions. The third category might be called "technocratic" and involves the formulation and analysis of specific state policies. This is the preferred arena of experts who can use their technical knowledge to define goals and design the means to achieve them. The final category of activity or political skill may be called "organizational" or the politics of palace coups. These politics occur purely within the walls of the bureaucracy and involve the informal exchange of favors and loyalties. This is the world of "grey eminences," of hidden deals and whispers. Each type has its favored locales, tactics, and practitioners. In Mexico the first three categories were associated with *políticos, burocratas políticos,* and *técnicos* and *tecnócratas* respectively. But while all practiced the last, the new elite demonstrated their mastery of it on their climb to the top. The following section discusses the first three categories, while Chapter 6 will analyze the last.

The political activity of the bureaucratic elite reflects the changing relationship between the Mexican state and the PRI. Whereas previously the typical career ladder for a politician hoping to reach the cabinet had involved service as a PRI delegate or functionary, time served in the Congress or the Senate, then governorship or membership in the party National Executive Committee (CEN) and then and only then cabinet minister, as of the 1970s the ladder to power came to be based almost exclusively in the federal bureaucracy.[39] In the last twenty years the traditional career pattern has been reversed, with many prominent bureaucrats finishing their careers in the Senate. This does not mean that their previous service was training and preparation for the high point of their political lives but that the Senate has become a safe holding area for those personnel who no longer are significant political players. It also indicates that the traditional *políticos* were being replaced even in those institutions that they had previously dominated. In the words of Rafael Segovia, three years in Harvard were now worth more than three years in the Congress; any doctorate was worth more than a municipal election.[40]

Grass-roots experience within the party (for example, local elections or work with sector organizations) was never a major factor in determining access to the cabinet. Most of the cabinets since Cárdenas did not have a single representative of the labor CTM, the peasant CNC, or the middle-class CNOP. Thus, *políticos* (as defined earlier) were never a major factor in the bureaucracy. The form of political experience that was rewarded (at least until the early 1970s) was "stability maintenance," associated with the *burocratas políticos* and involving either management of the national machine (CEN) or representation of the president in the states (governors and senators). Beginning with the Echeverría *sexenio,* however, even this limited political participation lost

---

39. In the 1970s Peter Smith perceived a professionalization of the executive and administrative track with an accompanying closing of high-level positions to those with purely political backgrounds, while Wilfred Gruber concluded that "[Mexico is] becoming a polity that is governed by an oligarchy of professional politicians and technocrats." See Smith, *Labyrinths of Power,* Table 4.1–4.5 and pp. 114–116; and Gruber, "Career Patterns in Mexico's Political Elite."

40. "El fastidio electoral," in Soledad Loaeza and Rafael Segovia, eds., *La vida política mexicana en crisis,* 1987, p. 15.

**Table 5-3.** Political Activity of Elite

| | Executive | | | |
|---|---|---|---|---|
| | 1983(a) (%) | 1986(b) (%) | 1989(c) (%) | Graduate Degree(d) (%) |
| Party militancy | | | | |
| No PRI membership | 25.9 | 25.0 | 23.7 | 27.2 |
| PRI member but not active(e) | 33.2 | 34.3 | 32.8 | 33.9 |
| Active in party | 40.9 | 40.7 | 43.5 | 38.9 |
| *Total*(n) | 100.0 | 100.0 | 100.0 | 100.0 |
| Types of activity(f) | | | | |
| IEPES/campaign(g) | 24.8 | 24.6 | 27.3 | 21.7 |
| Traditional activity(h) | 29.6 | 30.9 | 28.8 | 29.1 |

| | Legislative | | Provincial |
|---|---|---|---|
| | 1983(i) (%) | 1989(j) (%) | 1989(k) (%) |
| Party membership | | | |
| PRI | 75.0 | 57.3 | 97.8 |
| PAN | 13.0 | 17.9 | 0.3 |
| PPS | 3.0 | 5.2 | 0.0 |
| PARM | 0.0 | 5.5 | 0.0 |
| PDM | 3.0 | 0.0 | 0.0 |
| PRD(l) | 7.0 | 5.7 | 0.0 |
| PFCRN | 0.0 | 7.5 | 0.0 |
| Other/DK | 0.0 | 1.0 | 1.9 |
| *Total* (n) | 100.0 | 100.0 | 100.0 |
| Party activity(m) | | | |
| Posts in party | 82.9 | 78.4 | 73.6 |
| Unions/syndicates | 73.8 | 53.8 | 38.6 |

(a) Data bank of bureaucratic personnel (Director Generals or above) based on 1984 edition of *Diccionario biográfico* with N=1278.

(b) Data bank of 1983(a) list also appearing in 1987 edition of *Diccionario biográfico* with N=606.

(c) Data bank of 1983(a) list also appearing in 1989 edition of *Diccionario biográfico* with N=381.

(d) Sample is those in 1983 bureaucratic elite with graduate degree, N=420.

(e) Party activity involves any listing of posts or participation in *Diccionario*.

(f) Categories not mutually exclusive.

(g) Includes IEPES, CEPES, and work on any presidential campaign.

(h) Includes CEN membership, work as a delegate. work in the party bureaucracy, or elected post.

(i) Statistical Summary of Legislative Branch (Senate and House of Representatives), *Diccionario biográfico* (1st ed.). N=451.

(j) Statistical Summary of Legislative Branch (Senate and House of Representatives), *Diccionario biográfico* (3rd ed.). N=560.

(k) Statistical Summary of State Governments (Governors and staffs), *Diccionario biográfico* (3rd ed.). N=311.

(l) I have collapsed the numbers for the individual parties that became the PRD after the 1988 election.

(m) This includes those parties other than the PRI. Categories not mutually exclusive.

(n) May not equal 100% due to rounding.

its significance. By the 1980s, with one exception discussed below, the majority of cabinet members had not even had remote contact with the party or any of its organs.[41]

Given the monopolistic status of the PRI in Mexican political life, it is not surprising that no representatives of other parties may be found in the bureaucracy. Yet a quarter of the bureaucratic elite during the 1980s did not even belong to the PRI. This is particularly significant given the low relative costs of belonging. As almost all bureaucrats, no matter their political persuasion, are encouraged to contribute to party funds[42] and attend rallies, not belonging to the party can provide few savings while possibly exacting high career costs. While joining the party has little significance, not belonging is a relatively strong political statement. That a significant minority feels safe enough to make this decision indicates that the PRI's ability to control access to and success in the bureaucracy must be severely limited. Moreover, of the 1983 sample who did belong to the PRI, nearly half played no role in the party and were merely "card carriers" with no active participation in party life.[43] Nearly half of the party members joined after entering the civil service, again indicating that membership is no longer the necessary condition for entry into government service that it once was.

The significant exception to the lack of party activity is the number of cabinet members in the 1980s with experience within the Institute for

41. Basáñez's study also shows a drastic drop in representation in the elite of those with party militancy or electoral experience after 1982 (*El pulso de los sexenios*, pp. 125–127).

42. For example, an area director (one level below director general) was expected to contribute thirty thousand pesos (a significant part of a typical salary) toward the election in 1988. *Proceso*, no. 589, September 28, 1987, p. 9.

43. My evaluation of party militancy is based on membership in any one of various party organizations. A more rigorous measure would certainly provide even lower results. I did, however, analyze the same variables with a parallel measure based on years in the party and percentage of adult life within it. The results were practically identical with the two measures. The importance that most bureaucrats assign to party membership and activity was indicated by the results of an earlier survey of this personnel conducted before that used by this study. In this survey no explicit mention was made of political life. Rather, respondents were asked which organizations they belonged to and what activities they were responsible for within those organizations. Less than half mentioned belonging to the PRI and less than one-third discussed political activities. President de la Madrid was apparently quite embarrassed by these results coming as they did when his administration was being attacked for being too technocratic. He directed the Office of the Presidency to make political participation a separate question in the next questionnaire (from which the first edition of the *Diccionario biográfico* was compiled) and also let it be known that he wanted "better results" on this issue (interview, Mexico City, February 1988).

Political, Economic, and Social Studies (IEPES), the party think tank that assists the PRI presidential designate in writing a platform during the election year. This was widely considered the technocratic arm of the party which played a very small role in the actual politicking of the election but served more as a shadow cabinet for the "president select." It was also recognized as the fast-track party institution for leading positions in the government.[44] Nearly half of both the de la Madrid and Salinas cabinets had worked in IEPES prior to assuming their positions. This reflects two trends: first, it indicates the increasing technocratization of the party leadership as those in charge of preparing formal policy documents and platforms replaced those in charge of actually managing the vote; second, more than any other party organization, IEPES was staffed by the inner circle of the presidential candidate and, as we will see in the next chapter, these personal connections increased in importance over the past two decades. The decision to replace IEPES with a new foundation (called Cambio XXI) after the party convention of 1991 indicated that it largely served as a focal center for network connections and not as an institutional power in and of itself.[45]

Not surprisingly, we find a much greater level of party activity among governors and legislators. In 1989 half of the senators and governors had worked in the party's CEN. In the case of the governors, IEPES was also popular. The legislative and provincial political elites were also much more likely to have participated in one of the sector organizations where the CNC and the CNOP were strongest. The labor sector appeared to be represented less by exofficials of the central CTM than by those who had worked in specific unions.[46]

The differences in political participation seem to verify the existence of a *político/técnico* split. The distinctions, however, are not as clear-cut as is often assumed.[47] While there is a definite generational effect, this would appear to contradict the notion that the new bureaucrats are becoming less "political." In the 1983 sample the two youngest genera-

---

44. Of the thirteen assistant directors of IEPES in 1982, three went on to become undersecretaries (and one subsequently made it to the cabinet), three became federal deputies, one became a senator and another became a governor (*Mexico Journal*, March 28, 1988, p. 21). Carlos Salinas was the director of IEPES in 1982.

45. This is not surprising since it only really functioned during presidential campaigns and had little permanent staff or resources.

46. The figures for governors, for example, are 6.5 percent CTM, 22.6 percent CNC, 29 percent CNOP, and 22.6 percent specific unions.

47. Nor is there any clear relationship between social origins and party activity.

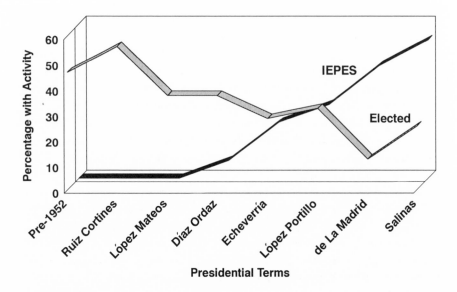

**Presidential Terms**

Fig. 5-4. Party activity in the cabinet. (Source: Roderic Camp, *Mexican Political Biographies, 1935–1981,* 1982; Presidencia de la República, *Diccionario biográfico del gobierno mexicano,* eds. 1st, 2nd, 3rd. "Elected" includes electoral, administrative, and corporatist activity.)

tions appear to be much more active in the party than their older counter-parts.[48] The younger politically active bureaucrats, however, tend to be more concentrated in the technocratic activities such as IEPES than their older counterparts.[49]

This last finding would therefore qualify the contention by Grindle and Camp that the traditional PRI politician-bureaucrats are being re-

48. One possible explanation of this phenomenon is the link between certain types of technical-scientific training and longer job tenure. Engineers and natural scientists have the lowest percentage of party members and militants. These are also the groups with the oldest members. However, even if we control for educational field, age remains a significant variable in determining political activity.

49. There is no evidence of the simple dichotomy of education and party activity, and we cannot divide the bureaucratic elite into a group of antiparty experts and another of unedu-cated party hacks. There is a slight positive relationship between obtaining a master's degree and attendance of schools outside of Mexico (including the United States) and party activity (even stronger for IEPES alone). Those who studied engineering and science have the least proclivity for party action, while those who studied law (concentrated in electoral and control activities) and economics (concentrated in the technocratic sectors) have the most.

placed by a new "técnico-politician" or "political technocrat." Grindle concludes from her study of CONASUPO officials that it is those with "political skills who are increasingly important in policy-making functions, and it is this type of actor who is increasingly found in positions of power and influence."[50] For Camp the critical development is the combination of both political and technical skills that defines what he calls "political-technocrats."[51] Again it is important to keep in mind the different types of political skills involved. As we will see in the next chapter, the new generation has succeeded in playing internal politics well enough to come to power. Unlike the classic *técnicos,* they did not shrink from the challenges of the game as played in Mexico. They also did not, however, have any experience in the types of politics outside the walls of the bureaucracy.

The decline in the extent of certain types of political participation may reflect the changing distribution of power between political institutions in Mexico. The most significant aspect of the elite's political participation (or lack thereof) is that the persons in control of the state had little experience dealing with popular demands and complaints. Their isolation inside the bureaucratic ivory tower was practically complete. This made it easier for them to impose the draconian measures of the 1980s. This is not to deny that they learned very quickly after 1988 and used resources such as PRONASOL with a mastery that would have made the most jaded *político* proud. As in the case of social origins and education, the central point is not a set of skills per se but a process of professional socialization that was conducive to a revolution from above.

## Professional Experience in the Private Sector

The extent to which government bureaucratic personnel form a distinctly separate subgroup within the ruling class has been the subject of extensive debate in Mexico. While there remain clear divisions between the public and private elite, the data available indicates that this gulf may not be as large as was once supposed.

Since 1936 few cabinet ministers have begun their careers in the pri-

---

50. *Bureaucrats, Politicians, and Peasants in Mexico,* p. 402.
51. "The Political Technocrat in Mexico and the Survival of the Political System," 1985.

vate sector, but many ex-members of the elite do turn to private companies or professional practice after leaving the government. The most striking historical trend in private sector employment is that in the 1983 sample, the percentage of those with nongovernmental experience prior to entry into the bureaucracy increases dramatically with the Echeverría *sexenio*. This pattern remains even when we control for age cohorts and possibly indicates that precisely during their time of most virulent quarrel, the public and private elites had already begun to merge.[52] In 1983 large parts of the elite had worked outside of the public bureaucracy.[53] The numbers for private banking (8 percent) and private business (21 percent) are relatively low by U.S. standards, but in light of the supposedly revolutionary nature of the regime and the persistent conflicts that have arisen between private capital and the state since its creation, they indicate a much greater association between the two supposedly divided professional worlds.[54]

One could argue that a large part of that group with private banking experience was forcibly recruited with the bank nationalization of 1982 and that this reflects not the penetration of the private sector elite into the government but the expansion of the state. A similar argument applies for those from the private industrial sector whose employers were taken over by the government.[55] The reasons for the increased representation of those with private sector experience, however, are not as important as their growing domination of critical segments of the bureaucracy.

In 1983 the personnel with experience within the private sector was concentrated in those ministries most concerned with relations between it and the state. This could indicate a dramatic shift in the willingness or

52. Of course, such cohort trends figures cannot provide a perfect indication of the characteristics of previous administrations. Another possibility is that private sector employees who had entered the government before 1970 had already left because of age or in order to return to the private sector.

53. While I do not have equivalent data for the entire 1989 elite, an analysis of those from the 1983 elite still in the bureaucracy in 1989 indicated that these percentages had remained steady.

54. While the "revolving door" between private and public employment has not developed in Mexico to the extent that it has in the United States, there is some movement as 11.6 percent of the bureaucratic elite *inside the government* in 1983 had worked in either private business or banking *after their initial entry into the public sector,* while 9.3 percent had returned to professional careers. Data on private sector employment of those who left the bureaucracy are not available. *Anecdotal* information suggests that the number going into the private sector after a public career has increased in recent years.

55. This might also help explain the dramatic jump in the number of persons with this type of experience during the Echeverría *sexenio*.

ability of the government to control or challenge the policies of national and international capital. Moreover, claims that the public industrial sector was inefficient because it was dominated by political hacks were clearly inaccurate. A large part of public investment was in the hands of the same persons who would staff its private equivalent. The government may have owned these enterprises in 1983, but at least on the level of personnel, had not radically changed them. This is particularly significant given the relatively high number with prior experience with U.S. multinationals. In ministries such as Tourism, where the needs of international hotel chains and those of Mexican economic development were likely to clash, the potential conflicts of interest were considerable. Of even greater concern is the link between those who manage the payment of the debt and the institutions to whom it is owed. In Treasury and Banco de México, nearly a third of the bureaucrats in 1983 had worked previously in the private sector (31.6 percent in Treasury and 31.8 percent in Banco de México).[56]

While this data does not necessarily imply that the private sector had a significant influence over policy making in the bureaucracy, it would indicate an important connection between the two supposedly divided worlds. If we measure the 1983 personnel by possession of one link to the private sector (by family, school, or professional experience), over 60 percent would qualify as having a *potential* connection to capital. The most important element in this relationship is the possibility that from the early 1980s the government and private industry began to share a common set of political perspectives and policy criteria. That is, rather than exercising influence through direct control, private capital's rationales and definitions of efficiency had established an important position within the public sector at the very same time that those perspectives associated with the political arm of the party were declining.

## Professional Experience in the Public Sector

The most common entry post for those who formed the bureaucratic elite in 1983 was in middle-level management, the technical support

---

56. The connection between these institutions and private banking is a long-standing one. See Sylvia Maxfield, *Governing Capital: International Finance and Mexican Politics*, 1990.

Table 5-4.    Career Experience of Political Elite

|  | Executive | | |
|---|---|---|---|
|  | 1983(a) (%) | 1986(b) (%) | 1989(c) (%) |
| Worked in private sector(d) | 24.8 | 24.8 | 22.6 |
| Area of first govt. post(e) | | | |
| Banking | 20.6 | 23.6 | 24.9 |
| Planning | 13.1 | 12.4 | 14.7 |
| Management | 30.7 | 29.9 | 26.5 |
| Control | 19.2 | 17.3 | 16.8 |
| Military | 6.4 | 6.1 | 3.7 |
| Diplomatic corps | 6.0 | 7.3 | 9.5 |
| Other | 4.0 | 3.4 | 3.9 |
| Total(g) | 100.0 | 100.0 | 100.0 |
| Area of specialization(f) | | | |
| Banking | 12.7 | 14.7 | 17.1 |
| Planning | 12.5 | 11.9 | 14.4 |
| Management | 28.3 | 29.2 | 26.3 |
| Control | 16.5 | 17.0 | 17.1 |
| Military | 5.2 | 5.5 | 2.9 |
| Diplomatic corps | 4.5 | 6.1 | 7.4 |
| Other govt. functions | 13.7 | 11.3 | 10.1 |
| Outside public sector | 6.6 | 4.3 | 4.7 |
| Total(g) | 100.0 | 100.0 | 100.0 |

(a) Data bank of bureaucratic personnel (Director Generals or above) based on 1984 edition of *Diccionario biográfico* with N=1278.

(b)Data bank of 1983(a) list also appearing in 1987 edition of *Diccionario biográfico* with N=606.

(c) Data bank of 1983(a) list also appearing in 1989 edition of *Diccionario biográfico* with N=311.

(d) Does not include professional practice.

(e) See footnote 58 for details.

(f) Measured by amount of time spent in each sector.

(g) May not equal 100% due to rounding.

staffs, or as personal assistants. The bureaucratic elite therefore entered the civil service at relatively high levels of responsibility involving either personal contact with a high-level functionary or direct supervision of other employees. Those in the cabinet and subcabinet in 1983 tended to enter the government at even higher levels. Over half of those in the cabinet in 1983 began their public careers as personal assistants or directors and above (compared to 32.4 percent of the 1983 elite as a whole).

It would appear, therefore, that the ability to reach a certain hierarchical level is closely associated with beginning a career not far removed from it. In the Mexican bureaucracy, as in most complex organizations, vertical movement from the bottom is extremely difficult and rarely spans more than two or three hierarchical levels.

Combined with the figures for social origins and education, this further indicates that the top elite is a particularly favored segment of Mexican society, not only in social background, but also in professional experience. This could have a significant effect on policy formulation and subsequent implementation since a large part of the elite has never had to deal with grass-roots reactions and opposition to government decisions but has always been several steps removed from such concerns.[57]

Where a bureaucrat began his or her bureaucratic career does play a major role in determining future postings. The personnel are most likely to specialize in that sector through which they entered, indicating that each of the ministry categories produces its own staff.[58] Over 70 percent of the 1983 bureaucrats at the level of director general had spent the majority of their careers in the area in which they were currently serving.[59] Those who remained in one ministry or a single sector of the

57. The study by Basáñez found that his elite "plurality" index based on degree of contact with population either through origins or through professional/political experience declined drastically in the 1980s (*El pulso de los sexenios*, p. 181).

58. In order to analyze career patterns I separated the ministries into groups. My categorizationn scheme for the federal bureaucracy is partly borrowed from John Bailey's *Governing Mexico* (1988) and Miguel Basáñez's *La lucha por la hegemonía en México, 1968–1980* (1982). The functions, responsibilities, and names of the various ministries have changed drastically over the years, but I have used their names during the 1980s and refer to the distribution of responsibilities during that period. Note that this schema does not reflect changes in 1992. The banking sector includes Treasury, Banco de México, the development banks, and the nationalized banking sector. The planning sector includes SPP, Commerce and Industrial Development, the Energy and Parastatals Ministry (but not the individual firms), the presidential office, and the Auditing Ministry. Managing includes the ministries of Agriculture, Urban Development and Ecology, Communications and Transport, Tourism, Fisheries, the parastatals, the Social Security Administration (Instituto Mexicano de Seguro Social, IMSS) and its equivalent for state employees, the Ministry of Health, CONASUPO, and Infonavit. Control includes the Ministry of Government, the Ministry of Education, the Ministry of Labor, Agrarian Reform, Justice, and the Federal District. Two other major segments of the bureaucracy that cannot be classified along these lines but that make up their own minicivil services are the Military (consisting of the Defense Ministry and Naval Ministry) and the Diplomatic Service within the Ministry of Foreign Relations.

59. My measure of specialization was obtained by first separating those who had spent the majority of their careers in the government. Among these, I then assigned the personnel to the

bureaucracy, however, appeared to limit their career advancement to the level of director general. Of those in the cabinet in 1983, for example, 85.2 percent had experience in at least two different functional areas in the bureaucracy versus 58.5 percent for the entire sample.[60] We observe a similar pattern in the 1989 cabinet. Of nineteen Salinas cabinet members, for example, over half had *not* previously worked in the ministry they managed. This lack of experience contradicts those analyses of the Mexican elite that emphasize functional expertise as the critical factor in its development. A survey taken among public servants in 1975 found that "scientific expertise in one's functional area" was rated the *lowest* among a series of qualities desirable for the ideal administrator.[61]

There was a strong link between the social and educational background of the bureaucratic elite in 1983 and the institution through which they enrolled in the public sector.[62] The youngest generation was the most likely to have entered the government through what I call the planning sector, which became increasingly dominant in the 1970s. While bureaucrats with private and U.S. education appear to be widely

---

sector in which they had spent the most time. Those who did not spend the majority of their time in government were either assigned to "Business" or "Professions" categories. Note that because of missing data the Other/DK category includes a disproportionate number of individuals.

60. Age played no role in determining mobility, and thus the representation of such persons is independent of their cohort membership.

61. Reported in Jorge Barenstein, "Los administradores en el sector público mexicano," 1982, p. 115.

62. In order to better analyze the personnel structure of the individual agencies, I applied two clustering techniques to the means of various indicators for each agency. (I utilized Wards and Average Linkage methods. See SAS, *SAS Users Guide: Statistics*, 1985, pp. 255–316.) I clustered the agencies according to the percentage of their 1983 personnel who were in the two youngest age groups and whose fathers were peasants or workers or who were born in rural areas. Three different clusters were identified. The first cluster (defined by relatively old age) included the Diplomatic Service (but not those in the Foreign Ministry), Banco de México, SCT, Pemex, Pesca, parastatals, the Military, and Agrarian Reform. The second cluster grouped those ministries distinguished by the relative youth of their personnel: Tourism, Infonavit, Exterior Ministry, and SPP (which has the youngest personnel of all the agencies). Other ministries with a relatively young personnel that were not included in this cluster because of differences in social background include labor, SEMIP, Presidency, and Commerce. A third cluster included the rest of the ministries that did not have a particular age distribution. The only ministries with significant participation by the working class or by peasants were SCT, Agriculture, and Agrarian Reform. For origins in Mexico City, Health, Tourism, the Exterior Ministry, and SPP had the highest representation and the two agricultural ministries and Justice the lowest.

dispersed throughout the administration, those with non-Mexico experience were more likely to have begun in planning and banking.[63] These agencies also tended to recruit those who studied economics.[64] Finally, the planning sector tended to attract personnel with some form of party activity.[65] (Each of these relationships remained significant even when controlling for the independent variables).

Given these recruitment patterns, it is not surprising that each ministry or sectoral group of agencies developed an institutional profile. Looking at the personnel makeup in 1983, it is clear that those in planning represent a very different generation than those in the other major functional sectors. Bureaucrats in these ministries tended to have advanced

63. The data set does not include dates of educational experience and it is therefore impossible to determine the causal order of this relationship. That is, we cannot currently determine if those with graduate degrees are attracted to a particular set of ministries or whether experience in such ministries leads to graduate education (both by encouraging such training and through greater financial resources available for scholarships). An analysis of the raw data indicates that the latter may be the case, but there is the possibility that those who join the government through Planning were already interested in such education. Utilizing the same clustering procedures discussed above, but clustering for graduate degrees and study abroad, two groups were identified. The first was defined by high educational achievement and study abroad including SPP, SEMIP, Banco de México, SEDUE, Commerce, Agriculture, Tourism, the nationalized banking sector (SNC), the development banks (INC), Treasury, and Presidency. While this cluster does not perfectly follow the categories I have utilized, these agencies *are* the ones most associated with *técnicos* and *tecnócratas* and with formalized policy-making procedures. The agencies with the highest representation of personnel having studied in the United States or Mexican private universities were Banco de México, Commerce, SEMIP, Tourism, and SPP. Note that Treasury personnel does not study in the United States but that large numbers in the three institutions that I have characterized as critical for the development of the *tecnócratas* do so. The second cluster is composed of those agencies without particular educational achievements. The analysis using subjects produced three clusters: one defined by study of economics and administration (Hacienda, INC, SNC, Banco de México, Commerce, SEMIP, and SPP); a second defined by engineering, science, and administration (Agriculture, Health, SCT, parastatals, Pemex, and SEDUE); and a third dominated by lawyers, but not as concentrated in any single subject, which included all the other agencies.

64. Interestingly, when I analyzed the education data using institutional groups based on area of expertise (for example, finance, industry, welfare) the relationships were not as significant. This would suggest that educational credentials are associated with a particular function within the bureaucracy rather than a division along areas of concern.

65. If we cluster the ministries along lines of activity, the first group is characterized by personnel with a high degree of party militancy: presidency, SPP, Gobernación, DF, Agrarian Reform, Auditing, Education, Labor, Foreign Relations (but not the Diplomatic Service), SPP, and Health (the last entry is the result of the high number of those from Health that participated in presidential advisory groups on related issues during the 1982 campaign). A second cluster defined by lack of political activity included IMSS, Banco de México, the Military, and the Diplomatic Service (despite the presence of a subgroup of retired *políticos*).

degrees in economics from foreign universities[66] and were more active in the party than their counterparts in banking and managing. The political activity, however, was of a very different sort from those in control, focusing on formulation of policy documents rather than electioneering or the maintenance of political stability. The key institutions that would claim control over the bureaucracy in the 1980s therefore recruited strikingly homogenous personnel and were dominated by precisely the same type of persons found at the top of the political ladder.

The association between the various elite types and bureaucratic institutions is even clearer if we analyze the data at the individual ministry level. The personnel in SPP throughout the 1980s exemplify the characteristics I contend are critical for the *tecnócratas:* youth, U.S. training, graduate education, concentration in economics, political participation through IEPES, specialization in planning, and relatively high mobility. Their dominance of what became the central organization in the bureaucracy no doubt played a major role in their advancement toward control of the state as a whole.

Despite these institutional patterns, there was considerable mobility within the bureaucracy.[67] The most extensive flows of personnel occur within the control group of institutions. Not only do these ministries exchange personnel between themselves but they all share very strong ties to the traditional party organs. These connections would suggest that the *burocrata político* wing of the bureaucracy is still very well integrated and would indicate a high degree of coordination between the organizations in formulating and implementing policies. There is also a great deal of movement between those ministries in charge of banking, with each well connected to the others as well as to the individual

66. Scientists and engineers are concentrated in managing, lawyers in control, and a combination of lawyers and economists in banking. Those in control attracted those with the minimum educational credentials.

67. I obtained information on mobility by creating a dichotomous variable for experience in each agency. For each bureaucrat these measured whether the individual had worked in a particular institution during his or her career up to and including posting in 1983. I then generated a correlation matrix with the agencies representing both columns and rows where the ijth correlation is the relationship between working in both the ith and jth agencies. I then selected all those who had a *positive* relationship with a PROB < .01. While such a method is far from perfect both in terms of statistical method (the distribution for most organizations was heavily skewed) and quality of data (representing only the experiences of a select elite at one point in time), I believe that the results can provide an indication of the connections between the institutions. Precisely because of these problems I have not provided the actual figures for each association since this would possibly indicate a false degree of mathematical precision.

**Table 5-5.** Personnel Profiles by Bureaucratic Sector(a)

| | Banking (%) | Planning (%) | Manage (%) | Control (%) | Military (%) | Diplomat (%) |
|---|---|---|---|---|---|---|
| Born after 1939(b) | 50.3 | 72.1 | 45.3 | 49.4 | 3.6 | 33.9 |
| Birthplace(c) | | | | | | |
| Mexico City | 55.3 | 59.3 | 52.0 | 40.0 | 25.0 | 67.3 |
| Other urban | 13.7 | 12.8 | 15.0 | 16.0 | 14.3 | 13.3 |
| Rural | 31.1 | 27.9 | 34.0 | 43.0 | 60.7 | 19.5 |
| Total(g) | 100.0 | 100.0 | 100.0 | 100.0 | 100.0 | 100.0 |
| Graduate degree | 31.7 | 44.8 | 32.8 | 32.7 | 10.9 | 32.1 |
| Studied in Mexican private or U.S. school | 48.7 | 51.7 | 34.6 | 21.9 | 23.6 | 35.7 |
| Subject(d) | | | | | | |
| Law | 25.9 | 20.3 | 17.6 | 49.8 | 5.5 | 66.1 |
| Science/engineering | 13.2 | 25.0 | 50.2 | 16.7 | 14.5 | 13.4 |
| Economics/administration | 70.9 | 59.9 | 39.3 | 31.9 | 1.8 | 19.6 |
| Political activity(e) | | | | | | |
| Nonmember | 27.0 | 14.0 | 27.3 | 12.4 | 76.4 | 42.0 |
| Nonactive member | 38.6 | 33.7 | 37.0 | 27.5 | 18.2 | 25.9 |
| Active | 34.4 | 52.3 | 35.6 | 60.2 | 5.5 | 32.1 |
| Total(g) | 100.0 | 100.0 | 100.0 | 100.0 | 100.0 | 100.0 |
| Same specialization(f) | 59.8 | 64.5 | 64.2 | 64.9 | 96.4 | 50.9 |
| Have worked in 2 or more sectors | 48.7 | 65.7 | 57.9 | 76.1 | 16.4 | 50.9 |
| Percentage of 1983 elite | 14.8 | 13.5 | 38.8 | 19.7 | 4.3 | 8.8 |

(a) Based on position of personnel in 1983. See Table 5-1 and footnote 58 for details.
(b) Median DOB for 1983 elite.
(c) See Table 5-1 for details.
(d) Categories not mutually exclusive because some persons have studied more than one.
(e) See Table 5-3 for details.
(f) Percentage of those currently in this sector who have spent most of their time within it. See Table 5-4.
(g) May not equal 100% due to rounding.

**Table 5-6.**   Personnel Profiles of Representative Agencies(a)

|  | Banking (Treasury) (%) | Planning (SPP) (%) | Managing (Agriculture) (%) | Control (Gobernación) (%) |
|---|---|---|---|---|
| Born after 1939 | 52.6 | 85.3 | 46.0 | 51.5 |
| Born in DF | 66.7 | 68.3 | 39.7 | 42.4 |
| Father's occupation | | | | |
| Professional | 32.8 | 41.5 | 28.1 | 48.5 |
| Business | 39.7 | 29.3 | 39.1 | 39.4 |
| Government | 13.8 | 17.1 | 15.6 | 6.1 |
| Peasant/labor | 3.5 | 7.3 | 10.9 | 0.0 |
| Other/DK | 10.2 | 4.8 | 6.3 | 6.0 |
| Total(d) | 100.0 | 100.0 | 100.0 | 100.0 |
| Graduate degree | 36.2 | 48.8 | 46.9 | 33.3 |
| Studied in U.S. | 17.2 | 39.0 | 39.1 | 12.1 |
| Subject(b) | | | | |
| Law | 37.9 | 12.2 | 3.1 | 36.4 |
| Engineer | 8.6 | 19.5 | 21.9 | 12.1 |
| Science | 5.2 | 7.3 | 51.6 | 3.0 |
| Administration | 32.8 | 7.3 | 20.3 | 15.2 |
| Economics | 36.2 | 65.9 | 17.2 | 21.2 |
| Active in PRI | 29.3 | 61.0 | 37.5 | 72.7 |
| IEPES | 19.0 | 53.7 | 26.6 | 12.1 |
| Specialization(c) | | | | |
| Banking | 70.7 | 0.0 | 17.2 | 0.0 |
| Planning | 0.0 | 90.2 | 6.3 | 3.0 |
| Manage | 1.7 | 2.0 | 59.4 | 0.0 |
| Control | 0.0 | 2.4 | 1.6 | 67.0 |
| Other/DK | 19.0 | 7.3 | 11.0 | 23.9 |
| Outsider | 8.6 | 0.0 | 4.7 | 6.1 |
| Total(d) | 100.0 | 100.0 | 100.0 | 100.0 |

(a) Based on position in 1983. See Table 5-5 for details. Sample sizes: Treasury=58, SPP=41, Agriculture=64, Gobernación=33.
(b) Categories not mutually exclusive.
(c) See Table 5-4 for details.
(d) May not equal 100% due to rounding.

banking companies that were owned by the state for much of the 1980s. This would also indicate a high degree of coordination between these institutions, managed by a well-defined subgroup of financial *técnicos* well acquainted with the tasks and perspective of each organization. The personnel in those organizations that are in charge of the budget and development planning, while they are not as interconnected as their control and banking counterparts, form a third potential institutional network.

The relative isolation of those ministries that I have grouped under management illustrates the career patterns of classic *técnicos*. There is very little intrasectoral movement within the category, reflecting the specialization of this group. That is, if an agronomist does leave his agency, he is more likely to move to a ministry in charge of overall planning or to Agrarian Reform than to one concerned with another industry.[68] The most significant aspect of the isolation of these agencies is that it would inhibit coordination between them and limit their influence to their individual sectors.

What is perhaps most interesting is that the majority of the intrabureaucratic movements of personnel occur in one direction: from banking (particularly Treasury) toward the other sectors. The professional experience of those in the elite in 1983 reflects the dominance of particular institutions in the bureaucracy described in Chapter 4. For the elite in 1983 the most common place of entry was Treasury, accounting for 11.3 percent of the bureaucrats' first job in the government. Moreover, 25 percent of all nonmilitary personnel had spent time in that institution, while its 1983 personnel only accounted for 4.5 percent of the sample.[69] While the banking and planning sectors each only accounted for 13 percent of the personnel slots available in 1983, over a third of the elite population had experience in each while over half had worked in one or the other during their career prior to the beginning of the de la Madrid *sexenio*.

The data for the cabinets reflects the increasing importance of these institutions and their functional groups. Since 1970 the representation in

---

68. Most links reflect intraministry cooperation within a single policy area such as that between the Urban Development Ministry (SEDUE) and the Department of the Federal District with its subsidized housing projects. It is also not surprising to find a professional connection between SEDUE and SCT, which share some of the responsibilities of the now defunct SAHOP. Such "intradisciplinary" links, however, do not imply agreement on policy. The disagreements between Agriculture and Agrarian Reform, for example, are legendary.

69. Given its late institutional "birth," it is not surprising to find that there are very few bureaucrats at this hierarchical level who began their careers in SPP. However, if one were to include those from the "old" presidency and from those sectors of Commerce and Hacienda that subsequently became part of SPP (the latter two figures are unfortunately not available as the early career entries are often vague regarding specific departments in the agencies), this number would be much higher.

**Table 5-7.**  Background and Hierarchical Position(a)

|  | Cabinet (%) | Sub-Cabinet (%) | Mid-Elite(b) (%) | Director General (%) |
|---|---|---|---|---|
| Born after 1939 | 18.5 | 41.7 | 42.2 | 55.0 |
| Birthplace(c) |  |  |  |  |
| Mexico City | 54.2 | 53.5 | 52.7 | 52.0 |
| Other urban | 8.3 | 13.4 | 14.3 | 14.0 |
| Rural | 37.5 | 33.1 | 33.0 | 34.0 |
| Total(f) | 100.0 | 100.0 | 100.0 | 100.0 |
| Graduate degree | 37.0 | 35.4 | 29.4 | 35.4 |
| Studied in Mexican private or U.S. school | 29.6 | 42.5 | 37.6 | 35.8 |
| Subject(d) |  |  |  |  |
| Law/lib arts | 51.9 | 35.4 | 22.9 | 26.7 |
| Science/engin. | 14.8 | 22.0 | 32.1 | 34.2 |
| Economics/administration | 44.4 | 44.4 | 43.3 | 49.5 |
| Active in PRI | 66.7 | 54.3 | 42.2 | 41.4 |
| Specialization(e) |  |  |  |  |
| Banking | 37.0 | 13.4 | 20.0 | 12.8 |
| Planning | 14.8 | 11.0 | 15.5 | 13.5 |
| Manage | 18.5 | 32.3 | 32.7 | 31.5 |
| Control | 14.8 | 26.0 | 12.7 | 16.9 |
| Other/DK | 14.9 | 17.3 | 19.1 | 25.3 |
| Total(f) | 100.0 | 100.0 | 100.0 | 100.0 |

(a) Based on position in 1983. See Table 5-5 for details. Sample sizes: Cabinet=27, Sub-Cabinet=127, Mid-Elite=110, DG=850.
(b) Includes Official Mayor and *Coordinadores*.
(c) See Table 5-1 for details.
(d) Categories not mutually exclusive.
(e) See Table 5-4 for details.
(f) May not equal 100% due to rounding.

the cabinet of those with experience in organizations associated with political control declined from roughly 50 percent to less than a quarter in the de la Madrid cabinet. In the 1980s those with experience in the more financial side of government clearly dominated. Those who entered through banking and planning were dramatically overrepresented in the 1983 cabinet, accounting for 59.3 percent of these positions as opposed to 33.6 percent of the elite population. The figures for specialization and prior experience are even more striking with over 50 percent of the cabinet specializing in either banking or planning (as compared to

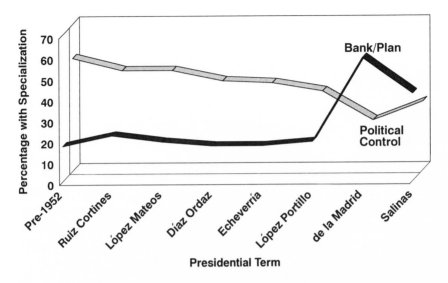

Fig. 5-5.   Cabinet career specialization. (Source: Roderic Camp, *Mexican Political Biographies, 1935–1981,* 1982; Presidencia de la República, *Diccionario biográfico del gobierno mexicano,* eds. 1st, 2nd, 3rd.)

25 percent of the elite as a whole) and over 80 percent having had prior experience in one of the two sectors. In 1989 a large number in the cabinet had experience in Treasury (33.3 percent) but even more so in SPP (50 percent).

In sum, the bureaucracy in the 1980s appears to have been taken over not only by a generic technocratic elite but by an even more exclusive and homogenous group of financiers. Again, as with the case of education, we must avoid simplistic functional assumptions that would equate their rise with the technical problems facing the state. The new elite often legitimated their rule by saying that the crises facing Mexico in the early 1980s were financial (for example, the debt). I would suggest a reverse causal order: the debt was defined as a financial problem (as opposed to a political or social one) because those in control of the state understood the world in those terms. The needs of the state did not define who would have power but vice versa. Their professional experience, however, was not completely irrelevant as it also shaped the elite's definition of the challenges faced by Mexico and the best means to overcome them.

# Change in the 1980s

Of those in the upper levels of the bureaucracy in 1983, 48 percent survived to the midterm of the de la Madrid *sexenio* and 29.8 percent survived into the Salinas administration. Part of the exodus reflects the budget cuts and reorganization undertaken during the de la Madrid *sexenio,* particularly in the parastatal sector. Some of those who did not survive to the end of the *sexenio* no doubt remained in the government but had been "elected" (more accurately, reassigned) to either Congress or provincial posts (for example, SEMIP head Labastida Ochoa became the governor of Sinaloa). Another small percentage may have been demoted, but given the rules of Mexican bureaucratic life, these would probably leave the government. In any case, a large number must have left public service completely, indicating much larger turnovers *within* a *sexenio* than had previously been predicted.[70]

As discussed in previous chapters, part of the turnover may be explained by Salinas's assault on the traditional *políticos.* Equally important, the late 1980s also saw dramatic declines in the representation of classic *técnicos.* Only four members of the initial Salinas cabinet could even remotely be characterized as such.[71] Naturally, the bureaucratic elite still had many representatives of this type of technical expert, but the influence of these persons was limited to their specific policy areas and to the implementation of directives from above. As in the cabinets since Echeverría, various ministries (for example, SEDUE, Tourism, Agriculture, Fisheries) were headed by men and women who had little previous experience, much less expertise, in the respective fields.[72]

Not surprisingly, the largest group in the cabinet consisted of *tecnócratas.*[73] What was really new in 1989 was not the domination of

70. See Smith, *Labyrinths of Power,* pp. 159–190. Part of this turnover may be explained by the purges that occurred in the Agriculture and Urban Development ministries as a result of both personnel changes at the top and the investigations in the aftermath of the 1985 earthquake. See Centeno and Weldon, "Small Circle of Friends," for an analysis of turnover in the 1980s.

71. Fernando Hiriart (SEMIP), Andrés Caso Lombardo (SCT), Jesús Kumate (Health), Miguel Mancera (Banco de México).

72. For example, the first minister of Tourism (later sent to Agriculture) did not speak any foreign languages.

73. Pedro Aspe (Hacienda), Ernesto Zedillo (SPP), Jaime Serra Puche (Commerce), María Elena Vázquez Nava (Auditing), Manuel Camacho Solís (DF), María de los Ángeles Moreno

this elite which, as we have seen, had been developing over the last fifteen years but the increasingly tight and closed access to decision making. It appeared that even more than in 1983, the bureaucracy had become increasingly homogenous by the end of the decade and was even more dominated by the new generation of *tecnócratas*. The state appeared to have been taken over by an inner circle consisting of presidential friends. Various participants and observers with whom I discussed this issue agreed that the Salinas clique was the smallest in the history of the regime. According to one study, "the members of the cabinet did not represent anyone, only the president."[74]

Yet the new elite did establish alliances with other bureaucratic sectors, especially with the *burocratas políticos*.[75] Much more so than in the previous administration, this elite group was relatively well represented in the initial cabinet.[76] This trend would appear to contradict the homogenization of the Mexican elite. I believe that this attempt to extend his network beyond the group of well-educated "*niños bien*" in the bureaucracy was both a strategy with which Salinas hoped to improve his chances for the nomination *and,* in light of the political crises facing the regime, an acceptance of the fact that the *tecnócratas* could not rule alone but required the assistance of those better capable of managing the political machinery. As one Mexican bureaucrat put it, "the technocrats treat the politicians whom they have recruited as political experts [that] should be represented on any management team."[77] In Mexico the re-

---

(Fisheries), Patricio Chirinos (Ecology), Fernando Solana (Foreign Ministry). This group should also include José Córdoba who while not officially in the cabinet is widely considered the president's most influential advisor. It could also include Héctor Aguilar Camín who while not in the government did serve as an influential advisor to the president. It could also include those who served in the cabinet after 1989 but were considered members of the presidential circle such as Emilio Gamboa Patrón and Emilio Lozoya Thalmann.

74. Manuel Villa Aguilera, *La institución presidencial,* 1987, p. 88. Also interviews in New Haven, Providence, San Diego, and Mexico City during 1988–1989.

75. Centeno and Maxfield, "The Marriage of Finance and Order."

76. Fernando Gutíerrez Barrios (Gobernación), Jorge de la Vega Domínguez (Agriculture), Arsenio Farrell (Labor), Manuel Bartlett (Education), Víctor Cervera Pachaco (marginal *político* in Reforma Agraria), Carlos Hank González (Tourism), Enrique Álvarez del Castillo (Justice), Ignacio Morales Lechuga (DF-Justice).

77. Interview, Mexico City, June 1988. Nowhere was this more apparent than in Salinas's alliance with Manuel Bartlett, even before the *destape*. According to various sources the two men had initially united to defeat the candidacy of Alfredo del Mazo and continued working together after the rise of the Cardenista movement threatened to disrupt the electoral performance of the PRI.

turn of these men, and particularly someone like Fernando Gutiérrez Barrios who was closely linked to the repressions of 1968 and 1971, was interpreted as signaling the regimes' fear of opposition and the recognition that it would perhaps require some strong hands to manage it.[78] The autonomy of these men and their independence from the president, however, was extremely limited. Their particular skills might be required in order to protect the status quo, but they would not be allowed to dictate policy.[79]

If the *tecnócratas* had invited the *burócratas políticos* into their bureaucratic haunts, it was also partly because the former were continuing their takeover of jobs previously considered the province of the latter.[80] The most obvious case was that of PRI chief Luis Donaldo Colosio, who was imposed on a very reluctant party and helped shape it in the president's image. Bureaucrats with little electoral experience (and somewhat acerbic personalities) were imposed on states that they hardly had visited in years (for example, Otto Granados in Aguascalientes). Those Salinistas with electoral experience (for example, Patricio Chirinos and Sócrates Rizzo) were imposed as governors over the objections of the local state political machines. Another trend included the nomination of men with little contact with the government at all but significant success in business (for example, Jesús Macías).

The complete domination by the new Salinas elite meant that the old distinctions between *técnico* and *político,* and their organizations and roles, were no longer relevant. Both sets of institutions were controlled by the *tecnócratas;* both essential functions of the state were under their care. Were Colosio and Camacho any less *tecnócratas* than Aspe? They now occupied traditional *político* jobs and probably could not manipulate econometric data with the same ease as their cabinet colleagues, but

78. Suprisingly, Gutiérrez Barrios developed a reputation after 1988 as someone willing to compromise and listen to the opposition. His replacement in 1993 by a much more hard-line politician was seen as a signal that Salinas would not allow a repetition of 1988.

79. This was especially clear in the case of Manuel Bartlett. As Minister of Education he should have been in the forefront of the negotiations with the dissident teachers organizations. At critical points during these negotiations, however, the regime's representative was the president's close friend Manuel Camacho, who as head of the Federal District had no organizational claim for involvement. The obviously involuntary departures of Jorge de la Vega Domínguez and Bartlett later in the *sexenio* gave a good indication of who was truly in charge (*Excelsior* [Mexico City], January 8, 1991, p. 1).

80. See, for example, Carlos Ramírez's column in *El Financiero* (Mexico City), September 25, 1991, p. 29.

they shared much the same background, spoke the same language, and, most important, owed their positions to one man. They were reflections of a single image and were oriented toward accomplishing a single goal. Lenin himself might have envied Salinas such a vanguard.

Two crucial attributes of the Mexican elite are the extent to which it is dominated by persons from extremely selective social strata and the increasing homogenization of the elite as a whole. The shared social, educational, and professional backgrounds of the elite fostered a common vision that, combined with the centralization of bureaucratic power and its insulation from external pressures, allowed the imposition of the revolution. These attributes, however, while significant in determining the characteristics of the elite and its policies, may have been less important in the climb to power than the personal relationships these men and women established with their predecessors. It is these relationships and the battles between various factions within the bureaucracy that best explain the rise of the *tecnócratas*. The next chapter addresses these relationships.

# 6

## Friends, Allies, and Families

The truism "It's not *what* you know, it's *whom* you know" is particularly relevant for Mexico. All observers familiar with Mexican bureaucratic politics have noted the critical importance of personal relationships in determining the composition of the elite.[1] No matter the educational and professional expertise, an individual's chances for success in government service, and the elite in particular, will be strongly associated with his or her connections to those on the higher rungs of the hierarchical ladder.[2]

This chapter describes the structure of network politics in Mexico. It demonstrates that the *tecnócratas'* rise to power had little to do with their functional expertise or the specific needs of the Mexican state. Rather, the new elite used their access to the presidential office to establish their network's predominance. Therefore, internal elite dynamics

---

1. See Samuel Schmidt and Jorge Gil-Mendieta, "La carrera por la presidencia en México," 1990; Roderic Camp, "*Camarillas* in Mexican Politics: The Case of the Salinas Cabinet," 1990; Peter H. Smith, *Labyrinths of Power: Political Recruitment in Twentieth-Century Mexico*, 1979; Miguel Basáñez, *La lucha por la hegemonía en México*, 1982; Merilee Grindle, *Bureaucrats, Politicians, and Peasants in Mexico*, 1977; and Miguel Ángel Centeno and Jeffrey Weldon, "Small Circle of Friends," 1979. For a summary of the literature on patron-client relationships in Mexico, see S. N. Eisenstadt and Luis Roniger, *Patron, Clients, and Friends: Interpersonal Relations and the Structure of Trust in Society*, 1984, p. 116, n. 59.

2. This is by no means unique to Mexico, as even a cursory glance at the composition of similar elites in practically any state will attest. See, for example, G. W. Domhoff and Thomas Dye, eds., *Power Elites and Organizations*, 1987; and Ezra Suleiman, *Elites in French Society*, 1978. For a wonderful analysis of networks and professional opportunities, see Mark Granovetter, *Getting a Job: A Study of Contacts and Careers*, 1974. Perhaps the strongest examples of the importance of intraelite networks were in the former Soviet Union where various authors have spoken of clans, cliques, and gangs within the bureaucracy.

helped determine the policies followed by the Mexican state. The political acumen shown by the *tecnócratas* also demonstrates the importance of distinguishing between different types of political behavior. As one member of the losing side of these struggles explained: "[The new elite] are very bad politicians on the stump, but no one knows how to climb organizational pyramids better."[3]

The nature of these networks also helps to explain the surprising cohesiveness of the elite that allowed the centralization of power, homogeneity of perspectives, and the resulting ability to impose an economic restructuring with great potential political costs. Analysts of economic transitions have noted that these moments represent a special problem to those regimes based on patronage networks since these will be strained by the need for budget cutbacks. The *tecnócratas* were careful to ensure that their particular networks were not adversely affected by the new economic policies and used the support of these privileged allies to impose more draconian measures on other sectors of the population.

## Camarillas

Professionnal and political networks in Mexico are known as *camarillas*.[4] *Camarillas* consist of a series of vertically and horizontally interlocking, roughly pyramidal, groups. Prospective politicians and bureaucrats attach themselves to a patron or "godfather" who will provide either a position or an introduction.[5] The basis of the relationship is a relatively simple one. The patron offers a job or increased influence, the client offers loyalty and trust.[6] At some moments the patron may help a client's career, at others the junior partner might provide resources or knowledge critical to the chief. In the absence of a civil service tradition or procedural guidelines, the management of these networks becomes particularly important

---

3. Interview, Mexico City, November 1989.
4. I would like to thank Maria Isabel Reuter whose excellent work on elite structures in Mexico as part of her research at Princeton contributed a great deal to this chapter.
5. Networks are also important among intellectuals. For example, Octavio Paz is considered the "godfather" of the *Vuelta* group led by Enrique Krauze. The Paz *camarilla* often fights with that associated with Carlos Fuentes for intellectual predominance.
6. For a list of the "rules of the game," see Smith, *Labyrinths of Power*, pp. 242–278.

for aspiring politicians.[7] If the aspiring politician remains at a relatively low level he or she will belong to only an initial *camarilla*. If the individual progresses, she will acquire more patrons whose networks she serves to connect. As she climbs the bureaucratic or political ladder, she will also begin developing her own *camarillas* consisting of those she has helped or sponsored in turn. The higher in the hierarchy the *camarilla*, the more interconnected it becomes.

While the exchange of favors represents the critical instrumental link in many *camarillas*, legal and ritual kinship ties (for example, the tradition of *compadrazgo*)[8] also help cement the relationships between members. It is important to note that *camarillas* do not involve one-time exchanges (although relationships *between camarillas* may be fleeting) but are based on long-term norms of reciprocity. They are relatively stable constructions on which all political players count. While it is important to develop trust and demonstrate loyalty, however, there are some limits: one cannot run the risk of being seen as too attached to a particular candidate, as the fall of a leading patron may lead to the disappearance of many of his or her clients from government. Since leading members of the political class belong to a variety of groups or may switch alliances, they may survive or even prosper after the fall of a patron. It is also important, however, to avoid a reputation as an opportunist as *camarillas* tend to have very long collective memories.[9]

*Camarillas* may be viewed as either the curse of Mexican politics or the savior of the system. On the one hand, they promote nonmeritocratic criteria for the selection of personnel, often lead to nonoptimal distribution of resources, and support the massive corruption that still characterizes Mexican politics.[10] On the other hand, they provide an element of stability, not only for individual actors, but for the political class as a whole. Of critical importance for the subject of this book is that they

7. See Susan Kaufman Purcell, "Mexico: Clientalism, Corporatism, and Political Stability," in S. N. Eisenstadt and René Lemarchand, eds., *Political Clientalism, Patronage, and Development*, 1981.
8. See Larissa Adler Lomnitz and Marisol Perez-Lizaur, *A Mexican Elite Family, 1820–1980: Kinship, Class, and Culture*, 1988, pp. 163–164.
9. Discusssing his father's failure to secure the presidential nomination in 1964 and his subsequent fall from grace, Salinas said that it had helped him know who his friends really were (*Los Angeles Times Magazine*, November 25, 1990, p. 16). In some ways his selection served as a vindication of the family. As he hugged his father at the announcement of his nomination he supposedly said, "It took us 25 years, but we made it."
10. See Stephen D. Morris, *Corruption and Politics in Contemporary Mexico*, 1991.

provided the channels through which the new elite rose to power, helped build the ideological cohesiveness that characterizes it, and prevented its complete isolation once they arrived at the top of the pyramid.

Because of the central importance of these networks, it is possible that the biographical attributes discussed in the previous chapter, such as education or political activity, may not be so critical in and of themselves but as indications of the existence of networks.[11] That is, a Harvard degree may not be as important as belonging to the Harvard network, while participation in IEPES may be important only because it allows contact with a subgroup of the elite. Similarly, the rise of SPP may not be as critical as the formation of an exclusive inner circle inside that ministry that then supported its members' rise to power.

As important as these relationships are, they are very difficult to define since they are based on a multitude of links including family connections, school ties, and prior working partnerships. The members of each group are naturally reluctant to discuss this politically sensitive area. Moreover, while most politically connected persons are aware of *some* of the connections between *some* individuals, few (if any) could confidently outline the complete set of links that make up a major *camarilla*. The information available is often anecdotal, but it can provide an indication of the relative importance and shape of these personal networks.

In order to understand these changes in the personnel makeup of the regime, it is first important to recall that the composition of the administrative elite is largely determined by the president. Each incumbent president is at the very apex of a pyramidical network, serving to unite the various sub*camarillas*. For example, one study has calculated that from 1946–1982, 59 percent of cabinet appointments were at least partly explained by personal contacts with the president.[12] Moreover, each president in turn shapes future administrations with the choice of a successor. While the actual mechanisms behind the selection are still clouded in mystery and not a small amount of myth, it is clear that the

---

11. It is important to also note that *camarillas* do not guarantee success. Mario Moya Palencia and Manuel Bartlett, for example, had developed extensive networks inside both party and government but were defeated in the "presidential sweepstakes." They also do not guarantee immunity. Two of ex-President Echeverría's relatives were arrested by the government for their corruption and possible involvement in the drug trade.

12. Rogelio Hernández Rodríguez, "Formación y trayectoria de las secretarios de estado en México, 1946–82," 1985, p. 101.

president remains the grand elector.[13] The term used to describe the announcement of the PRI presidential candidate, *destape* or unveiling, indicates that the decision is made internally with little participation by those outside the inner circle.

The first consideration in choosing a successor appears to be the contact that the candidate has been able to establish with the president by appearing to support all the latter's policy perspectives. This does not mean the successor will follow the same policies (witness López Portillo's refutation of Echeverría at his inauguration), but it does imply that any successful candidate must gain the confidence of the president. Moreover, the presidents tend to chose those who must resemble themselves. According to an expresidential confidant, Roberto Casillas, "the personnal characteristics of each president determine those of his team. . . . if the chosen one is a *técnico*, his cabinet will consist of *técnicos*."[14]

This effect is transmitted down the hierarchical ladder and reproduced across time. Thus, the "gerente de area" of Echeverría becomes a director general under López Portillo, subsecretary under de la Madrid, and enters the cabinet under Salinas, each time increasing the portion of federal functionaries that share his professional background. The recruitment and advancement of the new elite, therefore, has much to do with the political needs and preferences in personal style of those who preceded it.

## The Break in the Revolutionary Family

The rise of the currently dominant *camarilla* may be traced to the early 1970s. Previously, the composition of the Mexican government had been characterized by a considerable degree of continuity. Despite the person-

13. See speech by Roberto Casillas quoted in *Excelsior* (Mexico City), July 30, 1986. The president, however, cannot always have his own way. For example, Cárdenas was not particularly happy with Ávila Camacho, and Miguel Alemán favored Fernando Casa Alemán but had to go with Ruiz Cortines. In recent years, however, the president has been able to override the vetoes of other sectors as certainly de la Madrid had to do with his choice of Salinas. For descriptions of the process of *destape*, see Julio Scherer García, *Los Presidentes*, 1986; and Luis Suárez, *Echeverría en el sexenio de López Portillo*, 1983, pp. 205–251.

14. Quoted in Alejandro Ramos, José Martínez, and Carlos Ramírez, *Salinas de Gortari: Candidato de la crisis*, 1987, p. 335.

nel changes that occurred at the beginning of every *sexenio,* the pool of potential entrants remained relatively stable.[15] Even during the transition from Lázaro Cárdenas to Ávila Camacho, which represented perhaps the most critical ideological break experienced by the regime, a considerable number of Cárdenas allies survived the new presidency. A similar pattern is observed with the case of Miguel Alemán's clique.[16] At those organizational levels below the cabinet and subcabinet, the continuity was even more pronounced. One might have to shift offices or ministries depending on the fate of the *camarilla* leadership, but there was a general understanding that positions would be available for all those in the "family." The elite was composed so as to support the idea of "national unity." "The designation of various public posts during the period 1940–1970 was based on the idea of balancing and conciliating the diverse interests of political groups and *camarillas* within the national and local political spaces."[17]

The administration of Luis Echeverría produced a dramatic break with both the pattern of continuity and the functional division of the elite.[18] Although the first president not to have occupied an electoral post, Echeverría had a long political career within the party apparatus; he was widely regarded as a system man. His career certainly followed the standard path. He was first introduced to the "family" when he married the daughter of an exgovernor of Jalisco state. After spending several years in the party bureaucracy, he moved to Gobernación prior to being nominated for president.[19] Yet Echeverría came to power needing to distance himself as much as possible from the previous regime and

15. See Smith, *Labyrinths of Power,* pp. 159–190.

16. Francisco Suárez Farías, "The Political Elite of Mexico under the Presidency of Luis Echeverría," 1989, p. 102; Jorge Gil, Samuel Schmidt, and Jorge Castro, "La red de poder mexicana: El caso de Miguel Alemán," 1991.

17. Francisco Suárez Farías, "La elite política," 1988, p. 306.

18. Smith's calculations for the Echeverría *sexenio* indicate that the level of continuity from previous administrations was below average (*Labyrinths of Power,* p. 165). These figures understate the case as they only account for changes up to 1971, the year during which Echeverría purged much of the personnel. Another indication of the extent of the break is the seniority of public servants in 1975. The *Censo de recursos humanos del sector público* of that year calculates that 45 percent of the personnel in the federal administration had tenure of less than five years while 57 percent had been in their current posts less than three years. If one looks at the cabinet lists in Roderic Camp, *Mexican Political Biographies,* 1982, the break in the composition of the elite is equally striking.

19. See Samuel Schmidt, *The Deterioration of the Mexican Presidency: The Years of Luis Echeverría,* 1991, for more details on his career.

the repression of 1968 (largely managed by him as Secretary of Gobernación), and needing to purge the government of all those loyal to Díaz Ordaz, who in the closing months of his *sexenio* came close to repudiating his choice for successor.[20] Very quickly after assuming power, he replaced a considerable percentage of the old *políticos* with younger men whose loyalty was more assured and who would be more likely to support his policies.[21] By closing the access to government positions on which the old *político* networks depended for their influence, Echeverría largely decimated this wing of the ruling class.

Echeverría also limited the power of the traditional *técnicos* in the financial ministries. Not only did he replace the Secretary of the Treasury Ortiz Mena in 1970 (sending him into professional exile in Washington), he also removed almost all personnel associated with the old regime down to the level of director general. While such sexenial shifts were not uncommon in other parts of the bureaucracy, it was unheard of in Treasury.[22] The death of Rodrigo Gómez in the summer of 1970 also opened up control of the Banco de México. Initially, Echeverría relied on a slightly younger generation of *técnicos* led by Hugo Margáin at Treasury and Ernesto Fernández Hurtado at the Banco. But when these men also resisted presidential policies, Echeverría either fired them (Margáin) or removed a great deal of their institutional autonomy (Fernández Hurtado). From the beginning Echeverría also placed personnel who had no technical qualifications within the ministry to serve as his "guardians" (for example, Enrique Cárdenas and Gilberto Ruiz Almada).

Some consider that Echeverría favored the *técnicos*: "[Echeverría's]

20. Díaz Ordaz reportedly called the selection of Echeverría the biggest mistake of his life (Padilla, *Historia de la política mexicana*, 1988, p. 174).

21. Prominent losers in the PRI bureaucracy included party chief Manuel Sánchez Vite (replaced by Jesús Reyes Heroles) and Secretary General Vicente Fuentes Díaz (replaced by Enrique González Pedrero). Within the government political bureaucracy the major loser was the head of the DF, Alfonso Martínez Domínguez, whose personal and professional animosity toward Echeverría was legendary. For changes in the bureaucracy during this period, see Smith, *Labyrinths of Power*, pp. 278–313; Roderic Camp, "El sistema mexicano y las decisiones sobre el personal político," 1976; and Matilde Luna, "Las transformaciones del regimen político mexicano en la década de 1970," 1983. Echeverría appears to have been less successful in placing his men in the state governorships. See Roderic Camp, "Losers in Mexican Politics," in James Wilkie, ed., *Quantitative Latin American Studies*, 1977.

22. Similar changes occurred in the Ministry of Government Properties (today's SEMIP). In the case of this institution, however, the new personnel was characterized by a much more "nationalist" or populist ideology which would lead this ministry to contend with the more conservative Treasury during the *sexenio* of López Portillo.

statecraft emphasized the bureaucracy and youth over the PRI and party veterans, aggravating in the process the tensions between *políticos and técnicos.*"[23] Conversely, other analysts see it as the victory of political calculation: "The consequence of this political shift was that financial decisions came to be made not by financiers, but by politicians."[24] But, as discussed previously, the new elite generation cannot be understood within the previous pattern of bureaucratic divisions.

In some ways the entry of the new elite solved both a personnel and a political problem. A Mexican scholar with whom I discussed this topic believes that Echeverría used scholarships to foreign universities as a way of getting the radicalized generation of 1968 out of the country.[25] When the activists returned in the middle of his *sexenio,* he also used the traditional offer of government positions as a way of co-opting these dissidents. This view is supported by another observer who notes that "[Echeverría] admitted the heads of the '68 movement into the ranks of government *técnicos.*"[26] If this interpretation is correct, then the apparent economic and social conservatism of the present technocrats would imply a radical break from the beliefs of their youth.[27] Yet, the apparent failure of the student movements of 1968 and the deterioration of Echeverría's project after 1973 might also help to explain the fervor with which they adopted a more conservative ideology.

What is perhaps most important about Echeverría's recruitment strategies is that the new elite owed their positions to direct links to the president or members of his immediate circle. Echeverría began "the

23. John Bailey, *Governing Mexico,* 1988, p. 111.

24. Roberto Newell and Luis Rubio, *Mexico's Dilemma: The Political Origins of Economic Crisis,* 1984, p. 141.

25. Interview, Mexico City, April 1988. One of Echeverría's first policies involved dramatic increases in the education budget, particularly for technical training (Judith Adler Hellman, *Mexico in Crisis,* 1983). Professional degrees increased by 290 percent and the number of students in the university doubled from 1970–1976 (Secretaría de Programación y Presupuesto, *Estadísticas históricas,* 1985, 1:87). I have not been able to locate any solid figures, but it also appears that the number of scholarships for study abroad increased even more dramatically. One ex-employee at SPP said that in the early 1970s getting money for a Ph.D. in the United States was considered relatively easy (interview, Mexico City, June 1988). Of course, this only applied to the small percentage of the population with access to these resources.

26. Fernando Zamora Millán, *México: ¿Ahora hacia dónde?* 1987, p. 67. See also Schmidt, *The Deterioration of the Mexican Presidency,* p. 88.

27. Salinas's brother Raúl (now a mid-level bureaucrat) was very involved in the student movement, but apparently Carlos, while he did attend some meetings, never participated actively.

removal of functionaries with the old political know-how, representatives of a traditional, experienced and *institutional* political class, which he substituted with young men, without experience in these fields, but with *loyalty towards and the personal confidence of the president.*[28] While cliques and *camarillas* had always been important, none established as tight a domination of the government apparatus as that of Echeverría.[29] Moreover, while most of the previous cliques had been defined by shared institutional experience, the new group had not had the opportunity to develop an identity other than their link to the president.[30] Therefore, "the process of accomodating the *técnicos* took a peculiar turn when Echeverría passed over many qualified system regulars to promote a younger generation."[31] Where the cabinet positions had been previously divided among the various factions of the "family," the new elite represented nobody and no interests other than those of the president.[32]

Echeverría probably did not expect to create the bureaucratic elite that today controls Mexico and no doubt strongly disagrees with its policies.[33] What Echeverría did create, however, was the new clientelistic structure that would allow the new generation to assume their unprecedented control of the state apparatus. The organizational changes described in Chapter 4 combined with the assault on the "family" provided an opportunity for the new generation to take over the state apparatus. The first stage of that internal coup was the selection of his successor.

The choice of López Portillo surprised almost all observers, as he was the darkest horse in the race for the presidency. His opposition included some formidable politicians, each with a solid base of support in one of

28. Zamora Millán, *México: ¿Ahora hacia dónde?* p. 67 (my emphasis).

29. For an extensive analysis of the composition of the new clique, see Suárez Farías, "The Political Elite of Mexico," pp. 80–212.

30. According to Manuel Levi Peza the domination by the president after 1970 has prevented the bureaucracy from advocating policies other than those favorable to the leader's interests (*Por donde empezar,* 1987, p. 26).

31. Bailey, *Governing Mexico,* p. 33. The relative youth of these individuals led many observers to describe the system as a "youthocracy" (Smith, *Labyrinths of Power,* pp. 281–282).

32. Manuel Villa Aguilera, *La institución presidencial,* 1987, p. 88; and Schmidt, *The Deterioration of the Mexican Presidency,* p. 154.

33. Wayne Cornelius agrees that Echeverría is responsible for their recruitment. See "Liberalization in an Authoritarian Regime," in Judith Gentleman, ed., *Mexican Politics in Transition,* 1987, p. 23. See also Marcela Bravo Aluija and Carlos Sirvent, "La elite política en México," in Germán Pérez and Samuel León, *Diecisiete ángulos de un sexenio,* 1987.

the wings of the party.[34] Given his complete lack of experience with the running of the party (unlike his predecessor), López Portillo was a more dramatic indication that the PRI was no longer a factor in the selection of its presidential candidate. Nor did López Portillo possess the classical qualifications of a *técnico,* or at least not those associated with the powerful financial institutions. He had been trained as a lawyer (UNAM '46) and his contact with intellectual life outside Mexico was largely limited to a trip to Santiago, Chile (with Echeverría in the mid-forties). For the early part of his career he was associated with the intellectual circle within UNAM and had no more contact with the government than that normally expected of a lawyer engaged in private practice in Mexico City. He began his bureaucratic career in Sepanal (1959–1965) and spent much of the Díaz Ordaz *sexenio* in the Ministry of the Presidency under Emilio Martínez Manautou. In 1970 he became subsecretary of Sepanal and later moved to the directorship of the Federal Electric Commission.

The first hint of the future role to be played by López Portillo came when he replaced Hugo Margáin as Secretary of the Treasury in 1973. According to Margáin Echeverría was frustrated by Hacienda's fiscal conservatism and felt that it was endangering his governmental project.[35] As López Portillo did not have the professional or educational credentials, his nomination was a very clear signal that Echeverría wanted to be his own Secretary of the Treasury and believed his old friend would make an excellent stand-in. It is possible that the most important reasons for the selection of López Portillo as the presidential candidate had to do with Echeverría's hopes that he could re-create a *maximato* by appointing an outsider who possessed almost no contacts with the two traditional wings of the bureaucracy and who would depend on the expresident for political advice and support.[36] Therefore López Portillo was in many ways a perfect representative of the new generation of bureaucrats who had replaced the traditional *técnicos* and

34. They included the *político* Agusto Gómez Villanueva (Minister of Agrarian Reform and associated with the CNC), the *burocrata político* Mario Moya Palencia (head of Gobernación), who had the support of the army and of many governors, and Echeverría's speech writer and Minister of Labor Porfirio Muñoz Ledo, who had the backing of the CTM. Other candidates included Hugo Cervantes del Río and the *técnico* Luis Enrique Bracamontes. The PRI, however, remained in the hands of the political wing led by Muñoz Ledo and Gómez Villanueva.

35. Hugo Margáin, interview filmed in *Mexico 1940–1982: From Boom to Bust,* documentary aired on PBS, October 1988.

36. In his memoirs López Portillo goes to some trouble to deny this. One observer argues that Echeverría's fear of Moya Palencia's considerable independent power may have cost him the *destape* (Padilla, *Historia de la política mexicana,* p. 177).

*políticos:* little institutional loyalty to a particular ministry or subgroup within the bureaucracy and a close political and personal relationship with the president.

In order to avoid the domination of Echeverría who insisted on a more active role than was the norm for expresidents, López Portillo attempted to recruit his own elite and established alliances with those whom Echeverría had demoted. Within the party López Portillo reintegrated persons associated with Díaz Ordaz and the older generation of *políticos* and *burocratas políticos.*[37] However, he did place particular emphasis on those party institutions such as IEPES that were not associated with the traditional *políticos.*

The new president's circle was also notable for including a wide assortment of representatives from "both liberal and neo-mercantilist economic and social ideologies."[38] The conservatives were led by Julio Rodolfo Moctezuma Cid and, after his departure, Treasury Secretary David Ibarra. The populists were led by Carlos Tello and included the students of Horacio de la Peña and the so-called "Cambridge School" at the Ministry of National Property and Emilio Mujica Montoya at Communications and Transport. The Interior Secretary Jesús Reyes Heroles could be placed in the latter group, but he was more concerned with political reform and liberalization.

During the first three years of his *sexenio,* López Portillo refused to overtly show his favor and lend his support to any of the particular elite wings. For example, during the debate between Moctezuma Cid and Tello, López Portillo opted for a Solomonian solution by asking for both men's resignations and replacing them with the less adversarial David Ibarra and Ricardo García Sainz. Many observers noted, however, that while Moctezuma Cid had left an Hacienda shaped in his own image (monetarist), Tello had less impact on the new ministry, and the latter was therefore widely considered the loser. Certainly Tello felt that the government's policies were shifting to the right, declaring that the financial policy of Treasury was designed by "IMF functionaries."[39]

37. For example, Carlos Sansores Pérez, Juan Sabines Gutiérrez, Blas Chumacero Sánchez, and Joaquín Gamboa Pascoe. He also sought to include within his administration some representatives of this faction such as Carlos Hank González, Jesús Reyes Heroles, and Enrique Olivares Santana.

38. David R. Mares, "Explaining Choice of Development Strategies: Suggestions from Mexico, 1970–1982," 1985.

39. Carlos Ramírez, "Tello Macías, avance desde la nacionalización; Silva Herzog, marcha atras," *Proceso,* no. 306, October 1982, p. 8.

Despite his early openings to the *burocrata político* wing and his attempts at ideological heterogeneity, López Portillo followed Echeverría's example and continued the assault of both the traditional political *and* technical career ladders. López Portillo recruited and promoted those members of the new generation of bureaucrats who would provide the technical expertise required to manage the abundance of the oil boom and who did not have any links to powerful groups outside the bureaucracy. Even more than during the Echeverría *sexenio,* the administration was dominated by those who had personal links to the president.[40]

In a dramatic break with previous procedure very few of the major posts were occupied by personnel with prior experience in the relevant area. This is not to say that they were not well-educated or capable individuals but that they were not familiar with the specific problems and histories associated with the agencies under their command. For example, the potentially most important appointment, given the newly discovered oil reserves, was Jorge Díaz Serrano as head of Pemex. Much in the same way that Echeverría had met opposition from Treasury, López Portillo met opposition from parts of Pemex that did not share his faith in breakneck exploration. The answer: replace them with a group led by his old friend Díaz Serrano whose job it would be to remove the "generation of 1938" that had built the company after its nationalization. Díaz Serrano had no experience in the public sector or with the party, and while he had extensive expertise in matters dealing with petroleum, his major credential for obtaining the new post was his close and long-standing relationship with the president.

Some oil technocrats agreed to go along with policies with which they did not agree because managing the oil dollars represented a lifetime opportunity for both professional and financial success. Various groups of *burocratas políticos* agreed for similar reasons and also because they felt that the new money could regenerate the patronage machine and reassert the legitimacy of the regime. Once again personal loyalty to the president and intraorganizational infighting would replace bureaucratic service and institutional expertise as the central criteria for professional success. Observers would rightly conclude that political imperatives

40. Rogelio Hernández Rodríguez, "Los hombres del Presidente de la Madrid," 1987, p. 99.

were now controlling economic policy and that "policy came to rest in the hands of a political bureaucratic elite that had become increasingly narrow in its background and support base."[41]

# Miguel de la Madrid and the "Familia Feliz"

These shifts in recruiting patterns over the 1970s not only resulted in the changes in elite attributes discussed in the previous chapter but permitted the practically monopolistic control over the government by a subgroup in the elite with homogenous social, educational, and professional backgrounds. López Portillo's choice of Miguel de la Madrid assured that the new generation of bureaucrats would now dominate Mexican politics.[42]

De la Madrid's family had been influential in the state of Colima since the eighteenth century. While his branch of the family was not wealthy, it did have good connections with the political elite. Even more than López Portillo, de la Madrid was considered a pure bureaucrat since at no point had he demonstrated any interest in the electoral aspects of the Mexican system. After obtaining a master's degree from Harvard he had spent almost his entire career in Treasury and then moved to SPP in 1979. In some ways the *destape* of Miguel de la Madrid was a replay of 1976. The candidate was clearly a dark horse (after the announcement the most popular response was apparently "Miguel Who?" said only half in jest). As in the case of López Portillo he defeated men with much more solid links to powerful political wings or claims to expertise.[43]

The anger of the traditional wing over being shunned was expressed in the lukewarm support afforded de la Madrid by the CTM and its leadership. Some in the party went farther. Javier García Paniagua, for example, resigned his post in the PRI's Central Committee and attacked the

---

41. Bailey, *Governing Mexico*, p. 54; Judith Teichman, *Policymaking in Mexico: From Boom to Crisis*, 1988, p. 87.

42. Rogelio Hernández Rodríguez arrives at a similar conclusion ("Los hombres del Presidente de la Madrid").

43. These included the *técnico,* David Ibarra, and the *burócratas políticos,* Carlos Hank González, Jorge de la Vega Domínguez, and Javier García Paniagua.

domination of the party by "the technocrats of SPP."[44] Much more so than the selection of López Portillo in 1975, the *destape* of de la Madrid was a clear sign of domination by a new elite: "It introduced a man pre-occupied with the management of the economy and introduced a change in the governing political generation while sumultaneously establishing its distance from traditional politics."[45] Nowhere was this clearer than in López Portillo's description of de la Madrid as "a magnificent adminis-trator who has the *potential* to be an extraordinary politician"—this eleven months before this "potential" politician became president![46]

How can we account for the rise of the new elite represented by de la Madrid and his *camarilla,* the so-called "happy family"? First, it is important to remember that had the price of oil continued to rise Jorge Díaz Serrano would have probably been the leading contender for the presidential candidacy and today one might be speaking of an elite of "oil engineers" controlling Mexico. Second, why not a *burocrata polí-tico* in the traditional mold such as Paniagua or (less so) de la Vega Domínguez?[47] Given López Portillo's career it was unlikely that he would chose someone from an opposing elite wing to succeed him. There is always strong temptation to prolong one's *sexenio* by choosing a candidate that will continue previous policies. The *burocratas políticos* had made it very clear that they did not like the direction the regime was taking and from 1979 onward had broken the traditional taboos on criticizing the president.

There was also little indication in the fall of 1981 that the regime was in such a serious political crisis that it would require the return of some-one capable of managing repression. True, there were difficulties, but they were seen as originating in a different set of problems; ones that *apparently* required the type of skills that the new elite possessed. In his memoirs López Portillo claims that the decision came down to García Paniagua and de la Madrid. He would have chosen the former if he had felt there was the danger that "the country would come undone due to

44. Tomás Brito Lara, *La sucesión presidencial de 1910 en 1988,* 1988, p. 20.
45. Ramos et al., *Salinas de Gortari: Candidato de la crisis,* p. 167.
46. *unomasuno* (Mexico City), January 6, 1982. But López Portillo apparently did not think of politics as a serious calling. In a private party to celebrate his new book on the legend of Quetzacoatl, he reportedly expressed dismay that the "hobby" of politics had taken time away from his real vocation of writing (interview, Mexico City, February 1988).
47. While Hank González was a possibility, his selection would have created constitutional difficulties as his father emigrated to Mexico and the president must be a second-generation native.

the economic crisis" and that the government would need "leadership with a strong popular base." De la Madrid, on the other hand, was chosen because the root of the problem was "financial."[48] Note again that the interpretation of what Mexico required involved a subjective judgment that, coincidentally, reflected the very skills possessed by the new elite.

Purely functional explanations miss key personal dynamics. Why de la Madrid and not another financier such as David Ibarra? In the battle over the succession between the latter and de la Madrid, we may distinguish some of the behaviors which have characterized that wing of the elite I have called *tecnócratas* and which may account for a large part of their success. Unlike the *técnicos,* these men and women never forgot that they were functioning in an organization where the approval of the chief was always more important than the orthodoxy of the analysis. Given his professional pedigree, de la Madrid could be judged as a descendant of the *técnicos,* but he very quickly demonstrated a skill in bureaucratic politics that the traditional group had lacked. For example, he sought López Portillo's favor by placing both the president's son and his mistress in very high-level positions within SPP. If nothing else, both appointments indicated that de la Madrid's commitment to a functional meritocracy was flexible. Despite his reputation as an economic conservative, de la Madrid was also careful not to alienate his institutional clients, the president and the bureaucracy, by demanding budget austerity.[49]

While David Ibarra would constantly remind the president of the fiscal problems that his borrowing was creating, de la Madrid made an effort to assure that the president did not associate him with unpleasant news.[50] This was particularly important for a bureaucrat's professional success during the later years of López Portillo's *sexenio.* According to various observers the president refused to listen to practically anyone, including several in his cabinet, and only paid attention to those who said what he wanted to hear.[51] A functionary in the Banco de México

---

48. José López Portillo, *Mis tiempos,* 1988, p. 1109.

49. See Teichman, *Policymaking in Mexico,* p. 129.

50. For example, Ibarra and the head of Banco de México Gustavo Romero Kolbeck pressured López Portillo to devalue the peso, an act not only with severe economic consequences but rife with political symbolism in a country supposedly busy managing abundance. López Portillo responded by avoiding both of these bureaucrats and eventually firing them in 1982.

51. Benito Rey Romay, *México 1987: El país que perdimos,* 1988, p. 43.

described meeting David Ibarra and Gustavo Romero Kolbeck after they had a very frustrating conversation with the president. After informing him that it was impossible to keep the budget in perpetual deficit, López Portillo reportedly told them "not to worry."[52] While intransigence and refusal to compromise would be a critical aspect of the new elite's policy-making style, these men and women were also willing to be flexible in order to win access to power *within* the bureaucracy.

In his first days in office de la Madrid signalled an abrupt departure from the policies of his predecessor. Unlike López Portillo, de la Madrid did not seek to include a wide range of opinions and perspectives in his inner circle.[53] The composition of his cabinet reflected the personalizing or deinstitutionalizing trends begun with Echeverría. By 1982 the ministers no longer came from or represented political groups but instead owed their positions to having served as consultants or advisors to the president-elect.[54] Of the twenty-seven persons in the major positions in the bureaucracy, eighteen had worked with or under de la Madrid at some critical moment in their careers.[55] As in the case of the López Portillo administration, even when educational and professional credentials would hardly objectively qualify these men for leading positions in a ministry, links to the president were enough to impose a head on even the most "technical" agency.[56]

The connections between the men and women in the de la Madrid *camarilla* went back several decades.[57] In some ways the new elite represented a fourth generation of a single interconnected family that dominated Mexican economic policy for thirty years. The first cohort consisted of Ramón Beteta (Mario Beteta's uncle), Antonio Carillo Flores, and Rodrigo Gómez. The second included their students and assistants Antonio Ortiz Mena (Carlos Salinas's uncle) who studied with Carrillo Flores, Raúl Salinas (Carlos's father), and Eduardo Bustamante. The

52. Interview, Mexico City, May 1988.

53. Hellman, *Mexico in Crisis*, pp. 226–228.

54. These included members and associates of the "Familia Feliz": Manuel Bartlett, Bernardo Sepúlveda, Ramón Aguirre, Francisco Labastida Ochoa, Fransisco Rojas, Miguel González Avelar, Emilio Gamboa Patrón, and, of course, Carlos Salinas.

55. For a summary of these career intersections, see Hernández Rodríguez, "Los hombres del Presidente de la Madrid," pp. 25–32.

56. Examples include Eduardo Pesqueira Olea in Agriculture, Francisco Labastida Ochoa in SEMIP, and Mario Beteta in PEMEX.

57. See Roderic Camp, "*Camarillas* in Mexican Politics: The Case of the Salinas Cabinet," 1990.

next generation included Ernesto Fernández Hurtado (de la Madrid's uncle) who worked under Gómez for many years, Horacio Flores de la Peña who studied under Bustamante, and Hugo Margáin (student of Carrillo Flores and Beteta who worked under Salinas's father). While the changes brought about by Echeverría and López Portillo had decimated the traditional *técnicos,* their progeny utilized this opportunity to amass more power than their predecessors would have imagined.

This familial legacy provided the base for the relationships established within the fourth generation. For example, Salinas's father had promoted the career of Hugo Margáin, who repaid the favor by introducing young Carlos to Miguel de la Madrid.[58] As I mentioned in the previous chapter, the intergenerational connections also provided invaluable training for the new elite. These relationships equipped these individuals with a political capital that augmented their graduate degrees. Salinas admitted the importance of his background when he said that "in my house I saw Lázaro Cárdenas, Ruiz Cortines, López Mateos, and Luis Echeverría. That contact with those who shaped politics in Mexico was a daily political education in my house."[59]

Having inherited power, each member of de la Madrid's *camarilla* in turn placed members of his or her personal group in his agency. Of the five leading posts in Treasury under Silva Herzog, one was held by an exclassmate and another by a coworker who had moved from Infonavit with the minister. In SEMIP two of the four leading members of the subcabinet had worked previously under Labastida Ochoa in Presidency, Treasury, or SPP. Even in the most technical agencies such as Health, we find that most of those in the leadership had several professional connections before being named to the subcabinet.

Nowhere was this pattern clearer than in SPP under Salinas. Under-Secretary Manuel Camacho Solís had attended UNAM with Salinas and had worked with him in SPP since 1980. Javier Castillo Ayala had worked with both Salinas and de la Madrid beginning in 1973. Rogelio

58. I was told that Salinas had been one of de la Madrid's students and that they had begun their professional partnership at the university. However, given the specialization of Mexican Licenciados and the fact that de la Madrid taught law while Salinas studied economics, this seems unlikely.

59. Carlos Salinas de Gortari, interview with *Excelsior* (Mexico City), October 29, 1987, p. 1. Salinas was not alone in possessing an impressive familial background. Manuel Bartlett's father had been the governor of Tabasco in the 1950s. Alfredo del Mazo's father had been a senator, governor, and cabinet minister in the 1940s and 1950s.

Montemayor had served under Salinas since 1977 and had also worked with him at IEPES, as had María de los Ángeles Moreno and Marcela González Salas Petriciolli. Each of these persons, in turn, had a group of director generals working under them that again had followed them up the career path.

No matter one's professional qualifications, belonging to the wrong group exacted high costs. In 1983 there were hardly any individuals who had worked closely or been associated with such competitors to the current elite as David Ibarra, Carlos Tello, of Jorge Díaz Serrano.[60] As ministers were replaced during the de la Madrid *sexenio*, the personnel underneath them would also change. This was certainly the case in SEMIP, SEDUE, and Treasury after the departure of their respective secretaries.

The case of Silva Herzog of Treasury provides an excellent example of the manner in which personal alliances and power struggles helped determine the composition of the elite. In the summer of 1986 Silva Herzog, who had been on everyone's presidential short list and was the only member of the ruling elite with any apparent personal charisma, resigned and left public service. While there were some clear disagreements inside the cabinet regarding the best manner with which to renegotiate the debt, almost all analysts agree that Silva Herzog's exit was partly the result of his running battle with Carlos Salinas.

The defeat of Silva Herzog was particularly significant because he could lay claim to the same set of professional and educational qualifications as Salinas. Silva Herzog certainly enjoyed even more prestige in the international financial community as well as in the Mexican private sector, while having a less negative image among the public. Moreover, with Treasury he led one of the two organizations (along with Gobernación) that could possibly challenge SPP's control over the administration. One major, and I contend critical difference, was that Silva Herzog had not established alliances outside of the institutional network of Hacienda while Salinas had perhaps the most sophisticated support structure throughout the political system. More impotant, Carlos Salinas had been a member of de la Madrid's *camarilla* since the late 1970s and had served as the latter's

---

60. One prominent exception was Pedro Aspe, who had worked under Ibarra in Treasury. When López Portillo announced his choice, many of Aspe's colleagues at ITAM went to console him on having to leave the government so early in his career. Instead, he soon reappeared as one of Salinas's closest collaborators (interview, Mexico City, April 1988).

economic advisor during the crucial years of 1979–1981. Silva Herzog, on the other hand, had spent most of the 1970s competing with de la Madrid for leading appointments in Treasury. While Silva Herzog played no role in the electoral campaign of 1982, Salinas had served as the director of the party think tank, IEPES. Salinas had also followed the president's example in his relations with the incumbent. While Silva Herzog was pessimistic regarding the chances for recovery and would push for even greater austerity measures, the eventual winner would underestimate deficits and costs.[61] De la Madrid was apparently also uncomfortable with the degree of popularity that Silva Herzog enjoyed. According to one source de la Madrid distrusted anyone who was well-known outside of the bureaucracy and felt uncomfortable with Silva Herzog's popular touch.[62] In short, whatever their objective qualifications to suceed Miguel de la Madrid, the personal dimension was decisive.

## The Nuclear Family of Carlos Salinas

Even after the departure of Silva Herzog there was considerable competition for the presidential succession. By mid-1987 the contest was publically accepted to include six candidates.

The head of the Federal District, Ramón Aguirre, was perhaps the weakest candidate. Trained as an accountant, he had spent most of his professional life in financial agencies under de la Madrid and was reportedly a good friend of the president. The Attorney General Sergio García Ramírez was also without a powerful institutional base. He was associated with the liberal and "humanist" tradition of the party exemplified by Jesús Reyes Heroles. Secretary of Education Miguel González Avelar was most observers' favorite dark horse. He enjoyed the support of several leaders in the party, and his career was closer to the traditional political path than any of the other candidates. His first speech as a precandidate was notable for expressing the objections of the "populist-traditionalists" to technocratic control.

Alfredo del Mazo, the ex-Governor of Mexico state and Secretary of Energy, Mining, and Parastatals, was the leading candidate during much

61. Interviews with excabinet members, Mexico City, April 1988 and November 1989.
62. Interview, November 1989.

of the process.[63] Del Mazo did enjoy a very close relationship with the president, who once referred to him as the "brother I never had." Del Mazo was also widely considered the perfect compromise candidate as he had ties to both the technocratic wing (he had been a banker and had participated in some of the commissions in charge of economic modernization prior to coming to SEMIP) and the old *políticos* (partly through his father and also from his time in Toluca). Secretary of Government Manuel Bartlett had served in the central offices of the party and in the institution most associated with the political machinery of the system. Simultaneously, he was also seen as a potential leader of the democratization of the PRI, having worked closely with Carlos Madrazo who had attempted to rejuvenate the local and grass-roots arms of the party in the early 1960s. He did have the support of the leadership of the traditional wing that had been defeated and replaced by the new elite, but he also had some contacts with the technocrats having worked in the Treasury ministry at the start of his career.

While Salinas was one of the leading candidates, he was not the favorite. The Salinas family had long been politically influential. Carlos's first job came as an assistant to PRI legislative leader Gonzalo Martínez Corbala. While Salinas was at UNAM during the 1968 student movement, he was not very active within it. He went to Harvard on a government scholarship (courtesy of Hugo Margáin). After Harvard he joined the de la Madrid team in Treasury and later SPP and was named minister of the latter at age thirty-four. While many pointed out that he shared his immediate predecessor's lack of electoral experience, Salinas was no neophyte in intraelite politicking. As discussed earlier, he had learned a great deal from the visitors to his house and the salons held by his father. Moreover, he had been intensively involved in the de la Madrid presidential campaign of 1982. Was he chosen for this particular blend of talents?

De la Madrid was apparently obsessed with avoiding the fate of his predecessors, whose policies had been reserved by their successors. In his fifth State of the Union speech to the Congress, the president declared: "The renovation is an institutional goal. . . . we will not change course in mid-passage."[64] Since Salinas was the man responsible for the very policies that de la Madrid wanted to continue, he was the likeliest of the

---

63. In fact, it is possible that his confidence and that of his supporters might have played a role in his final elimination. One of the unwritten rules of the game is that ambition should be disguised. In the words of Fidel Velázquez, "If you move, you won't be in the picture."

64. Miguel de la Madrid Hurtado, *Quinto informe*, 1987.

potential successors to apply the economic restructuring that the president felt Mexico required. Salinas was also careful to reassure de la Madrid on this point. In his speech during the official presentation of the six leading candidates, Salinas promised to continue the current policies of the regime. Given the almost universal unpopularity of these policies, such a statement must have been directed at de la Madrid rather than any future constituency. Of his qualifications for holding the highest office in Mexico he said: "I have known how to be loyal"[65] and that he supported a "gradualism advised by political prudence."[66] Finally, the very absence of support for his candidacy outside of the government made Salinas more capable of maintaining the austerity program. Only Salinas, divorced as he was from the political pressures outside the government and not dependent on a social movement for support, could accept the social costs that the continuation of these policies entailed. In a perfect twist of technocratic logic, the fact that he was unpopular and a pure creation of the bureaucracy made him a stronger candidate.

As we saw previously, Salinas had also established a very strong personal relationship with de la Madrid.[67] If del Mazo was the "younger brother" of de la Madrid, Salinas was his favorite "son"; in Mexico one leaves the family business to the son, not the brother. Salinas had not only been a loyal assistant but had played a critical role in de la Madrid's success prior to the latter's designation as the candidate in 1981. Many believed that he was the real author of the Global Development Plan produced by SPP in 1980, which had first brought de la Madrid recognition as potential presidential material.[68] During the election of 1982 Salinas had served as the "point man" for the candidate, defending the latter's economic policies in a variety of forums. But, at the same time that he had been the strongest defender of the government's economic policies, he had also followed de la Madrid's game plan of removing himself from decisions and information that the president did not wish to make or see. According to one source in the cabinet, Salinas would consistently minimize the costs of various programs when discussing

---

65. *New York Times*, October 5, 1987, p. 8.

66. *Latin American Weekly Report (LAWR)*, September 10, 1987 (WR–87–35).

67. He was always careful, however, in covering his bets. When Salinas was working with de la Madrid in the late 1970s he also sought the support of another powerful sponsor and potential presidential candidate by asking David Ibarra to serve as his thesis advisor (special issue of the magazine *Lideres Mexicanos*, November 1991, p. 49).

68. Salinas appeared to admit as much in his approved biography in *Lideres Mexicanos*, November 1991.

alternatives with the president. No matter his brilliance and commitment to the new Mexico, Salinas was also familiar with the traditional rules of Mexican intrabureaucratic politics.[69] According to another observer Salinas had been very successful in the creation of what was variously called the SPP or Harvard Group and could count on the support of major bureaucrats, congressmen, and governors.[70] Despite the apparent lack of popular support for his candidacy, Salinas was not isolated *within* his ministry but had established an impressive group of supporters in all the various factions and institutions of the government.[71]

When he staffed his bureaucracy, Salinas was careful to reward his supporters. He first repaid some in previous generations to whom he was beholden.[72] But Salinas's most important concern seemed to be the creation of a tightly connected group who would follow his directions for restructuring Mexico. Even more so than in previous administrations, the relationship with the president became the most important factor in anyone's career. The extended "Revolutionary Family" was reduced to a nucleus surrounding the president.

69. Interview, Mexico City, February 1988.
70. Juan Ruiz Healy, *Novedades* (Mexico City), October 4, 1987.
71. In the bureaucracy these included Gustavo Petriciolli, Fransisco Suárez Dávila, and Jaime Serra Puche (SHCP), Miguel Mancera (Banco de México), Héctor Hernández Cervantes (Commerce), Eduardo Pesqueira Olea (Agriculture), Francisco Rojas (Pemex), Manuel Camacho Solís (SEDUE), Manuel Cavazos Lerma (Gobernación), Daniel Díaz and Javier Jiménez Espíritu (SCT), Otto Granados, José Córdoba Montoya, and Patricio Chirinos of SPP, and a potentially critical player, Emilio Gamboa Patrón, the personal secretary of de la Madrid. In the party those supposedly linked to Salinas included its president, Humberto Lugo Gil, Alfonso Martínez Domínguez, and its future chief Luis Donaldo Colosio. Among the governors his supporters included Enrique González Pedrero, José Ruiz Massieu, Fernando Gutiérrez Barrios, Heladio Ramírez López, Beatriz Ramírez Rangel, Genaro Borrego Estrada, and Luis Martínez Villicana. Other prominent Salinistas included María de los Ángeles Moreno, Emilio Lozoya Thalmann, Pedro Aspe, Manuel Alonso, Gonzalo Martínez Corbala, José Antonio Alvarez Lima, Sócrates Rizzo, Fidel Herrera Beltrán, Miguel Limón Rojas, Manuel Aguilera Gómez, Ricardo Carillo Arronte, Guillermo Jiménez Morales, Héctor Domínguez, Abel Arreguín, and Bruno Kiehnle. All these names were mentioned by at least two sources in various interviews, in Ramos et al., *Salinas de Gortari: Candidato de la crisis*, Brito Lara, *La sucesión presidencial de 1910 en 1988*, Bailey, *Governing Mexico*, and in the results of an elite survey cited by Elías Chavez in *Proceso*, no. 572, October 19, 1987, pp. 12–15.
72. For example, Antonio Ortiz Mena was brought back to head the largest of the nationalized banks, Banamex. In other cases it seemed more a case of loyalty to old friends. Salinas may have been willing to challenge tradition by dumping the head of the party that had failed miserably in July, but de la Vega Domínguez was a good friend of de la Madrid's so he was given a year as head of Agriculture. Salinas also sought to punish those who had slighted him. According to several sources in Mexico the assault on la Quina was partly motivated by the union boss's role in the publication of a book which claimed that Salinas and his brother had accidently shot a maid when they were children.

Table 6-1.    Bureaucratic Survival in Mexico, 1983–1989(a)

|  | Coeff. | Errors | t-stat. |
|---|---|---|---|
| Social origins |  |  |  |
| Father poor/peasant | −0.124 | 0.190 | −0.650 |
| Father in government | −0.059 | 0.134 | −0.434 |
| Education |  |  |  |
| Economics | −0.013 | 0.122 | −0.109 |
| Engineering | −0.013 | 0.127 | −0.102 |
| Science/medicine | −0.150 | 0.176 | −0.848 |
| Advanced degree | 0.181 | 0.098 | 1.848 |
| Party activity |  |  |  |
| PRI member | 0.051 | 0.129 | 0.393 |
| Electoral office | −0.183 | 0.132 | −1.385 |
| PRI bureaucrat | 0.046 | 0.121 | 0.376 |
| PRI campaigns | 0.314 | 0.162 | 1.937 |
| IEPES* | 0.337 | 0.110 | 3.061 |
| Career specialization |  |  |  |
| Banking | 0.169 | 0.203 | 0.832 |
| Planning | −0.011 | 0.222 | −0.049 |
| Control welfare | 0.254 | 0.238 | 1.068 |
| Maintenance welfare | 0.014 | 0.220 | 0.066 |
| Control order | −0.011 | 0.234 | −0.047 |
| Camarilla |  |  |  |
| In Agriculture 1983* | −0.865 | 0.248 | −3.485 |
| In SEDUE 1983 | −0.345 | 0.272 | −1.266 |
| In Treasury 1983 | 0.334 | 0.230 | 1.454 |
| In Labor 1983* | 0.586 | 0.288 | 2.033 |
| In SPP 1983* | 0.568 | 0.271 | 2.095 |
| Salinas Camarilla* | 0.835 | 0.272 | 3.076 |
| Losers Camarilla* | 0.463 | 0.222 | 2.090 |
| Constant* | −0.664 | 0.177 | −3.761 |

*Significant at .05.
(a) Data bank of bureaucratic personnel (Director Generals or above) based on 1984 and 1989 editions of *Diccionario biográfico*. N=867. See tables in Chapter 5 for details on categories.

The pattern of survival from 1983 to 1989 within the bureaucratic elite demonstrates the critical role played by *camarilla* politics. Table 6-1 summarizes the findings of a probit analysis of survival from 1983 (early in the de la Madrid administration) to 1989.[73] Many of the attributes

73. Taken from Miguel Ángel Centeno and Jeffrey Weldon, "Small Circle of Friends," 1991.

discussed in Chapter 5 appeared to play an insignificant role in determining survival. Social and demographic indicators were found to be completely insignificant. None of the variables for education predict much, indicating perhaps that Salinas was interested in things other than merely formal training when choosing the members of his administration. Given that the experts or technocrats have taken over and that credentials are assumed, the system has returned to a battle of cliques and networks, only now it takes place with well-trained personnel rather than traditional political hacks. The players have changed, but the game remains the same.

Political activity inside the PRI seems to have little influence in determining survival with the exception of having worked in IEPES. This would demonstrate that it is not political participation that matters but with whom one works in the party. The results for career indicate that experience with a set of policies or expertise in financial matters in and of itself did not contribute to one's chance for survival. The domination of a career pattern had little to do with the need for a particular type of knowledge but rather reflected the victory of an individual clique inside the financial/planning wing.[74]

The analysis uses several dummy variables to represent possible bureaucratic *camarillas*. Given the widely acknowledged ability of a secretary to determine the composition of much of the upper levels of his or her institution, it is assumed that presence in an organization in 1983 indicates membership in a particular clique. That is, while overall career pattern reflects association with particular institutional groups, employment in a specific ministry at the level of director general or above indicates a high probability of membership in the secretary's *camarilla*.

As previously discussed, belonging to a *camarilla* led by someone who fell from favor can have serious repercussions. The negative coefficients for belonging to Agriculture or SEDUE in 1983 reflect the purge that occurred in those two agencies in the middle of the de la Madrid *sexenio*.[75]

74. For details on career patterns see Chapter 5.
75. There was a major change of staff in both of these resulting from the demotion of their respective ministers. In Agriculture de la Madrid's longtime friend Eduardo Pesqueira Olea replaced the more traditional *técnico* Horacio García Aguilar. The purge in SEDUE was a direct result of the scandals resulting from the collapse of many public buildings during the 1985 earthquake. The deposed secretary had been associated with one of the largest privately held construction firms that had built those government office buildings. His group left with him, and Manuel Camacho brought in his own people. Changes in the leadership of a ministry do not always lead to purges at lower levels, however. We had included a variable for the Educa-

Interestingly, belonging to the *camarillas* of one of the losing precandidates for the presidency was not necessarily fatal.[76] This appears to reflect Salinas's strategy of establishing alliances with groups outside his own circle, while the latter maintained control over the important ministries. Choosing the winning side obviously had its benefits. Arsenio Farrell, the Secretary of Labor under de la Madrid, was the only cabinet member to remain in office under Salinas, and he was able to retain much of his staff. Having been in the Ministry of Planning and Budget with Salinas in 1983 increased the probability of remaining in the bureaucracy in 1989. Not surprisingly, one of the most important variables for predicting survival in 1989 was belonging to Salinas's *camarilla*.

These *camarilla* structures also helped to reinforce the interpersonal cohesion produced by the homogeneity discussed in the previous chapter. The regime was run by a very exclusive circle. Within the cabinet practically everyone had either worked, studied, or was related to other ministers, or was, at most, one network link away from such a connection.[77] The president, for example, had been at UNAM at the same time as three other ministers, he had worked with six of them on the de la Madrid campaign and with eleven during his climb to the presidency. Eight senators had worked with Salinas in IEPES, while nine had worked with him in Treasury or SPP. The same pattern is observed with the governors, ten of whom had studied or worked with Salinas prior to 1988.[78] Since members of the cabinet had also established some form of link with the legislature and the governors, and these, in turn, were also highly integrated, Salinas was assured a variety of channels through which to gather information or impose discipline.[79]

---

tion Ministry (SEP) in this period to test whether or not there was a replacement of bureaucrats when Secretary Reyes Heroles died. The coefficient was positive, though not significant. It does not appear that the new secretary, González Avelar, made many changes among the high-level staff at SEP.

76. The sources used for assigning individuals to these *camarillas* are the same as described in n. 71.

77. Deviant cases such as that of Fernando Hiriart could be explained by the president's policy needs. Since he meant to dismantle much of the parastatal system, Salinas could not afford to have a strong or well-connected minister in charge of SEMIP who might attempt to protect his bureaucratic base.

78. Both of these numbers would increase after the 1991 federal and 1991 and 1992 state elections.

79. While I do not have similar data for state-private sector networks, the president apparently had established a parallel network to capital (*Business Week*, July 21, 1991; *LAWR*, March 7, 1991).

Such a tightly knit family was perhaps destined to split and struggle over the succession. By 1992 there was increasing evidence of strife in the cabinet, not over policy issues, but over positioning for the next *destape*. Four "subclans" could be identified.[80] The first, led by José Córdoba, was supposedly the most committed to the restructuring of the Mexican economy. Since Córdoba was constitutionally prohibited from the presidency, this clique could play the role of "kingmaker" and even retain influence in the next *sexenio*.[81] The second group was based in the financial institutions that had proven so dominant in the past fifteen years. If for no other reason, this made its leader, Pedro Aspe, a leading presidential candidate.[82] A third group was led by Salinas's best friend Manuel Camacho and included most of those responsible for political control.[83] While these men and women had helped make the technocratic revolution politically feasible, their commitment to economic restructuring was unclear. The final group centered on Luis Donaldo Colosio. He had used his control over the PRI to place allies in several governorships, was reportedly close to the president, and could count on the resources of PRONASOL to develop strong support. It was unclear, however, what supporters, if any, he had in the upper levels of the bureaucracy. Each of these groups sought the support of potentially critical allies whose loyalty tended to fluctuate.[84]

While the experience of each of the leading candidates might appear to reflect the *técnico/político* split, it is important to recognize that they

---

80. *El Financiero* (Mexico City), February 4, 1992, p. 28.

81. This group included Ándres Caso Lombardo, Jaime Serra Puche, Francisco Rojas, Arsenio Farrell, and a "dark-horse" presidential candidate Ernesto Zedillo.

82. He did not, however, enjoy extensive support in the political bureaucracy other than from Gutiérrez Barrios, Hank González, and Ignacio Pichardo Pagaza, governor of Mexico State and one of the designers of López Portillo's administrative reform. He was also not a close confidant of Salinas. He did, however, have significant backing from the Mexican private sector and international creditors.

83. *La Jornada* (Mexico City), April 14, 1992.

84. For example, newspapers listed Carlos Rojas, who managed PRONASOL and was therefore very influential, as belonging to either Colosio's or Camacho's group. Emilio Gamboa Patrón and Emilio Lozoya Thalmann were also seen as potentially critical players, but it remained unclear whom they would support. As with Kremlinology at the height of the Cold War, each bureaucratic shuffle was analyzed for possible significance. The nomination of Chirinos to the governorship of Veracruz was seen as helping Camacho's efforts by eliminating an adversary from the cabinet. An article in the *Financial Times* praising Aspe and critizing Camacho's performance was traced to the Treasury press office (*El Financiero* [Mexico City], January 24, 1992, p. 27; *El Financiero* [Mexico City], April 13, 1992; interviews, Mexico City, December 1991, Princeton, March 1992).

all shared the common characteristics of the *tecnócratas*. Colosio, for example, was a graduate of Penn and had spent most of his professional life in SPP. Most important, they all belonged to the same *camarilla* led by the president and all appeared committed to the success of their revolution. The unity of the elite remained very impressive even during the height of the presidential "sweepstakes." No potential candidate dared to propose changes in policy or challenge the ideological cohesion of the elite. No matter which clan won the final contest, family control of the policies of the state seemed assured.

While the Mexican elite may legitimate its positions on the basis of formal expertise, the importance of personal relationships as described above contradicts the classic notion of technocracy as based on a functional meritocracy. As in any other political arena, personal alliances play a major role in determining the composition of the elite. While the challenges facing the regime may have helped define the educational and professional backgrounds of the elite, the results of internal power games were also critical. It is possible that the composition and structure of the personal networks may determine the distribution of the measures described in the previous chapter rather than vice versa. That is, instead of education playing a decisive role in and of itself, it becomes critical because certain *camarillas* won the political battles and their educational and career patterns became the norm. I would propose that the causal order flows both ways and that the most significant conclusion is that both patterns of career recruitment and advancement, "traditional" and clientelistic, and "modern" and technocratic, presently coexist within the Mexican bureaucracy.

What is most significant is that the centralization of power in bureaucratic institutions and the ascendancy of an exclusive clique assured that the Mexican state was dominated by a very powerful, cohesive, and homogenous elite who possessed the resources required to impose their policy prescriptions. The next two chapters analyze what these were.

# IDEOLOGY

# 7

# Modernity and Revolution

During his presidential campaign, Carlos Salinas made repeated references to *modernización* and to the need to create a new society. This term came to symbolize the various social, economic, and political policies of the *tecnócratas*, but it was never very clear what anyone, including Salinas, meant when they spoke of modernizing Mexico. To many in the opposition modernization meant counterrevolution: a betrayal of the principles associated with the great struggle that toppled Porfirio Díaz and created the contemporary Mexican state. To Salinas and the new elite modernization represented the best path to achieve the original Revolutionary goals. This chapter describes that path and the assumptions and attitudes which defined it.[1] The next chapter discusses the particular technocratic perspective on democracy.

At the heart of the debate over the Revolutionary heritage is the ambiguous legacy of the 1910 Revolution: it means "everything to everybody and something different to each."[2] The various armies and leaders certainly did not articulate a unified ideology or vision of Mexico's future.[3] Madero's initial revolt against Díaz focused on "effective suf-

---

1. I would like to thank Juliet Eilperin for her contributions to this chapter.
2. Robert E. Scott, *Mexican Government in Transition*, 1964, p. 101. On the political uses of the Revolution, see Ilene O'Malley, *The Myth of the Revolution: Hero Cults and the Institutionalization of the Mexican State*, 1986.
3. The academic literature on the Revolution is immense, but see Adolfo Gilly, *La revolución interrumpida*, 1971; John Mason Hart, *Revolutionary Mexico: The Coming and Process of the Revolution*, 1987; Friedrich Katz, *The Secret War in Mexico: Europe, the United States, and the Mexican Revolution*, 1981; Alan Knight, *The Mexican Revolution*, 1986; Ramón Eduardo Ruiz, *The Great Rebellion*, 1980; Jesús Silva Herzog, *Historia de la Revolución Mexicana*, 1960; and John Womack, *Zapata and the Mexican Revolution*, 1970.

frage and no-re-election" and while making vague commitments to so-cial justice certainly did not advocate a restructuring of Mexican society. The Flores Magón brothers, on the other hand, emphasized the plight of both peasants and workers and reflected the more radical demands of the Cananea and Rio Blanco strikers. The *Plan de Guadelupe* proposed by Carranza and Obregón made little mention of social change, while Zapatismo focused on the needs and aspirations of peasants and the need for land reform. There were disagreements even among those for whom the Revolution was supposedly fought. In 1915, for example, urban workers in "Red Battalions" fought an army of peasants for control of the capital. Consequently, the doctrinal testament of the Revo-lution, the Constitution of 1917, was "amorphous and contradictory,"[4] permitting perpetual reinterpretation and allowing the new state exten-sive ideological license.

Since the 1920s and the defeat of the Cristero Rebellion, Mexican governments have used that latitude to sustain a pragmatic balance be-tween social justice and economic growth, between political freedom and regime stability. The often-noted pendulum effect, whereby the dif-ferent administrations shifted from left to right (while never moving far from the center) reflected the divisions that existed within the "big tent" of the PRI. Rather than a commitment to an explicit ideology, the regime utilized the symbols of the Revolution to legitimize its institutionaliza-tion. The very name of the PRI reflected the ambiguity of the regime; how could it resolve the incongruity between institutional and revolu-tionary? But while most contradictions lead to instability, the Mexican state weathered crises that would have shaken the foundations of better-defined regimes. Precisely because it was so malleable, the ideological edifice could absorb assaults without crumbling.

During the past twenty years this ambiguous legacy provoked a "dis-pute over the Mexican nation" between two very different development strategies.[5] The "neoliberal" project favored the integration of the Mexi-can economy into a global marketplace through utilization of its com-parative advantages (low labor costs, natural resource exploitation, prox-imity to the United States, agricultural production for export as opposed to consumption). It treated inflation (rather than demand) as the domi-

---

4. Ramón Eduardo Ruiz, *Triumphs and Tragedy*, 1992, p. 335.
5. Rolando Cordera Campos and Carlos Tello, eds., *México: La disputa por la nación*, 1981; and Cordera Campos and Tello, "Prospects and Options for Mexican Society," in Clark Reynolds and Carlos Tello, eds., *U.S.-Mexico Relations: Economic and Social Aspects*, 1983.

nant axis of any economic policy and represented an assault on the Keynesian paradigm, calling for fiscal and wage austerity even, and perhaps particularly, during difficult economic moments. Its principal villains were protectionism and state intervention, which hampered the full development of market forces that were deemed the most efficient mechanisms for economic growth.

A very different "nationalist" perspective placed much greater emphasis on the economic role of the state. It contended that domestic production had been hampered by supply problems resulting from private sector speculation. This view rejected restrictive monetary policies and emphasized fiscal reform in order to capture the resources required by the state. Perhaps most important, it called for decreasing reliance on export-generated growth and for the development of a domestic market.

To a large extent *salinastroika* represented the victory of the Carranzista or Obregonista view of the Revolution over that exemplified by Zapata. The dispute was apparently resolved with the victory of a neoliberal project. Yet the *tecnócratas* were not simply Mexican variants of the infamous "Chicago Boys." While their policy preferences clearly reflected neoliberal assumptions, the technocratic revolution has to be understood as a product of both ideology and history, of method and substance, and of theory and practice. The government's use of Revolutionary symbols *was* partly a politically opportunistic strategy with which to legitimize its policies. But it would be incorrect to dismiss the new definition of the Revolution as a purely pragmatic disguise for neoliberalism. Salinas appears truly committed to the Revolutionary notions of nationalism, sovereignty, and justice. He is "trying to make sense of the Mexican Revolution at the end of the twentieth century. The world isn't the same as in 1910."[6] The definition of that world and Mexico's position within it, rather than a blanket acceptance of neoliberal prescriptions, is what shaped the technocratic revolution.

# From Stabilizing to Shared Development

In order to understand the new elite's vision for a "modern Mexico," we first need to analyze the policies followed by previous administrations

6. John Womack, quoted in *Los Angeles Times Magazine,* November 25, 1990, p. 16.

and the consequences thereof. For nearly three decades after World War II, Mexican public policy was dominated by a model that gave private capital the leading role in fostering Mexico's economic growth.[7] This perspective limited the government's economic role to assuring a stable exchange rate and an extremely favorable fiscal climate, to providing enough protection to assure the success of Import Substituting Industrialization (ISI), and, perhaps most important, to guaranteeing the political stability required by domestic and foreign capital investment.[8] While it is normally associated with a conservative economic dogma, Stabilizing Development did not follow the neoliberal line regarding free trade. It erected protectionist barriers and supported the development of national industries.[9] At the heart of Stabilizing Development was the orthodox principle of trickle-down growth; Mexico would first create wealth and then would distribute it. In the words of President López Mateos, "it is our objective to create abundance, the only solution to our economic and social problems."[10] Development was not defined in social terms but as consisting of "sustained increases in the volume of production per unit of labor."[11]

7. Officially, the policies of Stabilizing Development only began after the appointment of Antonio Ortiz Mena as Secretary of the Treasury in 1958, but almost all sources concur that there was a general continuity in the government's economic policy from the *sexenio* of Miguel Alemán through the 1960s. For a summary of the basic perspectives of Stabilizing Development, see Antonio Ortiz Mena, "Desarrollo estabilizador: Una década de estrategia económica en México," 1970, pp. 417–449. See also Carlos Tello, *La política económica de México, 1970–1976*, 1979; Fernando Carmona et al., *El milagro mexicano*, 1974; and Roger Hansen, *The Politics of Mexican Development*, 1980.

8. The economic policy of the government was shaped by two criteria: control of inflation and support for aggregate economic growth with emphasis on industrial versus agricultural investment. The former required that the government maintain a balanced budget. Given the need to provide incentives for private capital and the subsequent low levels of taxation, this fiscal constraint limited the amount of public expenditures to 9.2 percent of GNP (Ortiz Mena, "Desarrollo estabilizador," p. 433). This amount was largely devoted to the construction of a basic industrial infrastructure and neglected agricultural development.

9. Ibid., p. 424. In general, however, the policy met with the strong approval of the international financial community. Other than its emphasis on the protection of domestic industry, Mexican economic policy during these years was clearly a reflection of the proposals suggested by international financial institutions such as the IMF and IBRD. Both López Mateos and Díaz Ordaz, for example, expressed their allegiance to the models offered by these organizations and their satisfaction in having successfully participated in the Alliance for Progress. See Paulina Fernández Christlieb and Luisa Bejar Algazzi, "Le década de los sesenta," in Germán Pérez Fernández del Castillo, ed., *Evolución del estado mexicano, 1940–1983*, 1986.

10. Quoted in Fernández Christlieb and Bejar Algazzi, "La década de los sesenta," p. 115.

11. Ortiz Mena, "Desarrollo estabilizador," p. 420.

By its own criteria Stabilizing Development was a success. While inflation was minimal by Latin American standards (3.6 percent per annum from 1959 to 1967), the economy grew at a rate of 6.5 percent during those same years.[12] While prior to World War II Mexico was a rural and agricultural country, by the 1960s it had become urban and industrialized.[13] The benefits of this growth, however, were not distributed equally. While Stabilizing Development was extremely successful in meeting its stated goals, the social welfare side of the equation remained a secondary concern.[14] The social and economic inequality, which had always characterized Mexico, actually increased during this period.[15] The one exception to this pattern was the creation of a relatively prosperous urban middle class, but it probably never represented more than 20 percent of the population.

By the end of the 1960s the basic paradigms of Stabilizing Development were being challenged both from within and outside the government. First, despite some of the later claims made by its defenders,[16] by the late 1960s the "Mexican Miracle" had reached its limits. Import Substituting Industrialization was already beginning to falter, with "difficulties through the balance of payments, in overall industrial and agricultural productivity, and to a lesser degree, in public savings."[17] By creating a relatively large urban middle class, this policy was also partly responsible for increasing pressure on the government to open political institutions. Perhaps more important, the apparent contradictions between the government's priorities and the social ideals of the Revolution, combined with the growing frustration with the autocratic nature of the

---

12. Ibid., p. 426.

13. The agricultural sector, which accounted for 17.8 percent of GNP and 58.3 percent of the work force in 1950, declined in importance to 13.3 percent and 47.9 percent respectively in 1967. On the other hand, manufacturing's role in GNP increased from 18.5 percent to 20.7 percent and its share of the labor force increased from 11.8 percent to 16.6 percent. Total product per laborer increased from 9,000 pesos to 15,200 from 1950 to 1967 (constant 1960 prices). See ibid., pp. 425–426.

14. Ibid., p. 419.

15. See Ifigenia Martínez de Navarrete, "La distribución del ingreso en México," 1980; and Rolando Cordera Campos and Carlos Tello, eds., La desigualdad en México, 1984.

16. Ortiz Mena declared that "if Mexico had continued the same policies after 1970 and then had found oil, . . . it would already be a developed country." Quoted in Alejandro Ramos, José Martínez, and Carlos Ramírez, Salinas de Gortari: Candidato de la crisis, 1987, p. 129.

17. Roberto Newell and Luis Rubio, Mexico's Dilemma: The Political Origins of Economic Crisis, 1984, p. 111. This judgment comes from authors who are generally sympathetic to this model of economic development.

regime, helped create the conditions for the student demonstrations of 1968.

The events of October 1968 signaled the weakening of what Daniel Cosío Villegas identified as the three bases for Mexico's political stability: the status of the presidency, the legitimacy of the party, and economic growth.[18] The isolation and alienation of Díaz Ordaz challenged the first, the overt repression of 1968 and the growth of popular demands for real democracy weakened the second, and the third was faltering. Ever since 1940 "the regime's pragmatic justification for authoritarianism stressed results: stability, material progress, proven leadership"; all three were in doubt by 1970.[19]

Until the late 1960s the government could still count on considerable popular support and was able to make a legitimate claim to power as the heir to the legacy of the Revolution.[20] By the end of the Díaz Ordaz administration, however, the ability of the PRI to provide the political stability required by the regime and its economic project began to weaken. The Mexican "economic miracle" began to demonstrate its limitations at the very same time that various social protest movements began to challenge the closed political system.

When he came to power, therefore, Luis Echeverría had to resolve a critical double crisis: economic stagnation and political delegitimation.[21] Echeverría correctly noted that the crisis faced by the Mexican regime originated in the contradiction between the pretense of an inclusionary revolutionary dogma and an extremely exclusionary economic system. Even flowing profusely, trickle-down wealth had produced levels of inequality that clearly contradicted the promises of the Revolution. As the amount of wealth, or the growth thereof, began to decline, this placed greater pressures on the legitimacy of the system, which was still suffering the aftershocks of 1968.

18. *El sistema político mexicano,* 1975, pp. 22–52.

19. John Bailey, *Governing Mexico,* 1988, p. 7.

20. Juan Molinar Horcasitas, however, believes that analysts have overestimated the legitimacy and popularity of the PRI prior to 1968 and claims that much of the government's success was due to the disarticulation of the opposition (*El tiempo de la legitimidad,* 1991, p. 248).

21. There is general agreement regarding the very difficult tasks facing Echeverría in 1970. See Judith Adler Hellman, *Mexico in Crisis,* 1983, pp. 187–196; Miguel Basáñez, *La lucha por la hegemonía en México, 1968–1980,* 1982, pp. 186–192; Héctor Aguilar Camín and Lorenzo Meyer, *A la sombra de la Revolución Mexicana,* 1989, p. 242. Even Newell and Rubio, who are clearly not sympathetic to Echeverría's philosophy, recognize the importance of reestablishing consensus (*Mexico's Dilemma,* pp. 121–122).

Echeverría's response was to produce a new model called Shared Development which would combine growth and social justice.[22] Shared Development would resolve the double crisis by increasing government participation in the economy with greater emphasis on social expenditures accompanied by a new populist and nationalist rhetoric.[23] The latter became one of the distinguishing characteristics of the Echeverría *sexenio*. The president sought to break away from the dependent relationship Mexico had established with the United States by seeking a wider range of trading partners and also by becoming a leader in the calls for a new economic order and greater independence in the Third World. As part of these measures the government established stricter controls on foreign investment and profit repatriation.

While these policies received a great deal of attention in the United States, much more important changes were occurring in the domestic role of the Mexican government. Through the increase in public expenditures, Echeverría hoped to resolve the conflict between growth and equity by obtaining both simultaneously. To a large extent the new policy followed the traditional political strategy in Mexico: absorb the opposition through coaptation of its leaders and its ideology. Echeverría tried to reappropriate the "Revolutionary Mantle" by enlarging the scope of government activity and increasing the size of the bureaucracy. Rather than calling on the military to save the regime from its enemies, as in the case of the Southern Cone countries facing similar problems, Echeverría expanded the government, and altered its policy discourse, in order to include them.

The government became much more directly involved in generating economic growth and managing a public industrial sector. In these six years (even before the oil boom), the state almost replaced the private sector as the major economic investor. The number of state enterprises increased from 84 in 1970 to 845 in 1976.[24] The ratio of private to public investment declined from 2.65 in 1971 to 1.46 in 1976 and the

22. In the following analysis I have limited myself to summary descriptions of economic policies. For a detailed study of these see Robert Looney, *Economic Policymaking in Mexico*, 1985, pp. 55–124. For Echeverría's political philosophy see Luis J. Molina Piñeiro, *Estructura del poder y reglas del juego político en México*, 1984.

23. More than any of his predecessors, Echeverría used mass media to communicate directly with the population and replaced the cautious utterances of previous presidents with a rhetorical style that one analyst has described as akin to preaching (Cosío Villegas, *El sistema político mexicano*, p. 99).

24. Hellman, *Mexico in Crisis*, p. 200.

percentage of the GNP accounted for by the public sector increased from one-fourth in 1970 to close to one-half by 1982.[25] Beginning in 1970 the economic role of the government increased to the point that the management of the economy became more important than the management of politics. That is, despite (or perhaps because of) the disruptions of 1968, in the 1970s an administration's perceived success and legitimacy were more and more based on its ability to *directly* foster economic growth rather than merely provide the political stability required to encourage and protect that provided by the private sector.

This redefinition of the role of the state obviously supported the rise in importance and influence of personnel with economic expertise. Yet, there were clear divisions within the public sector regarding the advisability of Echeverría's programs. The most important of these occurred not between the so-called *técnicos* and *políticos* but within the institutions associated with formulating economic policy. These recurrent battles between "monetarists" and "Keynesians" *within the economic side of the government,* rather than between *técnicos* and the increasingly marginalized *políticos,* would define public policy making during the next decade.

The personnel in the Ministry of National Patrimony (Sepanal, later SEMIP), led by Secretary Horacio Flores de la Peña, favored the expansion of the government and felt that the policies of the financiers in Treasury were limiting economic growth.[26] Despite Echeverría's assault on the autonomy of the financial bureaucracy described in previous chapters, however, this sector was still able to frustrate many of the economic reforms that the president contemplated.[27] The most obvious example of this opposition came during Echeverría's attempts to restructure the tax system.[28] The Ministry of the Treasury and the Banco de México allied with national capital to prevent a thorough fiscal reform that would have increased state revenues to match the new expenditures.[29] According to Carlos Tello it was the failure of the Echeverría

25. Bancomer, *Panorama Económico,* December 1983, p. 268.

26. José López Portillo, *Mis tiempos,* 1988, p. 350.

27. Héctor Guillén Romo, *Orígenes de las crisis en México,* 1984, pp. 46–53.

28. See Sylvia Maxfield, *Governing Capital: International Finance and Mexican Politics,* 1990, pp. 88–93.

29. The reasons for this failure are not clear. Some sources interviewed suggested that Echeverría was unwilling to accept the political costs of increased taxation, but given the rejection of his leadership by those sectors that would have been most affected, it is difficult to understand this rationale.

administration to fundamentally challenge "the system of privileges and protection" that eventually led to the financial crisis of 1976.[30]

On some levels Echeverría was successful, particularly during the first half of his *sexenio*. The economy grew, wages rose, and indicators of living standards among the poorest improved.[31] Despite Echeverría's reputation as a populist, the *percentage* of public funds used for social expenditures did not increase significantly during this period, while, much like his predecessors, the president emphasized industrial and infrastructural investments. Nevertheless, given the dramatic increases in the size of the federal pie, the slice devoted to social welfare was much larger.

The new role of the public sector did have a price, however, and this eventually doomed Echeverría's project. The president was not able to match the increases in government expenditure with a parallel rise in revenues, and this led to a fourfold increase in the public deficit.[32] The decline in foreign and domestic private investment after 1973 and massive capital flight[33] forced the government to increasingly rely on borrowing in order to meet its new obligations. Annual public sector netindebtedness increased by over 700 percent while the external debt rose by 450 percent.[34] This massive influx of new funds had the expected inflationary effect, and consumer prices doubled between 1970 and 1976. Moreover, the trade deficit increased dramatically, and in the last year of his *sexenio* Echeverría was forced to devalue the peso. By 1976, in what must have been a humiliating experience for the president, Echeverría was forced to ask for assistance from the IMF and to accept its austerity package.

---

30. *La política económica de México, 1970–1976*, p. 125.

31. Between 1970 and 1973 the GNP grew by 25 percent, and while there was a slowdown after the oil crisis of 1973, the economy as a whole grew by 51 percent during his *sexenio*. The minimum daily salary increased (in real terms) by 32.5 percent, while state subsidies helped reduce the price of the basic nutritional basket. See Secretaría de Programación y Presupuesto, *Información sobre el gasto público, 1970–1980*, 1982, pp. 1–32, and Secretaría de Programación y Presupuesto, *Diez años de indicadores económicos y sociales en México*, 1982, p. 78. There is, however, a great deal of debate regarding the actual improvement in the living conditions of those in the bottom half of the population.

32. From 2.3 percent of GNP in 1971 to 8.0 percent in 1976 (Héctor Guillén Romo, *Orígines de la crisis en México*, 1984, p. 47).

33. One estimate is $4 billion (U.S.) in the last eighteen months of Echeverría's administration (Looney, *Economic Policymaking in Mexico*, p. 58).

34. From 7.5 billion pesos in 1970 to 53.6 billion in 1976 (constant 1970 pesos) and from $4.3 billion (U.S.) to $19.6 billion (U.S.). See Secretaría de Programación y Presupuesto, *Información sobre gasto público*, p. 65.

The search for a new legitimacy also had its political costs. As discussed in Chapter 3, private capital strongly resisted the government's policies and began the pattern of capital flight that was to haunt the economy for the next decade. The left, on the other hand, was frustrated by the failure of Echeverría to alter the economic structure of Mexico in any significant manner. Moreover, large elements of the intelligentsia remained suspicious of the president because of his participation in the repression of 1968 and his probable role in the killing of student demonstrators in 1971. After 1973, as independent labor organizations and peasant land appropriations became more common, Echeverría increasingly relied on the discredited corporatist apparatus to guarantee political control.

By 1976 Echeverría's attempts to shift government policy away from Stabilizing Development were widely considered a failure. His rhetorical rejuvenation of the "Revolutionary Mantle" had enabled him to co-opt some of the opposition, but at the cost of the support of private capital. Without more abundant resources the government would be unable to replace private capital or continue to support improvements in the living standards of the majority of the population. The failure of Echeverría's populism must have helped shape the attitudes of the young bureaucrats who would take power in the next decade. Even if they agreed with Echeverría's analysis and his prescriptions for Mexico, the early 1970s taught this group that government policy could not succeed without the support of domestic and international capital. This lesson would be of paramount importance six years later.

# The Management of Affluence

At the beginning of his administration López Portillo represented a return to more orthodox economic policies. He first rejected Echeverría's populistic faith in the power of the government to solve critical problems: "In the long run, the worst policy is to turn the economy into a utopia. Populism does not solve anything, but complicates and enlarges problems."[35] He began his *sexenio* with reassuring words for the private

---

35. José López Portillo, "Primer informe del gobierno," in Presidencia de la República, *El ejecutivo ante el congreso, 1977–1978*, p. 43.

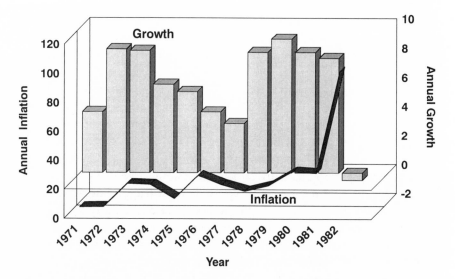

Fig. 7-1. The Mexican economy, 1971–1982. (Source: Secretaría de Programación y Presupuesto, *Diez años de indicadores económicos y sociales en México*, 1982; Secretaría de Programación y Presupuesto, *Agenda estadística*, 1979–1982; Banco de México, *The Mexican Economy*, 1992, 1992.)

sector that the confrontation with national and international capital would stop. López Portillo wished to create an "Alliance for Production" that would foster economic growth. This alliance would involve a tripartite cooperation between government, labor, and the private sector guided by the new economic plans that were being formulated, but it would be based on the traditional dogma that growth preceded distribution. Significantly, in López Portillo's set of promises to the Mexican people four words would stand out, only the first of which could remotely be linked to Echeverría's project: "justice, tranquility, security, and confidence."[36]

The appearance of two new sources of government revenue, however, freed López Portillo from the resource limitations that had constrained Echeverría's programs. First, it became clear that Mexico's oil reserves made it a potentially leading exporter. Second, thanks to the new discoveries the international financial community was willing and eager to give Mexico an unprecedented amount of credit. For López Portillo (and

36. Ibid., p. 27.

practically all observers at the time), oil (and the credit it could obtain) represented the answer to all of Mexico's problems. If Echeverría had not possessed the resources to break the conflict between growth and equity, the new affluence would allow Mexico to have it all.

The new wealth permitted López Portillo to temporarily quiet opposition from the left *and* the right by allowing him to satisfy the demands of both sides. Beginning in 1978 the economy grew at an unprecedented rate, eclipsing the best years of the "Miracle."[37] The private sector, which had opposed the Echeverría expansion, now found that it could profit handsomely from government investments in the massive infrastructure required by oil exploration and export. Few in the private sector were willing to sacrifice their share in the bonanza, particularly since López Portillo avoided the confrontational rhetoric of his predecessor.

The new affluence, however, did not reduce the conflict regarding economic policy *within* the public sector itself.[38] First, there were divisions regarding the rate of expansion, particularly increases in oil production.[39] On the one side, there was a group of expansionists centered around López Portillo's close friend and head of Pemex, Jorge Díaz Serrano, who called for increased production for export (largely to the United States) as a way of fueling industrial development. The "anti-expansionists" objected to the international integration and reliance on capital intensive (and expensive) technology that such a policy entailed and the large amounts of debt required.

The debate regarding the appropriate level of oil production paralleled discussions regarding the best policy the state should follow to promote economic growth. From the beginning of the *sexenio* there were constant battles within the Economic Cabinet between the structuralists, who wanted to stimulate production and reorganize consumption and distribution through state action, and the monetarists, who were more concerned with monetary controls and who opposed increased public participation in the economy. The two sides could not even agree as to

---

37. From 1976 to 1981 real GDP rose by an average of 6.9 percent per annum. See Secretaría de Programación y Presupuesto, *Diez años de indicadores económicos y sociales en México*.

38. See David Ibarra and José-Luis Alberro, "Mexico," in Joseph Pechman, ed., *The Role of the Economist in Government*, 1989.

39. For an analysis of oil policy see George Grayson, "Oil and Politics in Mexico," 1983; and Judith Teichman, *Policymaking in Mexico: From Boom to Crisis*, 1988, pp. 63–110.

the size of the government deficits that were being financed with new foreign loans.[40]

Each of the opposing sides were associated with particular institutions in the bureaucracy. The structuralists were linked to the Cambridge School (so called because many of its prominent members studied in the United Kingdom) associated with Flores de la Peña, Carlos Tello, and José Ándres Oteyza. This group was largely concentrated in the newly created Ministry of National Patrimony and Industrial Development (Sepafin) and, for the first year after its creation, the new supersecretariat of SPP. The monetarists were to be found in Treasury and the Banco de México. Miguel de la Madrid and his *camarilla* in SPP (after 1979) established a critical position in the strategic middle ground between these groups: they never challenged López Portillo's propensity to borrow but also did not emphasize the distributive policies suggested by Tello.[41] The overall policy guidelines produced by this last institution, however, were generally more in line with the preferences of the orthodox monetarists than with the more interventionist structuralists.

The divisions between these two groups were perhaps best exemplified by the opposing plans they produced for Mexico's development. These plans provide an insight into the groups' visions of Mexico's future prior to the constraints imposed by the debt crisis and also serve to define the critical differences between what might be called the left and right wings of the technocratic elite.[42]

Sepafin's National Plan for Industrial Development (PNDI) stressed state action but also emphasized a balance between economic growth and the welfare of the population. According to the PNDI the major problem facing the Mexican economy was the structure of the internal market and the unequal distribution of wealth. It proposed using the oil revenues to increase employment and to reorient production toward basic consumer goods. Although Carlos Tello had no official links with Sepafin, he served as an important spokesman for the structuralists in

40. López Portillo, *Mis tiempos*, p. 496. The fights continued throughout the *sexenio* (pp. 1148 and 1192).

41. David R. Mares, "Explaining Choice of Development Strategies: Suggestions from Mexico, 1970–1982," 1985.

42. The texts for the plans may be found in the *Antología de la planeación en México, 1917–1985* published by Secretaría de Programación y Presupuesto. See vol. 9 for the PGD and vol. 7 for the PNDI.

the government. He declared that the new economic strategy "would be based on the production of national goods and services which are socially necessary" and would focus on the "deficiencies in nutrition, health, education, and housing" that still plagued large elements of the population.[43]

The Global Development Plan (PGD), produced by Miguel de la Madrid's SPP under the direction of Carlos Salinas de Gortari, stressed financial control over the economy and considered that inflation, and the subsequent uncertainty, were the most important threats to development. Instead of the domestic market, it emphasized a greater integration into the world economy following the lines of the already booming Asian Pacific Rim NICs. Rather than supporting an increase in the size of the state, it emphasized efficient planning, frugality, and the need to resist populist pressures. While he played no role in its formulation, ex-SPP head Ricardo García Sainz best expressed the economic perspective of this sector of the elite when he declared that the political economy of the country would progress with "support for and incentives to capital and sacrifice and effort from the working class."[44] This explicit distribution of costs and benefits remained central to the restructuring of the Mexican economy throughout the 1980s.

In some ways each of the two plans represented a legacy from the days of Stabilizing Development. The PNDI retained the emphasis on the development of a domestic market but relied much more heavily on state intervention. The PGD, on the other hand, held that the external market represented the best hope for economic growth but, like its pre-1970 predecessors, rejected reliance on the public sector. A critical difference between the two documents is that the PNDI perceived the need for a radical restructuring of Mexican society while the PGD largely focused on improving the management of the economic apparatus without any dramatic change in the socioeconomic status quo.

The existence of the two plans and the battles that raged in the inner circles regarding which one should predominate indicated that there were serious divisions within the elite. However, they both shared a technocratic methodological bias.[45] In both plans the population largely

43. Quoted in Proceso, *Planes sin planificación*, 1980, pp. 31 and 39.
44. Ibid., p. 31.
45. One bureaucrat who had worked in SPP during these critical years dismissed the "quantophenia" of the PNDI by saying that the models utilized by Sepafin were very primitive. His assault on the PNDI was largely based on its lack of econometric sophistication, and he

remained a passive object in the strategies designed from above. Whatever the outcome of the battle between these two opposing visions, the decisions would be made by experts. Whether they were trained at Oxbridge or in the Ivy League might affect the particular models utilized but not the manner in which decisions were made.

During the boom years of 1979 and 1980, those who favored unlimited production and the expansion of the state's role in the economy dominated. Public sector participation in GNP grew at an even faster rate than during Echeverría's *sexenio,* while López Portillo remained committed to improving the social safety net provided by the government.[46] While the rate of increase in welfare expenditures was not as dramatic as during the Echeverría *sexenio,* enough of the oil boom was trickling down to temporarily satisfy most of the demands of the labor and peasant sectors. Even more than in the previous administration, however, expenditures for economic development far outpaced the welfare budget.

# Crisis and Austerity

Beginning in mid-1981 the expansion of the public sector was threatened by a decline in oil prices, a dramatic increase in the interest rates on the loans that Mexico had used to fuel its growth, and increasing signs of runaway inflation. Over the next twelve months the economy went into a tailspin. Annual production per capita declined by 2.9 percent, while capital flight (which may have reached $22 billion [U.S.] prior to the bank nationalization[47]) produced a liquidity crisis and a decline in private investment of 17.3 percent. The public deficit reached 16.9 percent of GDP, prices were increasing by almost 60 percent per annum, and López Portillo reluctantly devalued the peso.[48]

---

declared that "you don't ask Cambridge graduates for this kind of thing" (interview, San Diego, January 1990).

46. Secretaría de Programación y Presupuesto, *Información sobre gasto público,* and Secretaría de Programación y Presupuesto, *El ingreso y gasto público en México,* 1983.

47. Morgan Guaranty, cited in Stephen A. Quick, "Mexico's Macroeconomic Gamble," 1989. One estimate of total capital flight from 1975 to 1985 is $55 billion (U.S.). See Wayne Cornelius, *The Political Economy of Mexico under De la Madrid: The Crisis Deepens, 1985–1986,* 1986, p. 16.

48. Nora Lustig, "The Mexican Economy in the Eighties: An Overview," 1989, table 1.

Facing a new economic crisis, the Mexican government could have turned in two directions. The first, advocated by some in what we may call the technocratic left, included increasing state control over the economy and challenging the creditor banks. The second was a turn toward the new economic orthodoxy based on freer markets, less government intervention, and greater "fiscal responsibility" that would permit meeting Mexico's debt service requirements.[49]

At one point in 1982 it appeared that Mexico would follow the first alternative. In August the government announced that it was unable to make interest payments on the debt. Less than a month later, during his annual State of the Union speech, López Portillo accused the Mexican bourgeoisie of having "stolen more money from our country than the empires which have exploited us since the beginning of history." He announced that in order to prevent such a theft, he was nationalizing the banking industry and imposing foreign exchange controls.[50]

In the end, however, Mexico opted for the second strategy. The debt was rescheduled, and Mexico was soon on its way to becoming the "model debtor" that would meet its obligations no matter the circumstances. President-elect de la Madrid's displeasure with the nationalization was evident as he did not make any comment on the announcement for three weeks (in Mexican political protocol this amounted to disapproval). In a break with the usual monolithic unity of the bureaucracy, Treasury Secretary Jesús Silva Herzog came close to directly criticizing the nationalization when he attended the IMF meetings in September.[51] Immediately upon taking power, de la Madrid allowed "the public" to purchase up to 35 percent of the stock in the new corporations, and, perhaps more important, did not replace any of the management below the level of president. Miguel de la Madrid and his *camarilla* insisted that the time had come to end what they called a "fictional economy."[52] The fact that these same persons had been active participants in the expansion of the state sector and had, until the *destape* of Miguel de la Ma-

---

49. See Robert Kaufman, "Stabilization and Adjustment in Argentina, Brazil, and Mexico," in Joan Nelson, ed., *Economic Crisis and Policy Choice*, 1990, pp. 97–100; and Kaufman, "Economic Orthodoxy and Political Change in Mexico," in Robert Kaufman and Barbara Stallings, eds., *Debt and Democracy in Latin America*, 1989, pp. 113–115.

50. See Carlos Tello's *La nacionalización de la banca*, 1985; and Maxfield, *Governing Capital*.

51. Carlos Ramírez, "Tello Macías, avance desde la nacionalización; Silva Herzog, marcha atrás," *Proceso*, no. 306, 1982.

52. López Portillo, *Mis tiempos*, p. 1014.

drid, resisted previous warnings about the deficits, was apparently irrelevant. In place of debates on how to develop, the critical economic issue became how to divide the costs of decline.

Obviously, the pressure exerted by domestic capital and the international economy helped determine the policies followed by the Mexican state and constrained its autonomy. Continuing to challenge capital would have required a complete break with the economic status quo and a radical change in the nature of the regime. As I discussed in Chapter 3, however, it is imperative not to dismiss the policies of the regime through some reductionist method of "politico-economic arithmetic" where the state is nothing but the instrument of a dominant capital.[53] The important question is not whether capital forced the regime in a particular direction but why the government was willing to acquiesce.[54]

To answer that question it is important to recall where these men and women came from and how their lives helped shape their attitudes. The new elite was embedded in a social and professional world where economic autarky and contempt for property rights were inconceivable. The "methodological lenses" through which they analyzed the crisis were also based on the economic orthodoxy of free markets and trade. The educational background of the new elite would not have prepared them to consider other alternatives. That is, the new elite defended orthodox economic policies, not as a direct articulation of class interests, but because these programs appeared as the only rational option. The definition of that rationale was partly determined by social position and exposure to an economic ideology in the United States, but it is vital to distinguish between simple pursuit of class advantage and the identification of this with universal interests. As described by a Mexican bureaucrat familiar with these issues: "[T]he decision-making process relies more on the indirect scientific-economic rationale for the social construction of reality than on the direct political/ideological commitment to a given class."[55] The policies resulting from the two may be identical, but the differences in origin are critical.

53. Cordera Campos and Tello, eds., *México: La disputa por la nación*, p. 65.
54. For a detailed firsthand version of the elite's perspective, see papers by government representatives in Dwight Brothers and Adele Wick, *Mexico's Search for a New Development Strategy*, 1990. See also Javier Beristain and Ignacio Trigueros, "Mexico," in John Williamson, ed., *Latin American Adjustment: How Much Has Happened?* 1990.
55. Interview, New Haven, March 1986. (Perhaps the best indication of the extent of technocratification of the elite is that many of its members actually speak like this.)

The elite's own experience during the previous decade also played a role in their policy decisions. Having witnessed the collapse of Stabilizing Development in the late 1960s, the failure of populism during Echeverría, and the false promises of affluence during López Portillo, the new elite resolved to follow a "new realism," which accepted Mexico's position in the global system. Rather than fighting the system, the *tecnócratas* chose to make the best possible accommodation within it. This partly reflected a calculated strategy to assure the survival of the regime. The elite realized that without growth its political position would be severely threatened and it chose the model that would elicit the greatest degree of support from those who possessed the resources needed for economic dynamism.

In sum, the *tecnócratas* considered that the Revolution was seventy years old; it should be retained but adjusted to new realities. It had to be redefined to include a different type of state in a new kind of world. The next sections discuss that redefinition.

# The State as Rector

Miguel de la Madrid's inaugural ten-point program for meeting the economic crisis (Immediate Program for Economic Reorganization, PIRE) reflected the earlier concerns of the PGD by identifying inflation as the most important threat facing the country. According to the PIRE the way to resolve this was through a drastic cut in public expenditures.

Beginning in 1983 the government's participation in the economy as measured by percentage of GNP dropped for the first time since 1977 and continued declining. Welfare expenditures were not the only ones affected, as agriculture, infrastructure, oil and manufacturing investment by the public sector also declined. Not counting debt service, public expenditures declined by 62.9 percent from 1982 to 1987.[56] The downsizing of the state accelerated during the Salinas *sexenio*, which saw the share of GDP accounted for by federal expenditures decline from 31 percent in 1987 to 21 percent in 1990 and helped produce a fiscal surplus by 1991.[57]

56. *El Financiero* (Mexico City), February 1, 1988, p. 18. The biggest drop came in capital investments, which declined from 24.7 percent of expenditures in 1982 to 9.6 percent in 1987.
57. Presidencia de la República, *The Mexican Agenda*, 1991, pp. 77–78.

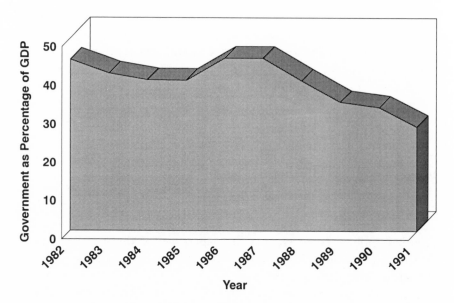

Fig. 7-2.    The shrinking of the state, 1982–1990. (Source: Presidencia de la República, *Primer informe de Carlos Salinas de Gortari*, Anexo, 1989; Banco de México, *The Mexican Economy, 1992*, 1992.)

Part of this reduction came from the privatization of the parastatal sector which had grown so dramatically since 1970. The state, while not renouncing its obligation to "regulate and manage" national development, would no longer be a proprietary institution. According to Salinas there was a basic contradiction between a just and efficient state and a state that had to manage a range of industrial enterprises. In his first State of the Nation speech, Salinas declared that "[T]he bigger state is not necessarily a more capable state; an owner state is not nowadays a more just state." For fifty years statism had been associated with development, but according to Salinas a larger state had "resulted in less capacity to respond to the social demands of fellow citizens."

Much of the parastatal industry disappeared during the decade.[58] By 1988 the government had ordered the sale or closing of 750 of the 1,155

58. The process began early in the de la Madrid *sexenio*. Of the 467 firms in which the nationalized banking industry had owned a controlling interest, 369 were sold by 1983 (Unidad de la Cronica Presidencial de la República, *Las razones y las obras*, 2:251).

parastatals existing in 1982.[59] As of November 1991 the government had divested itself of over 1,000 companies.[60] Most of these were marginal firms, but privatization did include several major enterprises including the steel mills Altos Hornos de México and Lázaro Cárdenas-Las Truchas, as well as previously sacrosanct entities like the phone company. Perhaps the most significant sale involved the banks nationalized by López Portillo. Now they could be united with brokerage houses to create very powerful financial syndicates. In general, the process of privatization contributed to the increase in the already highly concentrated control over capital.[61]

The restrictions on the economic role of the state and the privatization campaign seemed to indicate that Mexico was following an orthodox neoliberal program. A better guide for understanding the new elite's economic policy, however, was the experience of the so-called Asian Dragons that tempered their faith in the market with a commitment to the central role played by the state in directing the economy. The model was Taiwan or South Korea, not Friedman Chile. The new elite did not believe that the market, left to its own devices, would resolve all problems through invisible hands: "If the free functioning of economic mechanisms implied the achievement of national goals, planning would be unnecessary. . . . the evidence indicates the inexistence of automatic equilibria and of spontaneous social harmony."[62]

Nor was de la Madrid willing to accept the complete autonomy of domestic capital: "We must regulate, orient, and induce the development of the private sector so that it supports national priorities and state policy."[63] He did not want to return to the limited state that the private sector encouraged: "We have changed the doctrine of the Liberal State. From a state which was a mere arbiter of particular interests, responsible solely for law & order, and basic public services, we defined a state . . . with the capacity to be the rector of national, political, economic and

59. María Amparo Casar and Wilson Peres, *El estado empresario en México: Agotamiento o renovación?* 1988, p. 156.

60. Presidencia de la República, *The Mexican Agenda*, p. 79; Pedro Aspe, "Mexico's Experience in Economic Reform," 1992, p. 6.

61. Tom Barry, ed., *Mexico: A Country Guide*, 1992, p. 126.

62. Carlos Salinas de Gortari, "La inducción en el sistema nacional de planeación en México," in Secretaría de Programación y Presupuesto, *Aspectos jurídicos de la planeación en México*, 1981, p. 169.

63. Speech, León, Guanajuato, May 5, 1982.

social development."[64] Obviously, this was a different type of state from that envisioned by Echeverría and López Portillo. Nevertheless, the new presidents shared with their predecessors the conviction that society should be directed from above.

The key to understanding the government's economic policy lies in the word the new elite most often used to describe the ideal role of the public sector: rectorship.[65] The government should not directly control the economy but rather serve as an overseer that would impose the discipline, order, and efficiency the system required. For example, according to Pedro Aspe the privatization effort was not limited to state firms but also included the elimination of financial and material subsidies for the private sector.[66] The defining moment of that new role came at the end of the de la Madrid *sexenio* with the creation of the Pact of Economic and Social Solidarity (Pacto de Solidaridad Económica y Social).[67] Begun in December 1987 and essentially continued through the Salinas *sexenio,* the Pacto was a perfect reflection of the particular structures and apparent contradictions that defined Mexico's technocratic revolution. Despite their association with orthodox, market-driven mechanisms, the economic decision makers opted for a mixed program. On the one hand, orthodox elements included tighter government spending, greater efforts at increasing revenues, and monetary and credit controls. On the other hand, the Pacto included a wage and price freeze meant to reduce inflation. The Pacto demonstrated that the *tecnócratas* were not generic neoliberals who applied monetarist policies indiscriminately but were willing to utilize a variety of mechanisms to establish control over the economy.

But more than the mix of policies, what characterized the Pacto was the willingness and ability of the regime to control various social ac-

64. Speech, Tuxtla Gutiérrez, Chiapas, June 23, 1982.

65. A prominent bureaucrat in SPP declared in 1984 that "the solution to problems must be found under the rectorship of the state" (Rogelio Montemayor, comments in panel discussion or planning published in Secretaría de Programación y Presupuesto, *Planeación en tiempos de crisis,* 1986, p. 242). According to another prominent member of the elite, the National Development Plan was intended to strengthen this same rectorship (Sócrates Rizzo, quoted in ibid., p. 188).

66. Aspe, "Mexico's Experience in Economic Reform," p. 6.

67. See Laurence Whitehead, "Political Change and Economic Stabilization: The Economic Solidarity Pact," in Wayne Cornelius, Judith Gentleman, and Peter Smith, eds., *Mexico's Alternative Political Futures,* 1989; Beristain and Trigueros, "Mexico."

tors.[68] Obviously, the acquiescence of the CTM and its mastery over the labor movement allowed the regime to impose much of the costs of adjustment on the bottom two-thirds of the population. The key to the success of the Pacto, however, was the enforced cooperation of private industry. When the government did not receive the required cooperation from producers and retailers, it reportedly threatened major business leaders with sanctions, audits, and loss of government contracts.[69] As in the cases of the East Asian economies, the state demanded discipline not only from labor but also from capital. The technocratic state would organize all segments of Mexican society to meet the challenges of the 1990s.

## The New Nationalism

The elite's relationship with the international environment and its attitudes toward national sovereignty are complex and often contradictory. These men and women had spent a great part of their youth outside of Mexico, most spoke at least one foreign language fluently, and they admired many aspects of Japanese, European, and American societies. Both their attitudes and behavior often seemed to imply that Mexico would be better off if it could be a bit more modern and, more important, a bit less Mexican. Yet the elite was not a technocratic caricature of their Porfirian counterparts whose national loyalties were always divided or in question. A better parallel (and one that the new elite might approve of) would be with the elite of Meiji Japan, searching the globe for models in order to strengthen their own state. It was clear that the *tecnócratas* were committed to Mexico's sovereignty and devoted to improving the economy. It was only a question of how one defined independence and development. That these definitions were acquired at Harvard and not in Mexico is significant, but the mode of ideological isomorphism was subtler than international determinancy models would suggest.

It may be worthwhile to remember that many of the new elite completed their studies at the height of the *dependencia* boom and were no

68. Enrique Cárdenas, "A Reflection on Mexico's Contemporary Economic Problems in Historical Perspective," 1989, p. 26.
69. Interview, San Diego, December 1989.

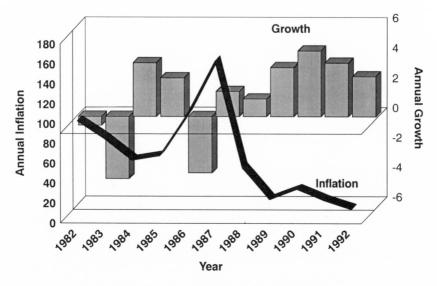

Fig. 7-3. The Mexican economy, 1982–1992. (Source: Presidencia de la Repúblicalica, *Primer informe de Carlos Salinas de Gortari*, Anexo, 1989; Banco de México, *The Mexican Economy, 1992*, 1992.)

doubt partly shaped by this perspective. I suggest that they took the message of dependency to heart, but with a special technocratic twist. Committed as they were to Mexico's future, they sought the best possible strategy among those available. Since international economic relations were determinant and autarky was impossible, Mexico had little choice but to accept the rules of the game. In the elite view the most they could hope for was tactical autonomy in a strategy dominated by others. The public pronouncements of Miguel de la Madrid, even before he assumed the presidency, emphasized that a "country cannot realize the growth that it wants, but that which it can obtain."[70] A nation-state must play by the accounting rules of the international markets, and there was no escape from its measures of efficiency.

The technocrats' relationship with the international economy could be understood as the pursuit of efficiency (as defined by them), without which Mexico's future as a nation would be imperiled. According to the new elite the reality of the global economic system forced Mexico to abandon its protectionist isolation and accept the limits of its role as a

70. Cited in Proceso, *Planes sin planificación,* p. 101.

supplier of cheap labor and as a mendicant in the world financial market. From the perspective of the new elite the country could not afford its attachment to anachronistic notions of independence. If it were to maintain control over its future, Mexico would have to accept the limits of its autonomy. According to Salinas: "[N]ations that do not know how to adapt creatively to the new conditions will not be able to preserve their integrity."[71]

Part of that adaptation included the acceptance of the debt burden. While all other government expenditures (with the critical exception of the military) were drastically reduced, the amount devoted to debt service (domestic and international) increased every year and accounted for 60 percent of the public sector's budget in 1988. From 1982 to 1988 Mexico was regularly sending $10 billion (U.S.) annually to the international banks, while receiving practically no new investment capital, and simultaneously increasing its external debt by close to 50 percent. Even opportunities to plead for debt relief, such as the earthquake of 1985, were ignored in favor of continuing interest payments. The Mexican government went from promoting internal development to assuring its continued acceptance in the international markets. In the words of Guillermo Ortiz, Salinas's Under-Secretary of the Treasury: "In order to pay the external debt, the government had to affect an internal transfer. It had to gather resources from the society and transfer them abroad."[72]

In 1990 the government announced a new debt agreement, which continued Mexico's commitment to its financial obligations in exchange for concessions that reduced the debt by roughly 10 percent and could save the country over a billion dollars a year.[73] The Baker-Brady agreements also allowed Mexico to borrow new money on the international market. Despite the claims of the government that the agreement meant the end of the debt crisis, however, Mexico still had to use nearly half of export revenue to pay international obligations and had to devote a quarter of its budget to debt service.

71. *Los Angeles Times Magazine*, November 25, 1990, p. 14.
72. Miguel Ángel Centeno, *Mexico in the 1990s: Government and Opposition Speak Out,* 1991, p. 32.
73. It did little, however, to resolve the perhaps larger problem of the internal debt. In the 1990 budget, for example, external debt service was supposed to absorb 2.6 percent of GDP, but domestic debt would account for 7.8 percent. See Secretaría de Programación y Presupuesto, *Criterios generales de política económica*, 1990. Since those who were buying the new banks also tended to be those holding the domestic debt, the relative power of private capital again increased.

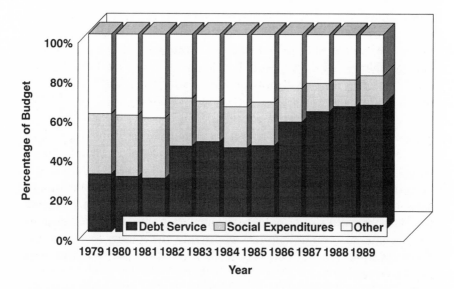

Fig. 7-4. Government priorities (debt service includes domestic and foreign debt). (Source: Banco de México, *The Mexican Economy, 1992,* 1992; INEGI, Sistema de Cuentas Nacionales 1992; Presidencia de la Républica, *Primer Informe de Carlos Salinas de Gortari,* Anexo, 1989.)

Mexico "behaved" in part because it needed the resources available in the international markets. The resumption of lending, the debt renegotiation, new foreign investment, and the repatriation of Mexican capital meant that the regime had the resources to spur growth and ameliorate some social dislocations caused by a move toward a new economy. In order to accomplish their restructuring of the Mexican economy, the *tecnócratas* needed massive amounts of money, and it was impossible for domestic savings to generate the necessary capital.[74] Much like Cárdenas before him, Salinas accepted that there were limits to his actions.

An equally important reward for Mexico's behavior was the international legitimacy granted the Mexican regime in the 1980s and 1990s. The PRI as a political organization appeared to be more palatable in the

74. Presidential aide José Córdoba, for example, told a meeting of stock exchange leaders that the key to the Mexican economy would be obtaining $150 billion (U.S.) of foreign investment during the 1990s (*El Financiero* [Mexico City], May 8, 1992, p. 35). *The Financial Times* of November 21, 1991, also noted that the government's economic policy required continued inflows of foreign capital. Foreign investment was welcomed in what had been sacrosanct sectors totaling $24 billion by 1992 (*The Economist,* Mexico Survey, February 13, 1993, p. 7).

international arena than other much less repressive and more democratic regimes with a "leftist" bent (for example, Alan García's Peru). Therefore more limited political reform was acceptable. With his economic policies Salinas helped support the "blind eye" that the United States often turned to obvious flaunts of democratic principles. The approval of the United States was also critical to maintaining the flow of labor across the Rio Grande that was estimated at over one million Mexicans per year. Migration arguably served as a political "safety valve," which allowed disaffected persons to leave Mexico while the migrant laborer's wages in dollars became an important source of capital. External supporters also provided a convenient scapegoat for explaining the limited accomplishments of the regime, particularly in the area of social inequality. The elite could always point to the limitations imposed on Mexico by an international economic system whose rules the country had to accept, while insisting that the best way to defend nationalism was to accept these contraints.

The central element of the "new nationalism" was the integration of the Mexican economy into world trade. Both de la Madrid and Salinas sought to emulate the economic success of the Pacific Rim NICs by emphasizing exports. Since the mid-1960s the government had supported the creation along the border of "export-processing plants," or *maquiladoras,* which allowed firms interested in the United States market a cheap source of labor literally feet away from the border. The precipitous decline of the peso after 1982 made *maquiladoras* even more attractive. During the 1980s *maquila* production increased by 350 percent and accounted for 13 percent of all manufacturing sales.[75] The *maquiladoras* served as a symbol of the new Mexican economy: they created jobs and prosperity around the border, but these jobs paid little and required working in very unsafe conditions while producing little auxiliary growth. In the 1990s, however, the *maquiladoras* were more a symbol of a general strategy of international integration than a principal factor in the Mexican economy. Internationalization had gone far past the border zone.

The *tecnócratas* also considered that Stabilizing Development had created disequilibria by giving too many incentives for the utilization of capital as opposed to labor, had protected the domestic market for too long, and had deferred economic adjustments. While Stabilizing Develop-

---

75. Barry, ed., *Mexico: A Country Guide,* p. 143.

ment had directly fostered the creation of a modern national manufacturing sector in Mexico, the new elite sought to "impose the discipline of international markets on [the previously protected] domestic producers."[76] This internationalization of the economy accelerated after 1986 when Mexico officially joined GATT. By early 1989 virtually all import permits were eliminated and those few tariffs that remained were limited to a maximum of 20 percent. With the exception of the auto industry, Mexico had become an open market. The new strategy obviously required continued sacrifices from the working class as much of Mexico's attraction was based on the low cost of labor. But the new trade rules also led to serious losses for segments of domestic capital.[77]

For the government's international economic strategy, integration into the U.S. economy was critical. According to a prominent journalist, the North American Free Trade Agreement "is not just the icing. It is the cake, the oven and the kitchen."[78] NAFTA officially recognized that despite some efforts to attract Japanese and European interest, the United States, accounting for 70 percent of exports, remained the most important factor in the Mexican economy.[79] NAFTA was meant to guarantee access to that market not only for domestic producers but also for third country actors interested in access to both rich American consumers and cheap Mexican labor. As discussed in Chapter 3, it also served as an institutional guarantee of the continuation of the Salinas policies. The triumph of *salinastroika* was increasingly tied to NAFTA not only for the actual, concrete benefits this would provide (always open to debate) but because so many expectations were based on its success. Again, this obviously made Mexico especially vulnerable to U.S. pressure as it could be required to sacrifice a great deal in order to obtain an agreement.[80]

76. Salinas Treasury Under-Secretary Guillermo Ortiz, quoted in Centeno, *Mexico in the 1990s*, p. 30.

77. Mexico's largest snack food manufacturer, for example, was unable to compete in the new economic environment and was bought out by Pepsico in 1991. There were reports of closings in the textile industry and increasing inventories in other major segments of the economy. A Mexican academic described the differences between Ortiz Mena and the new elite by saying that the former had allied himself with the *national* bourgeoisie, while the latter had done so with the *international* bourgeoisie (interview, Mexico City, November 1989).

78. Rogelio Ramírez, quoted in *The Economist*, Mexico Survey, February 13, 1993, p. 6.

79. The regime was apparently not interested in opportunities for greater Latin American integration. One official in the Secretariat of Commerce declared: "Mexico has never been part of Latin America." See *Latin America Weekly Review*, October 25, 1990, WR-90-41, p. 5.

80. At the time of writing, the fate of NAFTA is in the hands of a Congress and new administration with a less than overwhelming enthusiasm for the idea.

Therefore, the new nationalism did involve some loss of control, if not sovereignty. According to the new elite Mexico could aspire to an improvement in the living conditions of its population only by losing some of the trappings of independence. Moreover, even if the sacrifices required to pay the debt and internationalize the economy were greater than any benefits accruing to Mexico, the *tecnócratas* would have been favorably disposed toward these policies. Not only did these reflect their social and professional biases but the Mexican good behavior also bought noninterference. Economic interdependence allowed the elite to pursue internal politics autonomously.

## Social Liberalism

Despite the success of the government's economic policies as measured by GNP growth and price stability, the costs of the new order were disproportionally borne by labor, the peasantry, and the marginalized. The macroeconomics looked good, but the microeconomics looked awful.[81] Many of the *tecnócratas* appeared to recognize this but felt that it was unavoidable given the "realities" of the situation as they perceived it.

Overall, an estimated 400,000 jobs disappeared during the 1980s, at the same time that the labor force expanded by 8 million.[82] Combined with government pressures on the unions, this had the expected results: the real minimum wage declined by 25.2 percent in 1983 and continued declining through 1988.[83] By 1987 the minimum urban wage was 58 percent of that in 1980, the average daily wage was 62 percent of that in 1970, and the share of GNP accounted by wages declined from 42 percent to 30 percent.[84] Despite some improvements in the wage picture by 1992, the living standards of the majority of the population were still lower than in 1980. How did the government respond to this suffering?

In each of their inaugural addresses, de la Madrid and Salinas both

81. Francisco Cardenas Cruz, *Excelsior* (Mexico City), January 6, 1992, p. 1.

82. Quick, "Mexico's Macroeconomic Gamble," p. 9.

83. Lustig, "The Mexican Economy in the Eighties," table 1.

84. Rolando Cordera Campos y Enrique González Tiburcío, "Percances y damnificados de la crisis económica," in Rolando Cordera Campos, Raúl Trejo Delarbre, and Juan Enrique Vega, eds., *México: El reclamo democrático*, 1989, p. 114; Miguel Basáñez, *El pulso de los sexenios: Veinte años de crisis en México*, 1990, p. 71; Aguilar Camín and Meyer, *A la sombra de la Revolución Mexicana*, pp. 269–271.

declared that the provision of basic necessities was a fundamental preoccupation of the government. But the manner in which this social project was defined was very different from the perspective of Echeverría's Shared Development.

As we saw in the PGD, the new elite refused to consider any radical changes in the socioeconomic structure of the country. Beginning in 1982 discussions of social inequality largely disappeared from the official discourse, which emphasized justice but without reference to social structures. The new elite defended conservative interests because they saw social hierarchies and stratification as natural.[85] Dramatic social injustices existed, but governments could do little about them other than promote growth and hope for the best.

The new elite, however, did not appear to share the policy of "benign neglect" that had largely characterized Stabilizing Development. During his presidential campaign de la Madrid declared: "We are no longer in those times in which it was thought that by letting them be and letting them happen, things would resolve themselves."[86] Others in the elite criticized the "developmentalism" that had neglected social justice and that had increased the dichotomy between "modern" and "traditional" Mexico.[87] Early in the de la Madrid sexenio, Carlos Salinas also criticized the pre-1970 emphasis on financial stability without explicit social criteria.[88] Interviews with both members of the elite and informed observers, as well as the public pronouncements of these individuals, revealed a deeply felt commitment to improving the living standards of Mexico's poor.[89] For example, the several months Salinas spent working with peasants in Tlaxcala state during his thesis research did reflect a genuine commitment to the improvement of living standards in the countryside. One may disagree with the new elite's policies toward the poor, object to the often explicit paternalism and to the politically opportunistic uses of PRONASOL, but to claim that the tecnócratas did not care is to miss a much more complex point.

85. Alejandro Ramos et al., Salinas de Gortari: Candidato de la crisis, p. 15.

86. Speech, Mexico City, June 13, 1982.

87. Manuel Camacho, "Los nudos históricos del sistema político mexicano," 1977, p. 202; and Pedro Aspe and Paul Sigmund, The Political Economy of Income Distribution in Mexico, 1984, p. 7.

88. "The Restructuring of the Mexican Economy," 1984, p. 16.

89. David Ronfeldt, for example, believes that the ruling elite still adhered to a very strong nationalist and left of center ideology. See "Questions and Cautions about Mexico's Future," in Susan Kaufman Purcell, ed., Mexico in Transition, 1988, p. 59.

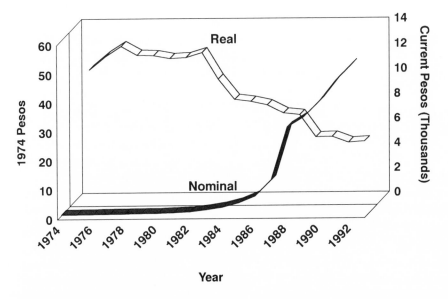

Fig. 7-5.   Minimum daily wage, 1974–1991. (Source: Banco de México, *The Mexican Economy, 1992,* 1992.)

It was the concept of "new realism" rather than an explicit rejection of social welfare programs that determined the policies of the regime. The new elite felt that "efficiency is not enough; an efficient but unjust system cannot endure."[90] Its concern, however, was directed toward the future; little could be done at present to relieve the misery of the poor, but future generations would benefit from the sacrifices of their parents. According to de la Madrid and Salinas, justice could only be achieved through increased efficiency, not through social change.[91] De la Madrid declared that the best strategy to reduce inequality in Mexican society was not through the redistribution of the economic pie but through growth and employment: "[T]he sustained increase in employment will allow for a better distribution of income."[92]

90. Pedro Aspe and Javier Beristain, "The Evolution of Distribution Policies during the Post-Revolutionary Period in Mexico," in Pedro Aspe and Paul Sigmund, *The Political Economy of Income Distribution in Mexico,* 1984, p. 17.

91. See, for example, the introduction to Secretaría de Programación y Presupuesto, *Plan Nacional de Desarollo, 1989–1994,* 1990.

92. Speech, Mexico City, March 11, 1980.

Given a "realistic" appraisal of the situation, there were clear limits to the ability of the state to affect inequality: "The Mexican experience with government action to promote social justice demonstrates that even with a political tradition that places a great emphasis upon government action against poverty, it is difficult to develop effective programs that alter income distribution."[93] The regime rejected populist measures; to offer "an easy solution would be irresponsible."[94] In his inaugural speech de la Madrid declared that the government would "support the weakest . . . but without false paternalism and without demagoguery." Salinas was also adamant in his rejection of what he called populism: "We have learned that populism hurts the interests of the majority and constitutes the worst enemy of our aspirations for the popular welfare."[95]

The new elite's position was best summarized by a declaration made by the PRI some weeks after Salinas's first State of the Union message: "It is intolerable that the rhetoric and actions to artificially elevate and disarticulate the living standards of Mexicans continue to postpone the creation of healthy and firm economic foundations."[96] These foundations would be built no matter the social or political costs. Given that "a strong government is needed to receive from society the redistributive assignment as well as the power and resources to carry it out," and that such strength came from efficiency and austerity, there was no choice but to impose the draconian measures.

The new social policy also emphasized individual responsibility. Prior to his selection as the PRI candidate, de la Madrid seemed to reject the concept of collective welfare, which had dominated much of Mexico's political rhetoric, in favor of a more individualized notion akin to U.S. liberalism.[97] Throughout his *sexenio* presidential messages deemphasized communal identities and prerogatives in favor of individual and property rights.[98] The move away from the *ejido* and toward agribusiness and a more "yeomanlike" peasantry clearly reflected these biases.

93. Pedro Aspe and Paul Sigmund, "Introduction" to their *The Political Economy of Income Distribution in Mexico*, p. 12.

94. Luis Donaldo Colosio, in Centeno, *Mexico in the 1990s*, p. 28.

95. Campaign Speech, November 11, 1987. Quoted in Carlos Salinas de Gortari, *Tesis de campaña: Ideas y compromisos*, 1988, p. 124.

96. Quoted in *La Jornada* (Mexico City), November 24, 1989, p. 7.

97. Secretaría de Programación y Presupuesto, *Aspectos jurídicos de la planeación en México*, p. xii.

98. See de la Madrid's second and third State of the Nation speeches in *Los presidentes de México: Discursos políticos*, 1989, 5:378–390.

Four years before the nomination of Bill Clinton, Salinas also emphasized personal responsibility of the individual: "The Mexican state is constitutionally committed to the welfare of the individual, . . . [but] the tasks of maintaining welfare and the research for a better quality of life are a shared responsibility."[99] According to Pedro Aspe Mexico would have a just system when: (a) inequalities would be attributed to individual characteristics and would only affect the less able, and (b) access to resources would be guaranteed.[100] While this limited liberalism is the norm in U.S. politics, it represented a radical break in the official pronouncements of the Mexican government.

Along with accepting and emphasizing personal responsibility, the new policies sought to target the limited welfare funds available to those at the very bottom of the socioeconomic ladder. The new elite judged that welfare policies, rather than helping the least advantaged sectors, had benefited the middle class.[101] Instead of providing blanket subsidies the regime increasingly emphasized the creation of a bare-bones safety net. Social development was apparently no longer considered a government priority but was replaced by a minimalist conception of a welfare state. During his first State of the Nation speech, Salinas emphasized that the government welfare programs were not oriented toward those "who make no effort, who do not work" but instead to the "*least* favored, . . . the *most* underprivileged, . . . the poor*est*, the needi*est*, those who try the hard*est* and struggle the *most*."[102]

This new focus helped shape the policies of PRONASOL, or Solidarity, the government welfare program described in Chapter 3. According to Salinas Solidarity "did not give away anything for free. It is not populistic. We do not print money as the answer to social demands. Neither is the program paternalistic. People must take the initiative and organize themselves."[103] Most important, Solidarity involved the creation of national cooperative effort; the ideology of the Solidarity Program emphasized coparticipation instead of class struggle.[104]

99. Speech in El Chalco, May 12, 1988, quoted in Carlos Salinas, *El reto*, 1988, p. 75.

100. Aspe and Beristain, "The Evolution of Distribution Policies," p. 18.

101. For this argument see Aspe and Sigmund, *The Political Economy of Income Distribution in Mexico*, p. 3. In a series of presentations at the University of California, San Diego, in the spring of 1990, various representatives of the government emphasized that they only wanted to eliminate those programs that were not targeted at the poor.

102. I have used the translation by the Office of the Press Secretary of the President (my emphasis).

103. Interview in *New Perspectives Quarterly* 8, no. 1 (Winter 1991): 7.

104. Denise Dresser, *Neopopulist Solutions to Neoliberal Problems*, 1991, p. 29.

The new philosophy, combined with the economic crisis, led to dramatic declines in social welfare expenditures. Despite the economic pressures on the population, the budget for social development, including education, housing, and health, declined by 22.1 percent in 1983 alone. Carlos Salinas would claim that government programs "had diminished the impact of the crisis among the least privileged sectors of the population,"[105] but clearly this was not the case. Welfare expenditures as a percentage of the *nondebt* budget did increase from 35.5 percent in 1982 to 37.1 percent in 1988. If we include debt servicing in the total, however, the percentage assigned to welfare declined from 19.1 percent to 12.7 percent. In real terms social expenditures declined by 35 percent during the *sexenio* and by 1988 were below those for 1974 (per capita).[106]

These changes helped produce dramatic declines in the basic nutrition and health of the average Mexican during the 1980s. By 1989 per capita meat consumption had declined by 50 percent from the levels of 1980 and was below those for 1975, while milk consumption had declined by more than 40 percent to below even those of 1970. The average caloric intake continued to decline and by 1990 was approaching half of that recommended by the World Health Organization. After decreasing steadily for decades, infant mortality rates increased during this period.[107]

The Salinas *sexenio* did bring some changes through PRONASOL. Expenditures for health, education, and social security increased after 1988, representing 26.5 percent of the federal budget in 1991 as opposed to 14.9 percent in 1988. These new expenditures were not meant to resolve the problems of social injustice so much as to provide the social stability needed by the regime to implement its plans.[108] In order to understand the social philosophy of the Salinas *sexenio*, it is worthwhile to remember that the doctoral thesis in which Salinas first proposed PRONASOL was not concerned with effectiveness of welfare delivery or with relief of poverty but with how social services could be translated into political support. Salinas's frequent visits to shantytowns

105. Comments in conference on planning, quoted in Secretaría de Programación y Presupuesto, *Planeación en tiempos de crisis*, p. 20.

106. Secretaría de Programación y Presupuesto, *El ingreso y gasto público en México;* and Presidencia de la República, *Primer informe de CSG*, 1989.

107. Cordera Campos and González Tiburcío, "Percances y damnificados de la crisis económica," p. 127. See also Barry, ed., *Mexico: A Country Guide*, pp. 93–99.

108. Dresser, *Neopopulist Solutions to Neoliberal Problems*, p. 6; *El Universal* (Mexico City), November 16, 1990.

and poor rural areas resembled more those of a benign monarch than of a politician seeking votes or a social activist seeking solutions.

In the end the technocratic social policies were based on a never-resolved contradiction regarding the balance between growth or the maintenance of "fiscal responsibility" and social equity. De la Madrid had declared that "[W]e cannot accept the theory that one first has to grow in order to later distribute,"[109] but others in his administration contended that efforts to combine a theory of economic growth with one of income redistribution had been fruitless. They considered that the problems of inequality could not be resolved through expansionary aggregate demand policies.[110] This is where the comparison with the Asian successes breaks down. In Taiwan, Korea, and Japan, the draconian welfare policies and control of labor were also accompanied by some of the lowest measures of inequality in the world. This equality had been partly the creation of state programs such as agrarian reform. The Mexican elite appeared to consider Mexico's rampant inequality as beyond their control and was unwilling to consider changes in social structure.

The result of this decision was to rely precisely on the growth over equity policies of their pre-1970 predecessors. While rhetorically recognizing the need to improve the conditions in which the majority of the population lived, the new elite emphasized the "attainment of maximal values of the traditional, basically quantitative indicators" through the "acceptance . . . of an economic realism that has no room either for the calculation of social or political costs or for questions relating to national independence."[111]

The administration was concerned that the austerity measures would produce a social revolt,[112] but in the end they decided that financial conditions did not allow the government to provide a welfare safety net and that other issues had priority. Again, they felt capable of accomplishing a better future with the sacrifices of the present, but in no way could the latter be avoided.

This perspective was particularly evident in the definition of agricultural policy.[113] Since the Revolution the development of rural areas and

109. Speech, Miguel Regla, Hidalgo, April 16, 1982.
110. Aspe and Beristain, "The Evolution of Distribution Policies," p. 16 and p. 28.
111. Cordera Campos and Tello, eds., Mexico: La disputa por la nación, pp. 72–73.
112. Aguilar Camín and Meyer, A la sombra de la Revolución Mexicana, p. 261.
113. The following analysis is derived from a series of interviews with experts on Mexican agriculture during my stay at the U.S.-Mexico Study Center at the University of California, San Diego, during 1989–1990.

the protection of the peasant had been one of the basic ideological themes of the regime. After several decades of neglect, however, the Mexican countryside, and particularly the south, remained disproportionally poor and underdeveloped. If one considered that many of the inhabitants of the shantytowns that surrounded the large cities (*colonias populares* was the official euphemism) were essentially rural refugees, the extent of peasant misery was even more obvious.

How was the government to respond? The Revolution, according to Salinas's first State of the Union speech, had never intended to create an agrarian reform structure that condemned peasants to "bureaucratism" and the "ignominity of living as an underdeveloped minority." In any case, the president declared that there was no more land to distribute and that the main stage of agrarian reform was finished. Those who denied this were simply lying to the 6 million landless peasant households. Two years later Salinas submitted to Congress a bill that would radically transform the communal *ejidos* and allow members of these farms to rent or sell their land. Combined with the increased flow of competing products from North American agribusiness, these policies probably would lead to the destruction of the peasant economy as Mexico had known it for seventy years. Whatever the merits of such a transformation in terms of the aggregate economy, the human costs would be substantial.

The attitude of the new government was essentially to treat the countryside as yet another factor of production that could benefit from Mexico's comparative advantage, instead of as the home of 20 million peasants who required immediate assistance. Mexico could not afford to improve their living conditions, and simultaneously it required the commercial agricultural income. The "populist" solution would have been to emphasize agrarian reform, credits to smallholders, and expenditures on hospitals, schools, and roads. The "realistic" approach was to accept the "fact" that Mexico did not need most of the 20 million rural poor and that they would have to incorporate themselves into the "modern" economy. Their suffering was recognized but, again, simply could not be avoided. Agricultural reform was no longer considered a Revolutionary commitment but an inefficient policy measure.[114]

In sum, the vaguely defined policy of "social liberalism" proposed by Salinas did seek to provide some support for the poor, but it largely treated this majority sector of the population as an obstacle in the way of

114. I would like to thank Juliet Eilperin for first suggesting this point.

*modernización.*[115] Such a process required sacrifices from the population. That these would be unequally distributed was as obvious as it was inescapable. If the new solidarity required more from those on the bottom than those at the top, this simply reflected the fact that the latter could, and had, exited from the national economy while the former remained imprisoned by it. Allegiance to the pursuit of social justice was secondary to the goal of economic prosperity, which alone could bring an improvement in living standards and avoid societal disintegration.

For the last twenty years there has been an ongoing battle to define public policy in Mexico. Since the 1970s, however, this debate has increasingly taken place within technocratic circles. The victory of the new elite has brought a redefinition of the basic economic and social policies of the government. Direct state involvement in the economy declined, but the government's capacity to enforce new policies appears to have remained constant. Mexico is in the process of an economic integration with the global system that while providing needed resouces has also required sacrifices and some loss of autonomy. The new policies are associated with, if they have not caused, dramatic social suffering. The new elite is aware of this price but believes that it is unavoidable. In recent years it has expanded the previously shrunken welfare apparatus but appears more concerned with assuring political stability than with supporting a more just social system.

The new elite has been able to use the symbols of the Revolutionary past to largely dismantle what many would consider the central social Revolutionary legacies. The next chapter analyzes the fate of the democratic promise of 1910.

115. *El Financiero* (Mexico City), March 26, 1992, p. 38; and *La Jornada* (Mexico City), March 9, 1992, p. 1.

# 8

## Democracy within Reason

Revolutions may begin by promising everything to all, but having achieved power, revolutionary vanguards must often choose between conflicting claims within their own manifestos. In much of contemporary Latin America and Eastern Europe, for example, the debate is about what mechanisms best promote the interests of the population. Do glasnost and perestroika support each other or does the cruel choice between political and economic rationales require privileging one over the other? During their respective campaigns de la Madrid and Salinas emphasized their commitment to a greater democratization in Mexico as part of the required modernization of the country. Yet, as we saw in the previous chapter, they were equally committed to a set of social and economic policies that could and did create political challenges. How did the new elite reconcile the often opposing goals of political and economic liberalization?

The key to the technocratic revolution is not necessarily the victory of a specific social or economic dogma but rather the triumph of a world view that is linear, formal, orthodox, and intransigent.[1] We must understand this perspective not as an ideology of answers or issues but as an ideology of method. The ideological cohesion of the new elite was not necessarily based on philosophical agreements on policy but an agreement on how such a policy ought to be pursued. That is, what the elite shares is an epistemological rather than an economic ideology, an agree-

---

1. Alejandro Ramos, José Martínez, and Carlos Ramírez, *Salinas de Gortari: Candidato de la crisis,* 1987, p. 339.

ment about the source and nature of policy knowledge, not its actual content. *How* the *tecnócratas* thought was more decisive than *what* they thought. The elite shares a cognitive framework, a unique way of analyzing social problems, formulating solutions, and implementing policy that limits the potential for public participation and that inherently denies the inevitability of conflicting social interests. This attitude, more than any specific commitment to markets or free trade, determined the fate of Mexican democracy in the 1990s.

While these men and women could change their minds or adapt policies to circumstances, they were not likely to alter the manner in which decisions were made or the basic rationale used in making them. The new elite considers itself above mass politics, which is seen as inefficient and possibly corruptive. Constituency demands cannot be satisfied if they contradict theoretically efficient solutions. According to their self-perceptions the *tecnócratas* have assumed responsibility for assuring the best possible policy for Mexico and they would be ignoring their fiduciary obligations if they were to allow democracy to pervert government decisions.

The Mexican *tecnócratas* shared many of the characteristics of their counterparts in Latin America in the 1970s. These experts were frustrated by the contradictions between the training they received (largely designed for conditions in the industrialized countries) and the social and political realities in which they functioned. A combination of their faith in their own expertise and their low tolerance level for the political system led technocrats to want to alter their social context.[2] Their self-image was of "pragmatic defenders and rationalizers of capitalist modes of economic modernization" who functioned as the "intellectual brokers between their governments and international capital, and as symbols of the government's determination to rationalize its rule primarily in terms of economic objectives."[3] They were convinced that "that which is efficient is good, and efficient outcomes are those that can be straightforwardly measured; the rest is noise that a 'rational' decision-maker should strive to eliminate from his decision premises."[4] The best manner

2. Guillermo O'Donnell, *Modernization and Bureaucratic Authoritarianism*, 1979, pp. 77–83.

3. Robert Kaufman, "Industrial Change and Authoritarian Rule in Latin America: A Concrete Review of the Bureaucratic-Authoritarian Model," in David Collier, ed., *The New Authoritarianism in Latin America*, 1979, p. 189.

4. O'Donnell, *Modernization and Bureaucratic Authoritarianism*, p. 81.

of achieving these goals was through the unbending application of principles from economics, "a positive science capable of providing policy
makers with a scientific answer to specific policy questions."[5]

As we saw previously, this scientific method is not applied in a political or ideological vacuum. The pressures of domestic and international
interests, the organizational structure of the Mexican state, and the logic
of bureaucratic politics around the presidential throne all helped shape
the manner in which it was applied. Moreover, such a method relies on a
set of ideological assumptions regarding the role of the state and the
market that will help determine its application. The results of such a
policy process will not be politically neutral; choices will be made that
will benefit some social sectors at the costs of others. Nevertheless, the
definition of the specifically technocratic aspects of government policy
must focus more on the process of decision making than on defining a
particular economic orthodoxy.

The first section of this chapter discusses the changes in styles of
policy making in Mexico during the 1970s. The second half analyzes the
implications of this change for Mexican democracy.

# From Corporatism to Planning

Prior to the 1970s the Mexican government and its party had served as
an institutional arena in which various interest groups were represented,
and both sought to limit conflict to these organizational walls. Despite
their authoritarian rule the leading elites did engage in the bargaining
and compromises that are at the heart of "political" decision making.[6]
Mexican corporatism had always sought to placate various interest
groups through the formal and informal mechanisms set up by Calles
and Cárdenas. There did exist a limited pluralism within the PRI based
on a complicated system of regional and sectoral constituencies. At the
heart of both party and government was the idea that politics was a

5. Alejandro Foxley, *Latin American Experiments in Neoconservative Economics*, 1983,
p. 92.

6. See Lorenzo Meyer, "El estado mexicano contemporáneo," in Colegio de México,
*Lecturas de política mexicana*, 1977, p. 36; Fernando Zamora Millán, *México: ¿Ahora hacia
dónde?* 1987, p. 35.

process of compromise.[7] The regime took into account the political needs of the labor and peasant leadership and sought to combine its support for the private sector both with the creation of a relatively privileged subclass of unionized workers and with the continuation of agrarian reform. According to all sources the process of decision making in the government was dominated by a pragmatic acceptance that each sector had interests to represent and defend and that these had to be incorporated into government programs. Accordingly, politics prior to 1970 were defined by "[t]he predominance of political over administrative criteria in decision-making, the dispersion of power within the government, the absence of a formalized structure, and the domination by a pragmatic case-by-case approach to the items on the state's agenda."[8]

This changed radically with the 1970s. López Portillo appeared to believe that the rationalization of the administration through planning would be enough to resolve and diffuse the political and economic crisis he inherited from Echeverría.[9] In the words of a leading proponent of administrative reform, "One had to organize the government in order to organize the society."[10] According to one Mexican academic the major change in the system was a search for a "new legitimation of the system through knowledge" and a "new process of integration into the system by government personnel."[11] The pursuit of efficiency, rather than redistribution, became the focus of government policies: "Our goal is to program . . . in an attempt to rationalize and optimize the government's functions."[12] López Portillo attempted to relegitimate the regime by a "project of absolute rationality" in which economic and administrative logic superseded any political negotiation.[13] The ideological project of the regime was based on the assumption that the state needed more

7. For an excellent description of this pattern, see Daniel Cosío Villegas, *El sistema político mexicano*, 1975, p. 53.

8. Matilde Luna, "La administración estatal y el regimen político," 1988, p. 253.

9. As part of this process López Portillo had several prominent Echeverrístas arrested such as the exheads of Agrarian Reform, Communications and Transport, and the Coffee Institute. This was not a new phenomenon, however. Ruiz Cortines had also prosecuted some of the worst offenders during the incredibly crooked Alemán administration. De la Madrid and Salinas were to follow with the same attempt to establish legitimacy through "moral renovation."

10. Alejandro Carrillo Castro, *La política y la administración pública en México*, 1982, p. 22.

11. Interview, Mexico City, June 1986.

12. José López Portillo, in Presidencia de la República, *El ejecutivo ante el congreso*, p. 14. See also his "La función de control en la administración pública," 1971.

13. Germán Pérez and Samuel León, "En busca de la legitimidad perdida," in Pérez and León, *Diecisiete ángulos de un sexenio*, 1987, p. 17.

efficiency and rationality in order to legitimate itself as the focus of economic, social, political, and cultural development.[14]

Planning required a new manner of relating the state and the society, a new manner of practicing politics. The form of politics that the new elite introduced *was* very different from that of their predecessors. The creation and imposition of the new planning apparatus symbolized the victory of a new form of rule, one that explicitly denied the inevitability of conflict and asserted the existence of an optimal solution to social problems. It is the faith in their ability to first define and then obtain this ideal state that makes technocratic systems so antithetical to democratic participation. Even more than a commitment to planning or to a particular economic orthodoxy, it is this faith in their own abilities and a refusal to recognize the legitimacy of conflicting interests that best characterizes the political thought of those who took over the Mexican state during the 1980s. In this, as in many other attributes, they most resembled the developmentalist elites of Japan and East Asia.

The new definition of politics was particularly clear when members of the new elite defended themselves from the accusation that they were technocrats. All the persons interviewed who might have been classified as such because of education, functional position, career patterns, or network membership adamantly rejected such a label. Their desire not to be called technocrats is partly explained by the negative connotations the term acquired in Mexican political discourse after 1982. More important, these persons appeared to truly believe that they were politicians, just more modern and efficient ones than their predecessors. Yet those very same interviewees who rejected the idea that technocrats were in control, and who wished to be described as politicians, would proudly agree when asked if the government should attempt to impose optimality.

Their definition of politics clearly indicated that they envisioned a very different role for public servants than had been the traditional case in Mexico. According to Alejandro Carrillo Castro, the father of the administrative reform project that so radically changed the bureaucracy, a true politician was "[a] person who is concerned with social life, with the life of a community . . . who is fundamentally concerned with understanding which are the problems facing *the population as a whole and not only on the level of individuals.*"[15] López Portillo claimed to be such

14. Susan Street, "Burocracia y educación: Hacia un análisis político de la desconcentración administrativa en la SEP," 1983, p. 240.
15. *La reforma administrativa en México*, 1982, 3:165 (my emphasis).

a politician, and not in the traditional Mexican sense of "the pact or shady deal, involving a game of loyalties, rhetoric but no proposals. Playing with names and games, lying even with the truth."[16]

The job of the new type of politician was not to represent any one person, not to make deals or compromises, but to formulate the best policy for the whole.[17] The old corporatism that involved compromises, gestures, political spaces, and the exchange of social spending for support had no role in the new political project.[18] Where previously politically sensitive measures were negotiated, now they were formalized and bureaucratized. From this perspective the technocratization of the regime would make it more democratic since it would eliminate the institutional fiefs, corrupt practices, and political privileges of the old system.

The new elite also shared a frustration with representational politics because the opposition of individual groups or interests often prohibited them from attaining the optimal solution. The answer was to empower a group with no such prior commitments who would choose what was best.[19] In 1974 Manuel Camacho, who would be one of the leading contenders for the presidency in 1993–1994, had called for the development of a strong state that would be able to challenge the hegemony of the interest groups. According to Camacho, Mexico needed to create a "compact, organized, efficient" group to reorient the state.[20] Much of his political writing, and that of other members of the elite, reads more like Lenin on the state than the Friedmanesque dismissal of public rectorship usually associated with neoliberalism.

Significantly, the new elite appeared to assume a complete and univer-

---

16. *Mis tiempos*, 1988, p. 749. One analyst of Mexican politics described his shock at hearing López Portillo's inaugural speech when he realized that the new president was essentially rejecting traditional notions of politics and suggesting rule by "truth," which of course would be defined inside the cabinet (interview, San Diego, November 1989).

17. On this point see Francisco Suárez Farías, "Normas y prácticas del liderazgo político en México," 1988, p. 26.

18. Pérez and León, "En busca de la legitimidad perdida," p. 27.

19. A Mexican politician told me that López Portillo saw himself as being able to create a new Mexico and insisted on "imposing himself on history" (interview, Mexico City, February 1988). That is, psychological rather than political factors may be most important in this case. Certainly, López Portillo, more than any other president before or after, attempted to create a "personality cult," for example, staging huge demonstrations in Teotihuacan while he landed on top of the Pyramid of the Sun in a helicopter.

20. Manuel Camacho Solís, "El poder: Estados o 'feudos' políticos," in Centro de Estudios Internacionales, *La vida política en México*, 1974. See also his "Los quehaceres de la renovación nacional," in *Nexos* 86 (February 1985), pp. 33–41.

sal consensus regarding national goals. These persons felt, for instance, that social and political conflict originated in erroneous policies that sought to reflect special interests rather than in structurally determined opposing perspectives on the same issue. With optimality, conflict and contradiction would disappear. The application of scientific rationale would guide Mexico to this optimality. In a speech to the Economists League López Portillo declared: "Economics is a science which allows us to conduct and guide the transformation of our society."[21] Science had no interests, it only presented the truth; with enough data and with enough analysis, the best answer could be found.

Planning was not intended to reflect the union of interests but would serve to *explain* the program and policy of the government.[22] The new politics required new forms of político-economic participation that *without becoming disruptive* would help transform the political system.[23] The formal planning system was to allow for popular participation in the policy-making process, but this was based not on the public voicing of preferences through voting on various proposals but on a series of conferences during which interested persons could comment on the government policies. According to the elite this promoted democracy: "In the process of democratic planning over 15,000 papers and articles were collected, which detected sincere social preferences."[24] The president would confront the petitions and suggestions collected throughout the nation, but then "decisions of economic policy would be executed, according to a precise calendar which had been drawn up previously."[25] Not surprisingly, the so-called democratic planning became nothing more than a series of round tables whose function was to legitimate decisions already made.[26]

21. *Mis tiempos*, p. 821. Often the new elite would forget that not all of its audience understood macroeconomics. The speeches of Pedro Aspe were particularly noted for being practically incomprehensible for anyone with less than a master's degree in the discipline.

22. Miguel de la Madrid, speech, Mexico City, April 18, 1980.

23. Carlos Salinas de Gortari, "Production and Participation in Rural Areas," in Pedro Aspe and Paul Sigmund, *The Political Economy of Income Distribution in Mexico*, 1984, p. 537 (my emphasis).

24. Secretaría de Programación y Presupuesto, *Planeación en tiempos de crisis*, 1986, p. 187.

25. Carlos Salinas de Gortari, "The Restructuring of the Mexican Economy," 1984, p. 9.

26. See Héctor Aguilar Camín and Lorenzo Meyer, *A la sombra de la Revolución Mexicana*, 1989, p. 262. Interviews with persons who had been invited to participate in these conferences revealed that no one had apparently ever assumed that their comments would play any important role in the policy-making process.

The new elite expected that there would be opposition to this new form of politics. There would be "the normal resistance to all improvements from those who wish to place their personal interests over and above the global interests of the society."[27] Since they considered themselves capable of optimizing means to the agreed-upon ends, the new elite personnel were not interested in recognizing the legitimacy of the different perspectives and social positions of the various political actors. Mexico simply could not afford the internal instability or the conflict between proposals that such "selfish" politics entailed.[28] The government had to reject such assaults from interest groups that did not have the formal recognition as institutional players.[29] According to de la Madrid it was important to distinguish popular voices that were not organized and institutionalized and who did not consider the long term from those that were and did; only the latter deserved the government's attention.[30] Since unorganized opposition could only represent a selfish desire to frustrate progress, there was no need to incorporate its criticisms. Obviously, how one determined which interests were organized and subsequently should be heard made all the difference in the world.

According to the elite the major problem with the opposition was that it refused to accept the economic reality now facing Mexico, which, again, the *tecnócratas* felt uniquely qualified to define. The technocratic faith saw the definition of social problems and the formulation of their solutions as relatively simple and obvious. If a business lost money, it should close; if the government could no longer afford to provide a social safety net, nothing could be done about it.

A reasonable democracy would recognize such limits. This perspective became particularly clear during the 1982 campaign. In a major speech in Guanajuato, de la Madrid declared that realism would be the focus of economic policy and rejected "populism and any form of demagoguery."[31] Partly, this strategy was designed to distance himself as much as possible from both Echeverría and López Portillo, but it also reflected the new elite's distrust of attempts to alter the status quo. Those who sought to do so were readily criticized: "It is very easy to

27. Carrillo Castro, *La reforma administrativa en México*, 3:172.

28. Manuel Camacho Solís, "La reforma democrática," in Rolando Cordera Campos, Raúl Trejo Delarbre, and Juan Enrique Vega, eds., *México: El reclamo democrático*, 1989, p. 442.

29. Interview with Jorge de la Vega Domínguez (n.d.), in ibid., p. 428.

30. *Excelsior* (Mexico City), May 29, 1992.

31. May 24, 1982.

ask for modifications to the political economy of the Mexican government when one does not have the responsibility to face the consequences of irresponsible options bereft of any technical sense (as do those who blame our policies for the social costs of the crisis). . . . We must be realistic. . . . any other way, the results are ephemeral."[32] Of course, the costs of this realism were not evenly distributed, but to rail against this was, naturally, unrealistic.

## The Monopoly on Truth

The key to the technocratic discourse that dominated after 1982 was precisely the perfectly closed logic of the new politics: we are the best at what we do, therefore our policies are the best possible solutions given present circumstances, therefore anyone who opposes them is simply unrealistic and not worth listening to. Realism also absolved the technocrats from any moral responsibility for their policies; Mexico was undergoing a process of modernization that was imposed by the reality of the international economy and there was no other choice but to continue.[33] The emphasis in the official discourse was on the inevitability of the government's policies. As Minister of SPP, Salinas would consistently defend the regime's policies by referring to their "coherence with the reality facing" Mexico and by claiming that the crisis had imposed inescapable conditions on the country.[34]

Given only one solution to Mexico's problems, there was no room for ideological conflict, interest struggle, or political critique: "The logic of science-technology-necessity-truth is proposed as the unifier of divergent perspectives to which all ideologies would have to submit."[35] This perspective supported an ideological homogeneity within the elite that inhibited internal criticism. One observer, who *did not* accept the notion of a Mexican technocracy, told me that the regime of de la Madrid was much

32. Miguel de La Madrid, speech to the CTM, February 9, 1984.
33. Carlos Salinas de Gortari, "Introduction" to *Cambio estructural en México y en el mundo,* 1987, p. 13.
34. Interview in internal Secretaría de Programación y Presupuesto document (SPP no. 25.01.00.00/1.02.15.0) and speech before the National Congress of Economists (SPP no. 25.01.00.00/1.02.00.0), Presidential Archives of the Unidad de la Crónica Presidencial.
35. Federico Reyes Heroles, *Transfiguraciones políticas del estado mexicano,* 1986, p. 56.

less willing to compromise its policies in the face of popular resistance than any of its predecessors.[36] Similar concerns regarding the inability of the *tecnócratas* to accept criticism were noted by an exmember of the Mexican cabinet who stated that while previous elites were used to bargaining, the *tecnócratas* were more comfortable lecturing.[37] According to Peter Smith the policies of the regime originated not so much in the specific ideology of the *tecnócratas* in and of itself but in the increasing exclusivity of the ruling circle.[38]

The most significant aspect of the new politics was that the elite and their institutions came to be considered as the only source of truth and objective reason. According to de la Madrid his administration would listen and analyze the critiques and proposals that were offered, would then judge their reasonableness and relevance, and *if they were viable and valid* would alter government policies. But if these were not convincing, the government would defend its theories and actions and attempt to explain and justify them.[39] Or in the words of another elite member discussing privatization: "If we are convinced that it has to be done, then it has to be done."[40] The job of the executive branch, according to a leading functionary, was to "above all, limit the demands and the possibilities of political opposition."[41] Of course, the corporatist system that this elite wanted to dismantle was not democratic either; however, their assault on it was not based on the desire to open up the political arena but rather on the perceived need to improve its efficiency.

Since they represented the only legitimate source of truth, members of the new elite became known for a dogmatic intransigence. They believed they were in power because they were simply the best at what they did and they did not feel that they should have to listen to those less able than themselves.[42] In his memoirs López Portillo consistently voices his

36. Interview, Mexico City, June 1986.
37. Interview, New Haven, February 1987.
38. "Leadership and Change, Intellectuals and Technocrats in Mexico," in Roderic Camp, ed., *Mexico's Political Stability: The Next Ten Years*, 1986, pp. 109–111.
39. Summary of Third State of the Nation Speech in Unidad de la Crónica Presidencial, Presidencia de la República, *Las razones y las obras*, 1983–1989, p. 478 (my emphasis).
40. *Latin America Weekly Review (LAWR)*, May 17, 1990, WR-90-18, p. 4.
41. Manuel Camacho, "Los nudos históricos del sistema político mexicano," in Centro de Estudios Internacionales, *La crisis del sistema político mexicano, 1928–1977*, 1977, p. 186.
42. Exstudents of various prominent bureaucrats (the majority of whom had taught for some years) universally referred to the capacity of these men to consider themselves above error. One told me that Pedro Aspe once flunked an entire class of over fifty students and never seemed to consider that his teaching may have had something to do with their inability to understand the material (interview, New Haven, December 1987).

frustration with the inability of the public administration system to implement his policies correctly. He said that the problem was never the
ideas but the incapacity of traditional politicians to carry them out.
Throughout the *sexenio* of Miguel de la Madrid, the government would
defend failures and economic mistakes by saying that, without its leadership, the situation would have been even worse. The point here is not the
common political practice of blaming others for failure but the apparent
inability of the new elite to consider opposing viewpoints.

Even when dealing with those whose professional qualifications would
appear to merit some consideration, elite representatives automatically
disdained those with whom they disagreed. Carlos Salinas, for example,
once arrived at a breakfast with leading economists only to tell everybody
present that they knew nothing about economics; he then walked out
without bothering to sit down.[43] The elite's strongest criticism was directed at the left opposition that was guilty of an "absurd infantilism."[44]
José Córdoba responded to a critique by Ifigenia Martínez, a widely
respected economist and at the time still a member of the PRI, by saying:
"Primitive, obsolete and decadent criticism leads to simplistic and incorrect analysis. . . . It appears that for the Licenciada Martínez, the sun
continues to revolve around the earth."[45] She, in turn, consistently objected to the autocratic style of Pedro Aspe and stated that the current
leadership "had once again demonstrated its dogmatism."[46] A more "realistic" approach would have allowed these critics to appreciate that all
earthly objects revolved around the global market and all followed the
inescapable laws that the "philosopher kings" mandated.

During his presidential campaign Salinas largely ignored the challenge
of the left and refused to respond to its criticisms of government policy.
An analysis of the presidential campaign press coverage by the seven
major newspapers in the capital turned up few isolated and general
references by Salinas to the opposition.[47] Even after the disaster of his
campaign stop in La Laguna when the official candidate was booed and
his convoy pelted with stones, Salinas refused to engage in a political
dialogue with the Cardenista camp. While this may have been a politi-

43. *Wall Street Journal,* August 31, 1988, p. 14.
44. Anonymous cabinet member quoted in the *La Jornada* (Mexico City), November 13,
1989.
45. *Proceso,* no. 572, October 19, 1987, p. 10.
46. Ibid., *Excelsior* (Mexico City), March 2–4, 1987, and Ramos et al., *Salinas de Gortari:
Candidato de la crisis,* p. 62.
47. Miguel Ángel Centeno, "The Press and Mexican Presidential Elections of 1988," 1988.

cally savvy method of denying the opposition any real role in the process, it also illustrated the *tecnócratas'* unique ability to ignore opposing viewpoints. A pro-Salinas billboard on one of Mexico City's major expressways in 1988 perhaps best expressed the perspective of the new elite: what Mexico needed was "less criticism, more solutions."

# The Limits of Reform

Throughout the 1980s it was increasingly clear that the new elite's definition of democracy did not necessarily conform to traditional notions of the term. The regime's understanding of democratic participation focused on the word *concentración,* with its implications of harmony and solidarity rather than conflict and compromise. Democracy involved convincing the population that government policy was right, not submitting it to popular judgment. In general, the new elite did not seem to understand that a real democracy did not only involve the articulation of views and the possession of "voice" but also the power of a vote and the possibility of "exit."

Democracy did have its uses. Manuel Camacho saw democracy not as an end in itself but as a means of promoting progress and gaining international legitimacy.[48] In a campaign speech Salinas declared his faith in a democracy that would make Mexicans more independent and that promoted development. In short, he had faith in a democracy founded on reason.[49] Manuel Camacho may have come closest to the new elite's version of democracy when he spoke of the attraction of the Singapore model.[50]

While Salinas may have wished to change the party and move it away from its reliance on the "politics of the sandwich,"[51] this did not mean a commitment to greater democracy. Few will mourn the disappearance of political gangsters such as La Quina or the CTM's Gamboa Pascoe, but while patronage politics may not have been democratic they did involve

---

48. Lecture at Princeton University, March 2, 1992.
49. Speech on November 9, 1987; quoted in Carlos Salinas de Gortari, *Tesis de campaña: Ideas y compromisos,* 1988, p. 49.
50. Princeton University, March 1992.
51. This refers to the custom of rewarding those who attend political rallies with a free lunch and describes the traditional exchange of largess for political support.

some sort of popular participation, or at least a form of reciprocity. The government wanted an authoritarian labor movement to control workers but did not want to pay the political price for maintaining it. As we saw in previous chapters, Salinas declared war on the patronage machine of the dinosaurs, but he did not intend to replace it with an independent labor movement that might hamper the implementation of his economic policies.

While the new elite spoke of democratizing the PRI, it was clear that they wanted to retain control of the process. At the PRI's sixtieth anniversary celebration in March 1989, party chief Luis Donaldo Colosio seemed to appeal for greater internal democratization. Yet Salinas also defended the need for a "strong and united" PRI that would help defend the strength of the presidency so as to prevent a "slide into parliamentarism."[52] The Fourteenth PRI Assembly in September of 1990 featured only one slate of candidates for national positions. Salinas declared that criticism of the party amounted to treason. He cautioned against making comments that could damage the country, and he admonished those who spoke of democratization but who "actually promoted division."[53] The "left wing" of the party was allowed some influence in preparing the official platform (which was largely ignored by the government), but significant numbers chose to leave the party soon after.

The two years following this assembly confirmed their worst suspicions. While there was little evidence that the party was becoming more democratic, its commitment to the traditional ideology practically disappeared. Governor José Fancisco Ruiz Massieu, a close friend of the president's, described the redefinition of the party as involving understandings with business, the Church, and intellectuals, but he never once mentioned the urban poor or the peasants.[54] One of his associates recognized the importance of two institutions that could pressure the government, the Church and the U.S. government, but neglected to mention unions, social movements, or grass-roots organizations.[55] The PRI had moved from an inclusive party designed to cover all segments of the society to an exclusive one in which only some sectors were represented.

The politics of PRONASOL reflected these trends. While the program

---

52. *Excelsior* (Mexico City), March 5, 1989.
53. *Los Angeles Times Magazine,* November 25, 1990, p. 42.
54. "El partido," in Diego Valadés and Mario Ruiz Massieu, *La transformación del estado mexicano,* 1989.
55. Mario Melgar Adalid, "Los grupos de presión," in ibid.

emphasized local control over development projects, that authority had its limits. Alternative organizations were not welcomed, participation in progovernment rallies was still required, and the omnipresent propaganda assured that all knew the source of the new wealth so that the relevant population could be appropriately grateful. PRONASOL could even be seen as moving the regime away from its traditional authoritarian willingness to accept passive acquiescence, by now requiring a more active mobilization and voicing of support more akin to totalitarian systems.

A real democratic opening would also require a willingness on the part of Salinas to either relinquish power or compromise his economic program with electoral calculation. Here lies the central contradiction in the president's dual project of economic *and* political liberalization. The ruling elite does not appear to realize the difficulty of winning votes without promises of short-term benefits. It refuses to recognize that there may be a basic contradiction between economic austerity and electoral success.[56] To ask a population to continue making sacrifices for some ill-defined future modernity is one thing, to ask for their vote is another. To ask for both simultaneously, however, is admittedly difficult. Interestingly, it is the supposedly "unrealistic" sectors of the political class that were most clearly aware of this dilemma. According to the traditional *políticos* the new leaders were trying to transform the system while at the same time refusing to accept the consequences of these changes.[57] A member of the DF Assembly complained that the "technagogues" were not prepared to change aspects of their economic policies in exchange for votes but still required that he maintain control over his district.[58]

Even if Salinas wished to democratize Mexican politics, he was not prepared to do so at the cost of his economic policy. The president would not allow democracy to pervert the economic reforms that he felt the country required. Salinas stated that "if you are introducing drastic political reform at the same time as strong economic reform, you may end up with no reform at all. And we want to have reform, not a disintegrated country."[59] He also made it clear that while he wished to

---

56. Representatives of both the ruling party and the government were asked whether they felt the austerity program would cause them political trouble. With few exceptions they appeared to believe that the population would understand the "necessity of sacrifice" (interviews, San Diego, January 1990.)

57. *LAWR,* March 1989, 89–08.

58. Interview, San Diego, January 1990.

59. Interview in *New Perspectives Quarterly* 8, no. 1 (Winter 1991): 8.

democratize the regime, "the priority is economics."[60] He was convinced "that as we move along the path of consolidating our economic reforms, political reform will continue to evolve."[61] Again, the similarity with the political pronouncements of East Asian governments is striking.

The policies of the new elite, therefore, were based on the continuation of authoritarian practices that assured the required social and political tranquility. Guillermo Ortiz, Salinas's Under-Secretary of the Treasury, recognized as much when he said: "It's very difficult to get the fundamentals [of a stabilization program] in place if you don't have the political mechanisms to make it work. How can you increase revenues and cut expenditures when you have political opposition or trade unions who are not convinced of the government's plans?"[62]

In general, the government seemed to envision a very selective democracy in which only votes for that opposition with whom it agreed could count and only those voters intelligent or "modern" enough to choose correctly would be recognized. The government would decide which democratic results were legitimate. Mexico included communities that were "backward and marginalized" and these perhaps could not be trusted with the responsibility of self-government.[63] The fraud perpetuated in July 1988 described in Chapter 1 signaled a limited commitment to democratic norms, but the special definition of democracy was more evident in the elections following the presidential race.

In 1989 the government recognized the victory of the PAN candidate for governor in Baja California (Norte). This was a significant break with the past as Ernesto Ruffo was the first opposition governor in sixty years. However, given the minuscule ideological distance between Salinas and the PAN, and the possibility of a quid pro quo between it and the government, few were convinced that this election represented a solid commitment to a real democratic contest between different views on Mexico's future.[64] The government's perspective on democracy precluded the acceptance of the left as a "responsible" opposition. Only the

60. *Newsweek*, December 3, 1990, p. 39.

61. Interview in *New Perspectives Quarterly*, p. 8.

62. Miguel Ángel Centeno, *Mexico in the 1990s: Government and Opposition Speak Out*, 1991, p. 18.

63. See ibid., pp. 17–19.

64. A joke in Mexico City during the 1988 election was that the PAN was the only party with two candidates: Clouthier and Salinas. According to the former "there was no one to the right of Salinas" (quoted in *Proceso*, no. 658, June 12, 1989, p. 27).

PAN, which agreed with the economic philosophy of the president, represented a viable alternative.

The results in other states confirmed the skeptics' doubts. In the 1989 local elections in Michoacán, for example, the PRD appeared to have magically lost the support of the majority of the electorate in the course of a year. The elections in Mexico State in November 1990 also witnessed similar displays of the electoral "alchemy" for which the PRI was famous. Since the new electoral law made it illegal to question the results of an election once official appeals had been exhausted (and the PRI maintained its control over the federal commission in charge of these), the government could impose its definition of democracy with apparent constitutional impunity.

The elections in Guanajuato and San Luis Potosí in 1991 were also meant to reflect a greater government commitment to democratic norms. And yet, despite the obviously important change heralded by these events (the first time that the central government admitted that elections might have been fraudulent), the manner in which opposition votes were recognized left much to be desired. In interviews in August and September 1991, PRI leader Luis Donaldo Colosio said that the *party* had decided what to do in Guanajuato; he never mentioned the voters.[65] The wishes of local *priístas* were ignored, and even the beneficiaries of the new policies seemed hesitant to rely on a defense of democracy by presidential dictate. The results of the local and state elections in July 1992 seemed to confirm the pattern: some democracy (when it suited the government's ideological taste), fraud in many cases, and continued imposition of decisions from above. Once again, PAN victories in Chihuahua were acceptable, but a PRD triumph in Michoacán was another matter.

The president claimed he wanted dialogue with the opposition, but on his own terms. He said that he "preferred to run the risk of diversity in democracy [rather] than the error of impossible uniformity of totalitarianism."[66] Salinas recognized the efforts of those who had compromised in order to achieve the electoral reform, but he also issued a warning: "The small groups that dogmatically insist on 'all or nothing' in the face of the State's democratizing attitude would be wise to reconsider their positions: adopting an anti-government stance as a philosophy only

---

65. See continual coverage in *Excelsior* (Mexico City) and *La Jornada* (Mexico City) during these months.

66. *Lideres Mexicanos*, November 1991, p. 53.

serves to raise tensions, to weaken the respect of the community that they require, and ultimately, to alienate them from the social bases that support them."[67] The message was clear to those who would listen: the government would prefer to negotiate rather than to repress, but it was prepared to repress in order to negotiate.[68]

Should electoral mechanisms prove inadequate, the government appeared willing and able to use violence. There remained questions concerning the murders of PRD activists Javier Ovando and Roman Gil in July 1988. PRD leaders and militants in Guerrero, Sinaloa, Michoacán, Mexico State, and Puebla were threatened and harassed when they contested election results. The PRD claimed that over one hundred militants had been killed by either the government or party groups. Journalists were either threatened (for example, Rodolfo Pena of *La Jornada*) or killed (for example, Guillermo Cosío Vidaum of Guadalajara's *El Diario*). The increase in the use of intimidation and "death squad" tactics, however rare in comparison to other Latin American authoritarian regimes, as well as the more frequent use of the military to resolve labor and electoral disputes led some intellectuals to refer to the "Gautemalización" or "Sudamericanización" of the Mexican political system.[69]

The changes in Gobernación in the beginning of 1993 clearly signaled that the years of compromises (such as they were) had ended as well-known political enforcers were placed in the critical jobs of electoral control. The results of state elections in 1993 also indicated that the PRI was still very much in control. The elections of 1994 would not be allowed to disrupt the plans of the president and his circle. Since experience showed that democracy could be irrational, the regime had to defend the sanctity of its reason.

In the apparently inevitable choice between political and economic rationales, the new Mexican elite clearly favored the latter. Its redefinition of government decision making and politics in general reflected the commitment of the *tecnócratas* to a single truth and their interpretation thereof. In the end the new elite's notion of democracy was similar to its concept of economic modernization: both were revolutions from above. *Sali-*

67. First State of the Nation speech.

68. Carlos Monsivais, "Del saber de los tecnócratas," *La Jornada* (Mexico City), September 28, 1989, p. 12.

69. Interviews in Mexico City, San Diego, and Princeton, 1988–1992.

*nastroika* represented not an expression of popular wishes and aspirations but the imposition of a model that allowed no criticism. The regime was not merely interested in governing the country but in remaking it, and this required authoritarian control. In this the *tecnócratas* sounded strikingly similar to another set of revolutionaries who also had absolute confidence in their monopoly of the truth. Their economics were capitalist, but their politics were Leninist.

# CONCLUSION

# 9

## How Much of a Model?

By 1993 Salinas and his project were the envy of much of the developing world. For the new rulers in the former communist block, the Mexican model certainly must have seemed extremely attractive. Among the ruins of other one-party regimes such as Algeria's FLN and the Soviet Union, Mexico's stability was especially impressive. The Mexican regime seemed to be weathering the 1990s better than even such previously steadfast institutions as Italy's Christian Democracy, Taiwan's Guomindang, and Japan's LDP. If imitation is the greatest form of flattery, the Mexicans must have been especially pleased to see one of the miracle countries of the 1980s, South Korea, creating an institution similar to the PRI in order to manage its transition to democracy.

What lessons did the Mexican model offer to those facing similar situations? What do the origins and foundations of this model imply for the success of similar projects outside of Mexico? What does the future hold for *salinastroika*? The first part of this concluding chapter discusses the model's lessons for other states and the final section discusses the chances of its survival in Mexico.

## Lessons for Comparisons

The preceding analysis focused on the various components of the Mexican regime: institutions, elites, and ideology. In this section the discussion emphasizes the three accomplishments that assured the success of the technocratic revolution: regime stability and bureaucratic autonomy, the control of legitimation, and international support.

Technocratic regimes may arise as a response to a general societal crisis that heightens the appeal of their emphasis on order, rationality, and apolitical decision making. Their rise often accompanies a rejection of the instability associated with democratic processes. Moreover, the economic and social restructuring involved in technocratic revolutions are often antithetical to democracy. We would therefore expect that such transformations are accompanied by authoritarian rule. The most successful examples of the rapid industrialization that is the goal of these revolutions have been based on the political and social stability that authoritarian regimes *appear* to provide. Certainly the experience of the so-called Asian Dragons appears to prove the axiom that perestroika must precede glasnost. The PRC is an even more dramatic example of political control combined with radical economic reform. While Eastern Europe may prove to be a significant exception to this unhappy rule, it is too soon to determine whether democracy and economic development can develop simultaneously in the late twentieth century.

The manner in which the Mexican government imposed its policies and the critical role played by its ability to control dissenting voices would indicate that authoritarian regimes do have an advantage over democracies in applying the economic model. The Mexican *tecnócratas* were lucky enough to inherit a system that had already established mechanisms through which to impose their policies. They could and did use the still significant political resources of the PRI and the threat of repression to defend their policies from populist "contamination."

The reliance on such authoritarian measures, however, presents a strategic dilemma to elites seeking economic change. Authoritarian technocrats, whether of the left or the right, require guardians to manage political repression. These, in turn, will constrain the autonomy of new elites to direct government policy according to their preconceived model. Those in charge of the repressive apparatus have a tendency to question why they should take the orders of those who depend on them for political peace. The Argentine technocrats of the late 1960s and 1970s, for example, could not control the ferocity of the military and its proclivity to support its own institutional interests. The fate of all the utopians who counted on Stalin to assure their dream of the future makes the costs of relying on repression to impose a new social order even more obvious.

The Mexican *tecnócratas,* however, did not have to make such an alliance with political watchdogs who could turn on them. They inherited a system of civilian control that also provided political security. Perhaps more important, the *tecnócratas* never had to dismantle a state in order to attain power, or challenge a well-established apparatus opposed to their policies. Instead they used traditional rules, such as the *camarilla* system, to usurp control over or establish alliances with those who could provide protection. The new Mexican elite, therefore, could concentrate much of their efforts on the implementation of *salinastroika* without having to create a new political order.

It is this relative stability rather than authoritarianism per se that differentiates *salinastroika* from its Soviet counterpart. Given the dominance of the bureaucracy over the party and his control of the former, Salinas counted on the apparat following his orders. Gorbachev, in contrast, faced a group of party leaders and bureaucrats who were not only opposed to his new policies and who had no loyalty to him personally but who also had their own bases of power from which to resist change. Unlike Salinas who came to power with a bureaucracy shaped in his own image, Gorbachev's task was more difficult in that he had to rid the apparat of older men who were beholden to the old Brezhnevite style. This may account for Gorbachev's choice of glasnost prior to perestroika: before he could institute any dramatic change, he essentially had to destroy the state apparatus.[1] Thus, the relationship between democracy and the market may have less to do with inherent contradictions between the two than with the ability of those leading the revolution from above to assert their control over the state. In fact, under certain conditions democracy may be a prerequisite to market reform as it may allow for the replacement of a political class beholden to the economic *status quo ante.*

The particular characteristics of Mexican authoritarianism, which I have called electoral-bureaucratic, would also support those who caution

---

1. I am basing much of my discussion on my observations during my eight-month stay in Moscow in 1992 and 1993. See also: Nancy Bermeo, ed., *Liberalization and Democratization: Change in the Soviet Union and Eastern Europe,* 1992; Ivo Banac, ed., *Eastern Europe in Transition,* 1992; Zbigniew Brzezinski, *The Grand Failure: The Birth and Death of Communism in the Twentieth Century,* 1989; Ralf Dahrendorf, *Reflections on the Revolution in Europe,* 1990; Ellen Frankel Paul, *Totalitarianism at the Crossroads,* 1990; Tatyana Zaslavskaya, *The Second Socialist Revolution: An Alternative Soviet Strategy,* 1990; John Gooding, "Gorbachev and Democracy," 1990; and the special issue of *Daedalus* on "The Exit from Communism," 1992.

against the use of vague criteria in constructing regime typologies. The Mexican government never opted for pure repression but used the resources available to co-opt and control much of the opposition. This not only assured that the *tecnócratas* could remain in control of the state without having to rely on a potentially threatening military but also eased the acceptance of the regime on the world stage. This model appears to be common among the most successful market-oriented economies of Asia. The equivalents of the PRI in Taiwan and Singapore provide that apparently optimal balance between stability and rigidity, insulation and isolation. These cases, along with Japan, until very recently shared a political system in which a dominant party is allowed to manage state-society relations, thereby avoiding isolation and providing some political stability.[2] The party, however, is not allowed to dominate the state bureaucracy that defines and manages the political economy the country pursues. The party serves as a buffer with which to insulate the technocratic core; it provides a channel for communication and coaptation. The dominance of the bureaucracy above it assures that policies will not be sacrificed for political needs.

A new conceptualization of state legitimacy also provided crucial support for the successful implementation of the Mexican technocratic revolution. The modern state's legitimacy claims appear to have shifted from those based on representation of some ideal (be it national identity, democratic representation, or revolutionary legacy) to those based on its ability to provide certain services.[3] The collapse of the Iron Curtain, for example, may have had more to do with the failure of the Soviet model to produce consumer goods on par with the West than with its authoritarian nature. Such an emphasis on economic growth and the management of a large industrial sector could therefore foster the rise of both technocratic personnel and institutions. Thus, the specialized expertise of the technocrat may only provide a potential entry into the power circle if such abilities are perceived as relevant to the main issues facing society. Certainly in the case of the *tecnócratas,* the shift in the definition

2. On the role of the state in Korea, Taiwan, Japan, and Singapore, see Alice H. Amsden, *Asia's Next Giant: South Korea and Late Industrialization,* 1989, and her "The State and Taiwan's Economic Development," in Peter Evans, Dietrich Rueschemeyer, and Theda Skocpol, eds., *Bringing the State Back In,* 1985; Chalmers Johnson, *MITI and the Japanese Miracle: The Growth of Industrial Policy, 1925–1975,* 1982; and Stephan Haggard, *Pathways from the Periphery: The Politics of Growth in the Newly Industrializing Countries,* 1990.

3. See Fred Block, *Revising State Theory: Essays in Politics and Postindustrialism,* 1987.

of legitimacy during the 1970s provided a unique opportunity to exercise power. Once it was accepted that the major role of the state was to promote growth, policies oriented toward that goal, even at significant social and political costs, were much easier to defend.

The definition of these goals and of the basic claim to state legitimacy, however, are not purely functional responses to changes in the environment. They also reflect the interests and perceptions of those climbing to power. Elites will often defend their privileged position by claiming that their expertise in a particular area is required by the challenges facing the state. Analyses of technocratic power that focus on technological development propose that the complexity of the tasks facing modern states supports the increasing power of technical institutions. It is important, however, to recognize that perceptions of complexity cannot be purely objective but may be dictated by political considerations. The way the goals of a state are defined, the model chosen for development, and the set of options available are not inherently given but reflect the biases of those who are doing the defining.

While technical influence may rise in response to technological change, it will also be a function of the desire and ability of an elite or set of institutions to limit participation to those fluent in the expert languages. The transformation of a political decision into a technical one may have less to do with the inherent complexity of the issue and more to do with the interests of those who benefit from excluding others. The mystique of expert knowledge can also serve as a powerful obstacle to any opposition. Those who wish to challenge the policies of such experts must engage them using the same professional discourse. Thus, while the acceptance of technical complexity does not necessarily imply the victory of a single policy or perspective, it does imply that the debate will be within technocratic circles.

The success of any elite's attempt to control state policy will therefore reflect its ability to shape policy agendas and the definition of problems. To the extent that they can portray themselves as uniquely qualified and in possession of the appropriate solution, technocrats will be able to exclude competing claims to participation. As discussed in the previous chapters, the rise of the *tecnócratas* was not a simple function of the state's need for their expertise but included their ability to frame the state's requirements so that only their skills were necessary. The decision to respond to the debt crisis as an economic/financial problem, for example, no doubt reflected the aspirations and qualifications of the new elite.

A reformulation of the debt crisis in terms of political stability, Mexican autonomy, or state-sponsored development would have enabled a very different faction to take over the state.

Efforts to redefine the role of the state and the requisite policies are also a function of the unity and cohesiveness of the elite. As discussed previously, one of the most striking characteristics of the de la Madrid and Salinas elites was their ideological congruity and absolute certainty regarding the correctness of their views. The acceptance of dissension or the willingness to engage in self-doubt might weaken a regime's resolve to impose often unpopular policies. If such homogeneity is not present, successful regimes may be forced to engage in purges of those who would represent a possible "fifth column." One key to the success of a revolution from above is not the simple possession of power but also the absolute conviction of one's right to such a position and the willingness to use available means to remain there.

The intellectual climate inside the country also may be decisive. If the type of goals advocated by the regime are those that are currently held to be feasible and desirable, it will be much easier to justify a specific set of means with which to accomplish them. The *tecnócratas* were helped by the apparent failure of both Echeverría's foray into populism and López Portillo's fictional abundance. The point here is not whether these policies were correct or incorrect. What mattered was the *perception* of failure that in turn supported the "realism" of the new elite. The decay and then collapse of the Soviet block and the subsequent problems faced by Cuba further strengthened those who focused on the capitalist alternative. Twenty years earlier it would have been political suicide to suggest an economic alliance with the United States (even if such an explicit admission would have merely confirmed reality). By the late 1980s it was not only acceptable but considered imperative. States facing a domestic environment less open to the market or to the constraints on sovereignty implied by international integration, however, may not be able to so easily legitimate the ideological shift these require.

It is also important to keep in mind the attitudes toward the leadership that help define the manner in which the population perceives government action. One of the most striking aspects of popular attitudes toward Salinas and the new elite in general was the almost universal (if at times grudging) admiration for their decisiveness. Salinas was considered *un hombre serio*—a serious man—with all the accompanying connotations of machismo and patriarchy. The president's arrest of La Quina early in his administration played a major role in fading his image as a technocratic wimp. The impressive educational pedigrees added a sophisticated veneer to this image of strength. For a nation dealing with a decade of disappointments and facing a confusing future, such a combination of images would be quite alluring. The benefits of these perceptions were especially important when the government had to justify its actions. The debt pact announced by the Mexican government in 1990, for example, was not particularly generous or advantageous to Mexico. Salinas, however, could sell it as the end of the debt crisis partly because he had already established a reputation as a strong leader whom the populace trusted to obtain the best deal possible. Public affirmations of strength, no matter how stage-managed or based on fiction, can therefore play a critical role in supporting the legitimacy of regimes managing economic and political restructuring. Such political theater is often considered the domain of populist or demagogic leaders quite antithetical to technocratic rule, but as the *tecnócratas* learned early in the rise to power, unpalatable practices may be necessary to achieve their goals.

PRONASOL may be the most important lesson in the management of legitimacy offered by the Mexican experience. Certainly the political successes of 1991 demonstrated that the president's doctoral thesis was largely correct. In his dissertation Salinas explained that simply spending money on a particular group did not guarantee its support for the government. Rather, the group had to become involved enough in the distribution and management of the funds to establish a clear relationship between benefits and providers. PRONASOL did not significantly increase the welfare expenditures of the government. It did, however, target these much more carefully and enable the regime to "buy more legitimacy for the buck." Acquiring the support of a critical social sector, be it urban marginalized, labor aristocracy, or small peasants, might therefore represent a better strategy for the success of revolutions from above than attempts to deliver benefits to the population at large.

If Salinas had to regain the confidence of the poor in Nezahualcóyotl, the support of the rich in Lomas de Chapultepec was perhaps even more important. In the end the legitimacy of the government depended on its ability to regenerate growth, no matter how unevenly distributed. Without the support of private capital the technocratic revolution would not have been able to deliver any economic improvement to partly offset the sacrifices of austerity and adjustment. The high interest rates on government debt, the sale of state monopolies such as the phone company, and the other financial opportunities offered by the regime may be seen as a form of PRONASOL for the bourgeoisie. The poor paid for their patronage with votes, the rich with capital.

The ability of the Mexican elite to retain control over the legitimizing symbolism of the Revolution is perhaps the most difficult accomplishment of the regime to explain. The new elite rejected important elements of the traditional Revolutionary creed such as the *ejido,* anticlericalism, and economic nationalism without necessarily discrediting the government's legitimacy. This success (at least until 1993) in maintaining the symbolic logic of the regime could also help account for the relative passivity of the population, which has undergone such traumatic changes during the past decade. While the repressive mechanism described in previous chapters was active, what is perhaps most understanding is how rarely (relatively speaking) the regime resorted to it. Perhaps Salinas was merely enjoying a calm before the storm and the millions who lived in the shantytowns surrounding Mexico City would rise much as their counterparts did in Caracas in 1989. But for the moment a significant part of the population was willing to accept that *salinastroika* was the only way to rescue some of the Revolution.

Thus, the Mexican regime was particularly lucky in being able to construct a legitimation strategy that could assure both the majority of the populace and the upper classes that their interests lay with supporting the new policies. This manipulation of symbols and strategic delivery of benefits requires extremely adept political management. In the pursuit of the new economic rationality, revolutionizing elites cannot afford to forget the equally important political base on which the market may rest. Transitions require a set of political skills that are impossible to predict or instill. As frustrating as it may seem to both the relevant populations and social scientists analyzing the process of transition, the idiosyncratic qualities of leadership may yet prove to be the decisive element in determining the success of a revolution.

Revolutions, however, cannot depend on purely domestic support. Few have been able to resist an antagonistic international environment. In the best of circumstances revolutions can count on the support of international sponsors that provide both the concrete resources and legitimation needed to solidify the new order. This was certainly the case in Mexico during the 1980s and 1990s. It would have been practically impossible for *salinastroika* to succeed without external assistance including financial support, diplomatic legitimation, and the accolades of the international media. This is not to imply that international forces dictated the choice of model, but they certainly influenced and helped support its implementation.

As discussed in previous chapters, the Mexican regime received considerable financial support. New lending, foreign investment, and the lowering of protection barriers partly provided the capital required by the new economic model. The multiplier effect of such assistance was also considerable as it helped reverse the flow of Mexican capital abroad. The potential of NAFTA certainly helped motivate foreign investors. Perhaps more important, the American willingness to accept a continued flow of laborers across the border meant that the Mexican economy had to create fewer jobs while also enjoying the repatriation of migrants' dollars.

The legitimacy bestowed by international recognition of the *salinastroika*'s successes may have been as important as the concrete support. The end of the Cold War appears to have momentarily assured an almost global consensus regarding the virtues of the market and the primary importance of development over distribution. Moreover, since the mid-1970s neoliberal economic dogma had replaced Keynesian policies as the dominant paradigm. The market revolutions of the 1980s, therefore, enjoyed a much more supportive environment than that faced by their counterparts in 1789, 1910, or 1917. Nowhere is the importance of international legitimation clearer than when we compare global response to the claims of the Mexican opposition versus those of Gorbachev's nationalist rebellions. While the opposition in Lithuania could take heart in the willingness of the United States' and the European powers' recognition of its aspirations, Cárdenas and the PRD gained little support from such quarters. With regards to the use of violence, a double standard was also applied to the two regimes. On the one hand, Salinas has not been taken to task for continuing and sometimes increasing repressive measures but has succeeded in deflecting attention away from such incidents. Gorbachev, on the other hand, reduced the Soviet government's traditional use of violence against the population yet was roundly castigated even for *relatively* limited repression.

The financial and political support, however, is not granted freely. In a post-Cold War world a variety of nations will be clamoring for such assistance. The last few years have clearly demonstrated that the advanced capitalist nations are not willing or able to bankroll every single transition. The Mexican regime was particularly successful in convincing the relevant international actors that its survival was crucial and that it required concrete support. Frustrated by their efforts to generate interest in Mexico among Japanese and European investors, the *tecnócratas* committed themselves to an American strategy. In this instance the ability of the new elite to speak the same language (both literally and metaphorically) as those in charge of the resources made a critical difference. When the Mexican elite sat down to negotiate with their American counterparts, there was a very good chance they were all wearing the same school ties. The Mexican *tecnócratas* did not only say and do the right things, they possessed the required credentials and cultural capital. Thus, the success of a search for an international sponsor might require a previous investment in the creation of an elite willing and able to serve as a bridge between the two countries.

The Mexican elite was also willing to accept the constraints that such relationships entailed. NAFTA required that Mexico accept the scrutiny of the U.S. Congress, public interest groups, and a myriad of committees and commissions. The price for allowing Mexican manufactured goods into the American market might include surrendering national control over mineral resources. In order for the agribusinesses of the northern frontier to sell winter vegetables in the United States, much of the Mexican peasantry would have to be displaced by American corn and wheat imports. In the political realm Mexico also could no longer allow itself the luxury of a foreign policy that would aggravate those members of Congress who might not like support for Cuba, to name one example. While few in the United States seemed to care about the PRD, the government also had to be much more careful in its relations with the PAN who had many supporters north of the border. The Mexican elite seemed not only to understand the rules of this game but was also willing to play even at a disadvantage. Countries wishing to impose their own technocratic revolutions may therefore have no choice but to accept membership in the economic empire of a world power. The nations of Eastern Europe, East Asia, and Latin America may not relish the thought of German, Japanese, or U.S. domination, but they may have little choice if they wish to participate in the new global system.

## The Future of *Salinastroika*

The Mexican government has survived over twenty years of predictions of its collapse. Practically every journalistic and academic article on Mexico in the 1980s featured the word "crisis" in the title. Yet, the regime has survived others whose solidity was taken for granted. Except in the case of some unforeseeable cataclysm, it will probably continue to do so. Will the technocratic revolution survive? Again, in the spring of 1993 there are few signs of strain. But it is important to recall the political and ideological gyrations described in the preceding chapters. No matter his acumen, no Mexican president since 1934 has succeeded in maintaining his influence after his term. The Cárdenas legacy, for example, was already in decline a year after the oil nationalization. Salinas has attempted to establish limits on the autonomy of his successor, but it is practically impossible to underestimate the potential power of a sitting president. Given the premium placed on loyalty, we cannot know the true views of those inside the Salinas elite. The next president may disagree with the policies of *salinastroika* or may find that a new reading of political reality restricts its continuation. The fate of the technocratic project, therefore, may rest on the simple choice of one man.[4]

Even assuming that Salinas's successor wishes to maintain the same policies or is constrained from changing them by the institutional changes described above, the future of the technocratic revolution is by no means assured. The regime's strategy in the early 1990s is based on the expectation that the economic and social restructurings will not translate into a political revolt. This expectation is based on several assumptions.

First, the new elite counts on the PAN continuing to prefer to support a government with whom it shares fundamental values than to run the risk of having the left alternative succeed in a democratic competition. Second, it assumes that the Cárdenas phenomenon was a historical aberration and that PRONASOL will continue to pacify the grass-roots discontent that produced 1988. Third, the regime expects that the disintegration of the traditional PRI and its replacement with whatever institution takes its place will be managed without a loss of control over the political process. Fourth, it counts on the continuation of the international approbation and support that provide the resources necessary to promote economic growth or, as in the case of migration, provide a political safety valve. Fifth, the economic model must continue to deliver growth with relatively low inflation. Moreover, the benefits from growth must come quickly and reach far down enough to satisfy what-

4. At the time of writing these conclusions no women candidates had been identified.

ever demands might arise should any of the above conditions not apply. Finally, the population must be willing to continue to accept an exchange of economic benefits for limited participation in government decision making. Each of these scenarios could be easily disrupted.

Even in the absence of a dramatic change in the democratic aspirations of the population, the PAN may not be willing to accept a secondary role in the power structure. The current leadership of the PAN appears willing to allow the status quo to continue as the party develops its regional strength. Rather than an opposition, the PAN often behaves as a reluctant coalition partner. There are three problems with this strategy. First, PAN governments in the individual states may have needs and goals that contradict national policies, and the party might have to take sides against the central bureaucracy. Second, the PAN leadership that enforced the alliance with the PRI is aging and the younger generation may not be so willing to remain a junior partner in a coalition. Finally, no political organization can permanently accept a glass ceiling on its aspirations. The challenges to the leadership of Luis Alvarez were defeated in 1990, but future presidential aspirants might and are likely to break the peace.

Salinas has also been blessed with a disorganized left opposition. Perhaps this was the price that the FDN/PRD had to pay for its initial dependance on Cuauhtémoc Cárdenas's singular appeal. There is no reason to suppose, however, that the fragile coalitions will not solidify over time. The disruption of the command by traditional labor *caciques* may provide an opportunity for more representative organizations to develop that could provide a base vote for the PRD or whatever party succeeds it. The generosity of PRONASOL has been partly funded by the proceeds from privatization, and once this unique bonanza is exhausted, its capacity to buy off enough groups to destabilize the opposition will decline. It is difficult to imagine that the many groups that have been affected by the economic policies of the regime and those whose lives will be disrupted by the NAFTA will remain disorganized and divided.

At this time it is difficult to define the future shape of the ruling party. Certainly it will not look like the traditional PRI. As discussed in Chapter 3, the territorial structure, the rise of a new political generation, the new (if limited) electoral pressures, and the patronage machine of PRONASOL will each contribute to changes in the way the regime manages political control. So far the transition has been relatively smooth, but the success of the PAN in the north and the Cárdenas phenomenon both imply that it cannot continue so easily. All the attempts to transform the Communist parties of Eastern Europe into new political animals failed. While the PRI does not carry as heavy a historical baggage, its disappearance will have to be carefully managed. Moreover, even if the president does succeed in creating a new political party, there is no reason to suppose that the bureaucracy can repeat the success of the 1930s and maintain control over it. In fact, the very nature of the changes required may force the new party to establish a more equal relationship. Those in charge of the party may demand a greater voice in policy in order to gain popular support and thereby curtail the bureaucracy's historical independence.

The continued support from the international environment is equally fragile. Bill Clinton has said that he supports NAFTA but wishes to change some clauses and add provisos. Will the Mexican government be able to give the United States the concessions it needs to make NAFTA politically viable north of the Rio Grande? Migration will remain a difficult problem and the Mexican regime will remain a hostage to the incapacity of the INS to seal off the border. A more active lobbying on the part of the Mexican opposition, or Latino political activism in the United States, may also force the American government to increase pressure on Mexico to finally hold truly competitive and fair elections. On the economic front Eastern Europe will still offer investment possibilities that are unavailable in Mexico. Latin America has been the fashion in business circles before, but it has failed to retain the attention of European or American investors for long. While the symptoms of the debt crisis have abated, the disease has not been cured. Mexico must still devote an inordinate amount of funds to maintain its status as a model debtor, and the increasing trade deficit might make it difficult for it to continue paying the dues for membership in a global system.

Even if the regime is extremely lucky and is able to meet the challenges discussed above, the policies of *salinastroika* may simply fail to create the economic boom they have promised. The reduction in the federal deficit and the increased investment have succeeded in simultaneously lowering inflation and in fueling economic growth. But the increasing trade deficit recalls some of the problems faced by the initial "miracle" of the 1960s. In any case, the quantitative indicators generally miss the increasing marginalization of large parts of the population. The type of investments occurring in Mexico, with their high technology and export orientation, have not and will not generate the massive increase in jobs required by the million Mexicans who join the work force every year.

The government policies have created an economy that, even more than in the past, is based on two separate countries. The first, including the commanding heights of capital, the urban middle classes, and selected segments of the working class, will benefit from the increased productivity and dynamism of the new economy. They will obtain the jobs created by new factories and enjoy the benefits of the consumption permitted by easier trade flows. But it is difficult to imagine what role the bottom half of the population will play in the new Mexico.

Nowhere is this clearer than in the countryside. On economic grounds the current structure of the agricultural system may make no sense, and the opening of the market in foodstuffs and the privatization of the *ejido* may increase the efficiency of Mexican agriculture. But agricultural policy in Mexico was never determined by economic criteria as much as by political rationales. The *ejido* vote was and is the most secure electoral base of the PRI. These communal lands, as well as the *minifundos* that are supported through price subsidies, also helped stem the flow into the already overcrowded cities. Neither one will survive a continued technocratic revolution.

Some of the millions who live on the *ejidos* may find work in the new factories and some will join their urban kin by surviving within the informal economy. But the government's policies of "modernization" prohibit the creation of an economic niche for this population, and the United States will not absorb them all. This permanent underclass will represent a potentially explosive challenge to the political stability of the regime and its ability to maintain the current policies. The Mexican government cannot afford to create a welfare apparatus large or rich enough to maintain such numbers on the margin. One cannot "PRONA-SOLize" the entire country. They may remain quiescent, but no government can depend on such luck. In the end the continued success of the technocratic revolution will depend on creating a more equitable distribution of wealth similar to that enjoyed by the Asian NICs. But such a policy would antagonize the very sectors on whose support the government relies. Moreover, as we saw previously, the new elite does not consider such an alternative feasible.

Paradoxically, the "East Asian Miracle" model that the *tecnócratas* sought to emulate might require precisely the democratic processes they disdain. If Mexico is to follow the model of Taiwan, Korea, or Japan, then it might have to accept the need for the relative social equality that characterizes these societies. It would appear that only a democratically elected government enjoying the support of large parts of the population would have the strength to even begin challenging all the forces that would oppose such a social transformation. Therefore, the economic model to which the *tecnócratas* are most committed may require a sacrifice of the political system on which they depend.

Finally, the events of 1989 in Eastern Europe demonstrated the unpredictable nature of democratic aspirations. Since 1929 the Mexican regime essentially has been based on the control of the population. The political passivity of the Mexican populace has puzzled more than one observer. Time and again compromises and deals struck by the elite have been accepted without systemic repression. Even if Salinas and his successor were able to provide economic benefits, there would be no guarantee that the population will continue to accept its political marginality. Should the populace insist on a more active role in defining the future of the country, the regime might have to accept the limits imposed on democratic governments. This would require a radical change in the manner in which decisions are made and the probable end of a revolution from above. The other alternative is to defend *salinastroika* through force. While it has so far succeeded in avoiding such a confrontation, the Mexican regime may soon have to face the consequences of its redefinition of the 1910 Revolution.

That Revolution defeated the last elite that attempted to "modernize" the country through "little politics, and plenty of administration." As the preceding chapters have demonstrated, there are many parallels between the new elite in control of the Mexican state and its *científico* predecessors. By 1904 the *científicos* also appeared to have succeeded in establishing their political predominance. Disdainful of the majority of the population, they basked in international accolades during the centenary of independence in 1910. Both the *tecnócratas* and the *científicos* came to power after the successful establishment of political stability by an authoritarian regime. While technical expertise played an important role in their initial entry into the government, both groups also possessed a considerable capacity for intrigue that allowed them to expand their influence versus other competing elites. But also saw the solution to Mexico's problems in the imposition of "efficiency" and the support of an international economic system that would lead the country toward "modernization."

Will the new elite be able to avoid the fate of the *científicos?* Again, predictions of the collapse of the Mexican political system are almost as old as the regime itself, but the main lesson of the last few years is that no political status quo can be taken for granted. Whether the "new *científicos*" will be able to survive the very crises that gave them power through a political and economic restructuring remains to be seen. Like the *científicos* whom they resemble in so many other ways, the new elite can no longer count on the guarantee of order provided by a now-discredited political machine.

The contemporary Mexican political system is certainly much more stable than that under which the *científicos* functioned, and the neo-Porfiriato will not disappear as easily as its predecessor. But it is likely that the new elite will have to fight to retain its power. The *científicos* did not survive the *pax porfiriana* to whose passing they contributed. It will be equally difficult for their successors to continue ruling after the *pax PRIana*. As he basked in the cheers proposing his reelection and in the worldwide tributes, did Salinas consider the fate of Díaz?

# Postscript[1]

As I was finishing the first edition of this book in the spring of 1993, I searched for some rhetorical flourish with which to indicate my pessimism regarding the ultimate fate of the Salinas revolution. For a few minutes I actually considered asking whether there might be "a young Zapata waiting in the jungles of Chiapas." I did so for absolutely no good empirical reason, but because I thought it sounded appropriately dramatic. I then decided that such an ending was too sensational; the Salinas *sexenio* would not end with a cataclysm.

While I may at times regret my lost opportunity at oracular fame, I would not have wanted to pretend that I could have predicted what happened in Mexico during the subsequent three years. The fall of Carlos Salinas was so deep and continuous that no single set of causes or events may be held responsible. Even those of us who did expect something to happen were completely taken aback by events. Many anticipated that the sacrifices endured by the poorer half of the Mexican population would result in some kind of urban revolt that would force the government to change its policies. Instead, an organized guerrilla army led by remnants of the largely forgotten militant Mexican left challenged the government from a base in one of the "safest" states for the PRI.

In a sense I was right. In 1994 Mexico did not have one, but several explosions. In January, Chiapas; in February, the threat from Manuel Camacho to split the party; in March, PRI presidential candidate Luis Donaldo Colosio's assassination. With these events, the technocratic revolution lost the patina of peace that had obscured the radical nature

---

1. With many thanks to Wayne Cornelius for his valuable comments.

of the changes undertaken. As in a nightmarish replay of the first half of the year, it all came apart again after the national elections of August 1994: first the assassination of José Francisco Ruiz Massieu; then the accusations of his brother that the PRI was involved in both the murder and a cover-up; finally, in December, signs of new violence in Chiapas followed by the virtual collapse of the peso.

That the *salinato* almost made it through the year is a testament to the political savvy of the president and the deep institutional roots of his macroeconomic revolution. Even after the initial Chiapas revolt and after Colosio's death, Salinas had the internal power and public prestige to impose his own candidate on the PRI and to help him win a largely clean (if unfair) election in August 1994. And even after the murder of Ruiz Massieu and the growing scandal associated with the investigation of the political assassinations, Salinas left office with his place in history apparently well secured and a job at the WTO still a possibility. What sank the *salinato* was not the opposition of those who had lost the most from the technocratic revolution, but the panic of those foreign investors on whom Salinas had lavished so much attention. Some of us had expected that the Salinas project would be challenged in slums like Chalco or Ciudad Nezahualcóyotl, but no one imagined that it would be defeated by Wall Street.

Salinas was brought down by a bizarre causal alliance: the masked Marcos and the equally anonymous traders of the global *bourse*. No one could have predicted such a combination, and it obviously shocked Salinas. Was the *salinato* a victim of some cosmic joke meant to compensate for the ex-president's hubris? Was Salinas merely the victim of a spectacular run of bad luck? How·aware was Salinas of the risks inherent in some of his key economic policy decisions? Did he cynically leave these festering problems on his successor's doorstep in order to protect his own image? In the following pages, I argue that the weaknesses of the technocratic revolution were fairly clear from the very beginning: a series of economic, political, and social contradictions that the *tecnócratas* refused to acknowledge, much less resolve. For a few years the system could sublimate these conflicts, but when strained, it could no longer live with the many contradictions of the technocratic project. Yet the spectacular collapse of the *salinato* should not blind us to its very substantial legacies. As in most revolutions, many of the original players are dead, discredited, or exiled and the original guiding ideology is perhaps more muted. But, for good or ill, the neoliberal revolution has left a very different Mexico.

A final introductory comment is in order. Having the opportunity to rewrite the ending of the book, I could have completely changed the focus of my analysis by moving away from the elite and the state, or by making use of the variety of methodological and theoretical alternatives available in political sociology. I have resisted since it would partly be intellectually dishonest to do so. More important, even if I have come belatedly to recognize that civil society may just "bite back" even the most powerful state, much of what happened in 1994 and afterward needs to be explained within leading political institutions. There are many other stories to tell of Mexico's "year of living dangerously,"[2] but this one is still worth telling.

## Transforming the Economy

The ultimate irony of the *salinato* is that it was partly brought down by mistakes right out of a final exam for intermediate macroeconomics. How could so much go so wrong so quickly?

Certainly the *sexenio* began well enough. After the collapse of the miracle in 1968, the Echeverria populism of the early 1970s, and the oil boom of later that decade, Mexicans had despaired of finding a stable economic model that married growth with low inflation. After 1987 the *Pacto* designed and implemented by the Salinas team appeared to work. If the economic growth was not extraordinary (an average of 3.0 percent p.a. and virtually flat per capita during the *sexenio*), at least inflation had been controlled (an average of less than 15 percent p.a.). Perhaps most important, there was a widespread belief that the economy had improved and there was considerable optimism about the future under NAFTA. If nothing else, Salinas had convinced Mexicans that good times were ahead.[3]

The economic strategy was deceptively simple. Mexico would attract large amounts of international capital (including some of the at least $50 billion that had fled the country since the 1970s). This capital would (a) help lower the debt burden and (b) be invested in new productive enterprises. The key to this scheme was to offer monetary stability and economic incentives such as cheap labor and access to markets. To ensure

---

2. I believe that Carlos Fuentes was the first to use this allusion in reference to 1994.

3. Jorge I. Domínguez and James A. McCann, *Democratizing Mexico: Public Opinion and Electoral Choices* (Baltimore: The Johns Hopkins University Press, 1996), pp. 126–30.

the first, government budgets were slashed (producing Mexico's first operating surpluses in decades) and the peso was pegged to the dollar. The second required opening the Mexican economy to world trade (and ensuring reciprocity). NAFTA was the obvious crowning touch as it promised investors access to the richest consumer market in the world. To a large extent, the policy was successful. Massive amounts of capital entered Mexico during the early 1990s.

As is now well known, this strategy was dangerous. Maintaining the dollar parity led to an overvalued peso[4] and thereby encouraged excess consumption of imported goods while making Mexican exports less attractive. It appears that economic policymakers were aware of this consequence, but believed that the continued entry of capital would balance the trade account for long enough to improve Mexican productivity and lift the economy into its supposed "First World" status. What the strategy did accomplish was to decimate large parts of the domestic bourgeoisie and industrial labor swamped by cheap imports, further impoverish significant parts of the peasantry not able to live without price subsidies or in competition with American agribusiness, and make the economy extremely sensitive to external capital markets. The long-term success of this policy was also hampered by the type of investments made. New capital was not being invested in schools, hospitals, roads, or business, but largely in the speculative gambling of the Bolsa. In 1992, for example, 72 percent of foreign investment was in the stock or money markets.[5] Domestic investment did not grow dramatically during any of the Salinas years and actually fell in 1993. Net job creation was disappointingly small.[6]

Given these conditions, the Mexican economy was effectively hostage to external perceptions. As long as the global capital markets judged it safe and profitable, the economy would perform. Much as the *tecnócratas* appeared to have convinced Mexicans that they were now in the "First World," they also convinced financial experts that Mexico was on the verge of the proverbial takeoff. In 1994, however, following the

---

4. This policy was also encouraged by the fixation of the economic team on controlling inflation and the political need to defend the government's greatest economic victory.

5. John Weiss, "Economic Policy Reform in Mexico," in Rob Aitken et al., eds., *Dismantling the Mexican State?* (London: Macmillan, 1996), p. 71.

6. A net one million jobs were created during the *sexenio*, roughly one-fourth of what was needed . Wayne A. Cornelius, "Designing Social Policy for Mexico's Liberalized Economy," in R. Roett, ed., *The Challenges of Institutional Reform in Mexico* (Boulder: Lynne Rienner Publishers, 1995), p. 140.

Chiapas uprising and the murders of Colosio and Ruiz Massieu, markets began to doubt the technocratic miracle. Moreover, as interest rates rose in the United States, the relative attraction of the Mexican money market declined. The interest paid by government CETES (the most common form of government bond) rose throughout 1994 in tandem with declines in reserves. Of greatest concern was the internationalization of the Mexican debt as peso-denominated paper was converted into dollar-indexed Tesobonos. Essentially, Mexico was relying on its reputation in order to borrow from Peter to pay Paul.

Beginning on December 19, 1994, the technocratic Ponzi scheme began to unravel. Precisely because so much of the economic policy had relied on a shallow optimism and the subsequent willingness of investors to ignore reality, the collapse was incredibly fast. Once the panic began, there was no safety net to catch the economy. As the peso lost half its value, debts denominated in dollars or with flexible interest rates bankrupted large parts of the middle class and thousands of businesses. The final result was that Mexico began 1995 owing more money than ever before, without parastatals to sell, and with a domestic manufacturing sector hard hit by nine years of open doors. How could such sophisticated policymakers with such impressive pedigrees make so many errors?

To an extent, they were not wrong. The failure of both the right and left opposition to formulate alternative economic strategies is indicative of the constraints under which Mexico was and is operating. The PAN may speak of better microeconomic interventions to save faltering industries and the PRD may criticize aspects of NAFTA and call for greater social spending, but neither one has proposed a paradigm significantly different from the technocratic revolution. As discussed in previous chapters, the apparent "inevitability" of the Salinas program was a major contributing factor to its political survival. But it also implied that the *tecnócratas* had few alternative options. Foreign capital was more available than domestic investment and had to be lured, no matter the costs and risks.

The collapse of the *salinato* was not brought about by Chiapas or the dramatic rise in political violence, but by the regime's failure to take on the central structural weakness of the Mexican economy: low domestic savings and investment. This is why the fall of the peso was such a cataclysmic event. Given the constraints on Mexico (porous financial borders, U.S. sensitivity, a fragile social system), it is frankly hard to imagine alternative feasible strategies without a much more dramatic political restructuring (which itself would have been "disruptive" to the markets). A radical solution would have required forcing the Mexican upper class to invest its cash in productive enterprises in Mexico. The failure to do so may partly be explained by the ideological sympathies of the *tecnócratas* or even by their relative class position. More important, they refused to recognize that the solution to Mexico's dilemma had a political and social component. The key to collapse of the *salinato* lies in that refusal.

## Alliances, Patronage, and Violence

What were the politics of the technocratic revolution? Carlos Salinas faced a series of political challenges, each with a respective audience and corresponding strategy. While he masterfully responded to each one, the variety of tactics used were bound to contradict and create complex interactions. The consequences of these became particularly clear in 1994.

The most immediate problem was from the left. The 1988 election made responding to the Cardenist opposition the single most important political problem for the regime. As described in previous chapters, PRONASOL was very effective in weakening the network of grassroots organizations partly responsible for the success of Cuauhtémoc Cárdenas. When more was required, Salinas was not above simple repression. Practically no one disputes that the PRI and the government countenanced extreme violence against PRD activists,[7] including murder. Certainly in Michoacán, the first two years of the *sexenio* saw a wave of repression. In part because of the threat from the left, Salinas remained dependent on the dinosaurs in the party (particularly on a local level) who could help guarantee the political peace he needed.

A second challenge came from the right. The rise of the PAN to at least regional competitiveness had been obvious since the early 1980s. Rather than fighting it, Salinas decided to make an alliance with this wing of the opposition. The support of the PAN came with the promise of allowing that party to continue growing as a national force and even to regional dominance. The gubernatorial elections in Baja California, Chihuahua,

---

7. It will probably always remain unclear how much of the violence was directed from Los Pinos and how much reflected local conditions that the national leadership decided to ignore.

SLP, and Guanajuato as well as the willingness to recognize PAN congressional victories indicated that the national leadership was at least willing to accept a two-party system in Mexico as long as the opposition was to the right of the PRI. The PAN seemed willing to accept this new democracy à la mexicana and was often reluctant to complain when fraud was perpetrated against the PRD.

The increasing centrality of NAFTA to the success of the government's economic policies created a third political challenge for Salinas. More than for any of his predecessors, American public and congressional opinion had to be courted. In many ways, Chiapas was an excellent example of the constraints faced by the government. It is now well established that the government knew of the guerrillas as early as 1992. The only explanation for the lack of action was fear that an unstable Mexico would make a less alluring destination for investment funds and certainly a less desirable partner. Even after January 1994 the government's actions were constrained by the wide media coverage. There had been guerrillas in Mexico before. There had been takeovers of municipal buildings and land seizures. Certainly there had been mutilated bodies of peasants on rural roadsides. The myriad reporters and cameramen were new, however. If Sub-comandante Marcos did not die in January as he fully expected, it was in part thanks to the *New York Times*. A "Guatemalan" solution might have been quick, but it would have led to congressional investigations in the United States and jitters on Wall Street. Salinas had to put up with Marcos.

A fourth constituency was the upper reaches of Mexican capital. In part because of the pressures detailed above, the walls between government and the PRI became higher and more forbidding. The *tecnócratas* must have realized that, increasingly, money would have to replace fraud as the decisive factor in Mexican elections. It is impossible to say to what extent Salinas expected a quid pro quo, but given that those he asked for PRI campaign support had also benefited from his policies, the assumption of reciprocity cannot be discounted. If Salinas was to replace the dinosaurs and their associated institutions with a "modern" party, he needed massive amounts of money and he needed the support and approval of those who had it. Jorge Castañeda has written that these sources of money might have included the *narcotraficantes* and that it was their inclusion into the political "family" that set the stage for 1994.[8] I would argue that, whatever their particular product, the important thing is that Salinas had a constituency of international businessmen

8. *The Mexican Shock* (New York: The New Press, 1996).

whose interests had to be taken directly into account when formulating public policy.

The biggest political headache for the technocratic revolution was not the PRD, the PAN, or even the EZLN (Ejercito Zapatista de Revolución Nacional). It was and is the PRI. Salinas and his party chairman, Colosio, tried to reconstruct it (if not necessarily in a more democratic direction), but the Salinistas discontinued their assault on the traditional party after the congressional elections of 1991.[9] This decision (no matter how involuntary) may be the key to the political legacy of the *salinato*. Beginning in 1992 and certainly after 1993 as the economy slowed and the opposition began to organize for the 1994 elections, the attacks on the dinosaurs and the party apparat stopped.[10] It became increasingly clear that the PRI as we have known it was not going to disappear quite as easily as the President (and many observers, including myself) had believed. How much this had to do with the move of Colosio to Sedesol, with the need to guarantee acquiescence of the CTM to yet another installment of the *Pacto,* or with the requirements of political security for NAFTA, we still do not know. The fact that Colosio, in his brief presidential campaign, felt the need to speak of political reform in much the same language Salinas had used six years earlier indicates that remarkably little had been done.

This was especially obvious after the assassination of Colosio. A great deal of political horse-trading had to be done to anoint Zedillo. The influence of hard-line *burocratas políticos* such as Carlos Hank González and Ignacio Pichardo Pagaza became more public throughout the presidential campaign. It appeared that in order to preserve their economic project Salinas, Zedillo, and Company had, however reluctantly, ceded responsibility for politics to those who had the expertise to properly manage it. Gone were the experiments of 1990 and 1991 and the talk of a new party. The PRI was back and looked much like its old self. Thanks to the dinosaurs, the PRI won its contest with the PRD for the Mexican countryside and the urban shantytowns.

Thus, if Salinas was constrained in his economic strategy, he appeared to be equally limited in his political choices. He had to satisfy the right, marginalize the left, keep the center, and placate clients, all under the

9. The end of the reform could be dated earlier to the March 1990 PRI Congress, at which sector leaders effectively blocked radical reconstruction.

10. Rumors still abound in Mexico City regarding what happened to the *reforma política.* One recurrent version is that PRI elders refused to sanction the creation of a Party of Solidarity, which would then change the constitution, allowing Salinas to be reelected.

watchful eye of the United States. For a few years he managed to keep a balance among the different strategies required by each of these "publics." Perhaps even more than August 1991, the election of August 1994 represented the apogee of Salinas's political gamesmanship. The PRD was humiliated, the PAN attained new status as the "official" opposition, the United States was satisfied with the degree of electoral transparency, and the PRI still won.[11]

The success of August 21 was particularly important because it was not purely based on old PRI tricks. It was a "modern" triumph reflecting the changes brought by the last decade. (The distinction between "old" and "new" ways of doing politics is nebulous. Where should one place the support of TELEVISA, for example?) The collapse of the left alternative could be partly blamed on strategic mistakes made by the PRD leadership and Cárdenas's less than charismatic performance. But it also reflected the ideological exhaustion of the left throughout Latin America. Nearly 80 percent of the population (give or take a few fraudulent percentage points) voted for parties advocating free markets and the sanctity of private property.

To an extent, therefore, the technocrats were politically successful: democracy had been made safe for neoliberalism. This rightward turn combined with another major element that Mexico shared with the rest of Latin America: fear of an alternative. Whether the fear was of violence perpetrated by the EZLN or the still-mysterious forces behind the Colosio assassination, or fear of the rapid exit of capital following any disruption in the Mexican political system, did not really matter. The technocrats had established the public equivalent of their own self-image: they were seen as the *only* choice, if stability and the promise of further economic improvement were to be ensured.

But the victory of August disguised the consequences of Salinas's delicate balance of forces and demands. "Modern" politics was expensive. Many were shocked when Salinas requested many millions from a gathering of prominent business allies. On the one hand, this could be read as a sign of the regime's continued power. On the other hand, the same event

11. Ernesto Zedillo won just over 50 percent of the valid votes while the PAN and the PRD reversed their roles from 1988: Diego Fernández de Cevallos received 27 percent and Cuauhtémoc Cárdenas 17 percent. In the Congress the PRI was able to maintain the dominance recaptured in 1991: 95 out of an expanded 128 senate seats and 300 of 500 deputies (including 278 of those directly elected). Despite the many observed and suspected frauds and illegalities, there was an almost unanimous consensus that the PRI really won this time. The election was unfair, especially in terms of campaign finance and media coverage, but it was clean.

could be seen as signaling the regime's dependence on these same persons to bankroll its victory. At least in theory, such a dependence might have played a role in the devaluation policy or in the timing of decisions in late December 1994.

Giving the PAN its regional victories (so that the PRI could focus its efforts against the left) also further alienated traditional forces in the party. As they considered whether they would be next on the presidential "hit list," these forces united and with increasing success challenged presidential power. As this postscript is being written in 1996, the traditional PRI appears to be making a significant comeback. The 17th Assembly of the PRI discarded much of the explicit ideology of the *salinato*, endorsing a return to "revolutionary nationalism" and rejecting calls for greater privatization in the oil industry. More significant, the Assembly could prove the end of the domination of the Mexican government by a technocratic elite. Challenging the leadership and following a raucous session on September 21, the Assembly imposed a requirement of a decade of party service *and* electoral experience on party candidates for president, senator, and governor.[12] It is impossible to determine at this point how stringently these new regulations will be enforced and how difficult it would be for leading candidates to achieve "electoral" victories prior to the more significant contests. No matter how cosmetic, however, these changes represented perhaps the most significant challenge to the technocratic revolution since 1988.

The legitimation strategy followed by Salinas was also particularly fragile since it depended so much on results in the economic sphere. The Mexican elite based their domination on a special claim to rule: they would deliver a modern, stable, and prosperous Mexican economy. They founded their hopes for "safe" future democratization on economic growth that would undermine popular radicalism. The fiction of a "First World" economy had to be maintained so that the "modern" technocratic leadership could justify its political recalcitrance. Salinas's handling of the potential financial panic following Chiapas and Colosio's assassination revalidated their claim to rule. But the December disaster called into question the legitimacy of the *tecnócratas*. If they could not deliver the economy they had promised, if they could not even guarantee the loyalty of Mexican and international capital, what purpose did they serve?

How did political considerations affect economic choices? In the first place, the continuation of authoritarian control allowed the *tecnócratas*

---

12. *La Jornada*, September 22, 1996, p. 1; *New York Times*, September 23, 1996, p. 3.

to maintain themselves in splendid isolation. As I have argued, this made the initial stages of the technocratic revolution possible. But it also made the revolution's success much more fragile since it made this success dependent on the elite's making the right choices at the right times. Finance Minister Pedro Aspe's fixation on inflation, for example, could only be transformed into government policy within the political isolation of technocratic rule, but there was no brake available when it became quixotic. By linking the success of the revolution to the political and economic wisdom of such a small number of persons, it increased the likelihood of disastrous errors. The isolation also closed potential sources of information. A more open debate about the consequences of government policies, for example, might have forced an earlier devaluation.

In an interesting paradox, their very isolation from opposition also allowed the *tecnócratas* to play politics with economic policy and not behave like the neoliberal monks many of us assumed they were. By early 1994 the danger signs were clear that the bet on global capitalization was not working, at least not in the short term. The peso had been arguably overvalued since 1992. The trade deficit was estimated at $20 billion. Yet the government never acknowledged the potential for problems and went so far as to disguise the situation by condoning strategic disruptions in the publication of economic figures and by allowing the growth of Tesobonos to conceal moves away from the peso. The collapse of the currency in December was part of the cost for the victory of August.

A more decisive move toward a democratic regime certainly would have had costs, but it might also have freed Salinas from these contradictory pressures and allowed a more gradual release of tensions. For example, an open abandonment of the PRI would have freed the dinosaurs to create their own political machine and created less pressure to stop the democratization of the party (such as it was) through violence. Alternatively, a more open relationship with the left, an acceptance of PRD victories, and a disavowal of traditional forces in places such as Chiapas might have convinced bodies such as the EZLN that there were electoral alternatives. By insisting on the continued imposition of authoritarian measures, Salinas ensured that often violence remained the only alternative. Perhaps more important, the need to construct a new electoral coalition might have forced Salinas to institute or at least consider a different set of economic and social options. A wider network of social support might have given him an opportunity to challenge the privileged position of the small minority who were able to hold the economy hostage.

Why was Carlos Salinas so unwilling to accept democratic constraints on his policies? In part the explanation may have something to do with his personality, which all describe as extremely autocratic. But, again, we have to appreciate also the constraints facing him. We should particularly emphasize the interactive effects of political and economic policies. If domestic politics forestalled a different economic strategy, the move toward the global economy may have also precluded democratic reform. A political opening might have frightened external capital. The now infamous memo in which Citibank advisers recommended a military response to the EZLN indicated that international capital did not wish its money risked on "democratic adventures." Salinas was appropriately loath to create a situation that would lead to possible investor hesitation. If the preservation of the legitimacy of the regime required economic performance through foreign dependency, this strategy demanded the maintenance of order through continued authoritarian measures.

To understand fully the collapse of *salinismo,* then, we have to understand why Salinas was so afraid of democracy, and for that explanation we must turn to the social context in which the regime operated.

## Solidarity and Inequality

Carlos Salinas well understood that his economic adjustment programs were going to impose social pain. He was aware of the latent tensions within Mexican society and the PRI and was reluctant to allow their overt expression. Solidarity was designed to ameliorate the political costs of neoliberalism by strategically targeting the poor and, more important, those groups and/or locales most likely to present a threat to the political order.[13] The general assessment of PRONASOL is that it did a wonderful job of securing support for Carlos Salinas and the PRI during the first half of the *sexenio,* but it did relatively little to relieve the misery of large parts of the population. Moreover, as Chiapas made abundantly clear, PRONASOL failed to resolve the long-term social problems of the country—inadequate job creation and growing inequality[14]. To use eco-

13. See Wayne Cornelius et al., eds., *Transforming State-Society Relations in Mexico: The National Solidarity Strategy* (La Jolla: Center for U.S.-Mexican Studies, University of California, San Diego, 1994.)

14. Kathleen Bruhn, "Social Spending and Political Support: The Lessons of the National Solidarity Program in Mexico," *Comparative Politics* 28, no. 2 (January 1996).

nomic imagery, PRONASOL was quite adequate at resolving a liquidity problem, but it could not fix a bankruptcy. The problem lay with the *tecnócratas's* assessment of what was wrong with Mexico and their refusal to accept the true extent of their difficulties.

The new elite seemed to view poverty as a temporary defect of the Mexican economy. An improvement in global markets, an adjustment in government services, an increase in efficiency, and a redistribution of the work force would begin significantly reducing the level of misery. Unfortunately, poverty in Mexico is not a question of management of economic performance, but reflects much deeper problems. Before Salinas came to power, roughly one-fourth of Mexicans suffered from some form of malnutrition, half did not have running water, and one-fourth had no electricity. Roughly half of the population was considered poor by the very low Mexican threshold.[15] In Chiapas, the figure was 80 percent.[16] Such figures indicate that poverty was not a temporary problem of a stage of Mexican development, but an innate part of Mexican society.

A budget of less than 1 percent of GDP could not hope to eliminate such poverty.[17] It did not. Nora Lustig's calculations indicate that simple trickle-down growth in imaginable quantities would not resolve the problem of poverty in Mexico.[18] Whether one uses a variety of consumption measures or the relative value of wages, during the 1980s and 1990s, the poor became poorer.[19] The already significant level of economic inequality actually increased during this period.[20]

Both the political and economic crises can be traced to the problem of inequality. First, the technocratic and neoliberal economic policies had as their implicit (and often explicit) models the East Asian miracles of the

15. Nora Lustig, *Mexico: The Remaking of an Economy* (Washington, D.C.: Brookings Institution, 1992).

16. Wayne Cornelius, *Mexican Politics in Transition: The Breakdown of a One-Party-Dominant Regime* (La Jolla: Center for U.S.-Mexican Studies, University of California, San Diego, 1996), p. 101.

17. This is the maximum estimate for PRONASOL expenditures (Cornelius, in Roett, ed., *The Challenges of Institutional Reform in Mexico*, p. 141).

18. Nora Lustig, "Solidarity as a Strategy of Poverty Alleviation," in Cornelius et al., eds., *Transforming State-Society Relations in Mexico*, pp. 81–82.

19. Philip Russell, *Mexico under Salinas* (Austin: Mexico Resource Center, 1994), pp. 276–81; Julio Moguel, "Salinas' Failed War on Poverty," *NACLA Report on the Americas* 28, no. 1 (July–August 1994): 38; Cornelius, *Mexican Politics in Transition*.

20. John Weiss, "Economic Policy Reform in Mexico," p. 76; Alejandro Guevara Sanginés, "Poverty Alleviation in Mexico," in Mónica Serrano and Victor Bulmer-Thomas, eds., *Rebuilding the State: Mexico after Salinas* (London: University of London, Institute of Latin American Studies, 1996), p. 154.

1970s and 1980s. While these societies are characterized by "strong" developmentalist states, they also saw the creation of relatively equal distribution of income at early stages in their development. The Salinas administration, however, sought to balance the government budget through cuts in subsidies and increases in regressive taxation while allowing the number of billionaires to increase severalfold. The new elite refused to consider any fundamental changes in the social and economic hierarchy of the country.

Questions of economic justice aside, Mexico needed to create a large enough domestic market so that its manufacturers (especially the small and medium-sized firms that were devastated by the trade opening) could attain the expertise and development needed to compete in the global market. More immediately, if Mexico were to entice long-term investment with significant economic integration and multipliers (as opposed to becoming one large *maquiladora*), it had to make its consumer markets attractive enough to merit the risk. The immense gap in wages between the United States and Mexico might lure some investment, but the possibility of millions of consumers outside the affluent enclaves of the major urban centers would have attracted much more.

Politically, the increasing inequality in income and wealth distribution produced a latent tension and at times explosions that made capital more expensive and that limited investors' willingness to make long-term commitments. Chiapas scared the financial markets because they recognized that Mexico could explode—hence the tendency to invest in short-term paper. Perceptions of a potentially more just Mexico might have made investors more willing to treat the EZLN as a local version of the American Indian Movement, with the same expectation of political marginality. Moreover, the need to control popular aspirations constrained the *tecnócratas'* ability and willingness to begin dismantling the authoritarian system. A practically colonial social structure could only be maintained through the traditional use of force or the threat thereof, and this required the continued frustration of democratic aspirations.

## How Much of a Revolution?

If I could change any significant part of this book, I would no longer call the *salinato* a revolution. It has become clearer that Salinas never had any intention of altering the fundamental distribution of power. He merely sought to improve the efficiency and sustainability of the political and economic machine that he inherited. This was his downfall. Without at least an initial questioning of the Mexican social status quo, the political and economic reforms would always be limited. As long as these could not develop according to their own dynamics, they would produce contradictions and conflicts, which not even the very politically astute Salinas could hope to resolve.

Essentially, Salinas wanted to build a "modern" economy upon an outdated political system and on an unstable social base. A modern economy could not rely on the whims of the international market, but the unwillingness and inability of the government to force domestic capital to invest made it the only alternative. Continued reliance on authoritarian measures prevented the creation of a deeper and more committed popular base, which would have allowed a softer landing or continued support even during periods of sacrifice. A more equitable social policy would have created a wider consumer base (and thus a more attractive site for investment) and a broader electoral coalition, but would have required challenging powers on which Salinas and his chosen successor had grown more dependent. The technocratic hubris was to believe that all these conflicting claims and pressures could be dealt with through centralized *dirigisme*. An exaggerated sense of their own wisdom (and others' faith in their expertise) allowed them to continue with their project despite the many warning signals, be they guerrillas in the Lacandon or the rush to Tesobonos. They were playing for time, and time ran out.

The events of 1994 were in many ways predictable, if not predicted. In hindsight, the high degree of social injustice and the miserable poverty of large parts of the population were certain to bring a Chiapas, the import boom had to be paid with a devaluation, and the disagreements within the PRI were bound to produce violence. The technocratic revolution could not be held responsible for all these events. But it could be blamed for refusing to recognize and address the problems all these entailed. The attributes that had helped the new elite attain power—concentration of resources within the bureaucracy, tightening of client networks, commitment to economic policy over and above democratic reform—created a series of contradictions that led to the explosion.

The contrast with another president who did lead a political and social revolution despite the limits on *his* autonomy is enlightening. Cárdenas, unlike Salinas, sought to reconstruct the political, economic, and social rules governing Mexican society in tandem. Agrarian reform, oil nationalization, the institutionalization of the PNR, and his voluntary departure from power fit into a synergetic strategy that gave Mexico nearly four miraculous decades. Salinas, on the other hand, appears to have sacrificed such coherence in favor of quick fixes and, lest we forget, his dreams of continued influence.

Despite the above and the fall of Carlos Salinas, however, the legacy of the technocratic revolution is undeniable. Salinas, like Calles before him, might see his reputation ruined and many of his policies changed, but the institutional base he designed basically remains. The economic collapse has actually strengthened the crucial aspiration of the Salinas elite to irrevocably link the Mexican and U.S. economies. This integration is continuing under NAFTA. In part because of these links and Mexican financial dependence on U.S. guarantees, it would be extremely difficult to dismantle the institutional bases of *salinismo*. For the medium term, the Mexican economy will remain open to global markets, respectful of private property, and dependent on both the attraction of cheap labor and the safety valve of emigration to the United States.

Politically, the Salinas legacy may be even more impressive. The possibility of a PAN victory in 1997 or in the year 2000 would provide exactly what the technocrats wanted—democracy without the possibility of dramatic social change and with continuity in macroeconomic policy. Even if the voting is freer in the future, the political spectrum of contenders will be increasingly narrower. (The wild card here is the degree of change brought about by the 17th PRI Assembly.) Much like its 1910 predecessor, the technocratic revolution is on its way to becoming institutionalized, and its ideology is increasingly accepted by all actors, including large parts of the PRD.

The central weakness of the technocratic revolution remains the same as it was in 1993. It is difficult to imagine how social misery and economic inequality can continue in Mexico without further popular explosions. It is important to remember that the attacks by the EZLN and the ERP (Ejereito Revolucionario del Pueblo) have been restricted to the countryside, where the ramifications are less immediate and control more secure. A revolutionary group in Chalco will be much more difficult to manage. We can only guess how many Maderos, Villas, or Zapatas await their moment.

# Bibliography

Adelman, Irma, and Taft Morris, C. *Society, Politics, and Economic Development.* Baltimore: The Johns Hopkins University Press, 1967.

Aguilar, Alonso. *La burgesía, la oligarqía, y el estado.* Mexico: Editorial Nuestro Tiempo, 1983.

———, and Carmona, Fernando. *México: Riqueza y miseria.* Mexico: Editorial Nuestro Tiempo, 1972.

Aguilar Camín, Héctor. *Transición política: El monstruo que vendrá en el desafío mexicano.* Mexico: Editorial Oceano, 1982.

———, and Meyer, Lorenzo. *A la sombra de la Revolución Mexicana.* Mexico: Cal & Arena, 1989.

Aldrete, José Antonio. "Hacia un nuevo enfoque para el estudio de la acción burocrática estatal: La política de vivienda del INFONAVIT." *Estudios Sociológicos* 1, no. 2 (May–August 1983).

Alonso, Jorge. *La dialéctica clases-elites en México.* Mexico: Editorial Casa Chata, 1976.

Americas Watch. *Human Rights in Mexico: A Policy of Impunity.* New York: Americas Watch, 1990.

Ames, Barry. *Political Survival: Politicians and Public Policy in Latin America.* Berkeley and Los Angeles: University of California Press, 1987.

Amnesty International. *Mexico: Torture with Impunity.* London: Amnesty International, 1991.

Amsden, Alice H. *Asia's Next Giant: South Korea and Late Industrialization.* New York: Oxford University Press, 1989.

———. "The State and Taiwan's Economic Development." In Peter Evans, Dietrich Rueschemeyer, and Theda Skocpol, eds., *Bringing the State Back In.* New York: Cambridge University Press, 1985.

Ascher, William. *Planning, Politics, and Technocracy in Argentina and Chile.* Ph.D. dissertation, Yale University, 1975.

Aspe, Pedro. "Mexico's Experience in Economic Reform." *Bildner Center Working Paper,* no. 12. New York: Graduate School of CUNY, 1992.

———, and Beristain, Javier. "The Evolution of Distribution Policies during the Post-Revolutionary Period in Mexico." In Pedro Aspe and Paul Sigmund, *The*

*Political Economy of Income Distribution in Mexico.* New York: Holmes and Meier, 1984.

——, and de León, José Gómez. "El crecimiento de la población en México." Paper presented at the Center for U.S.-Mexican Studies, University of California, San Diego, May 1985. Mimeographed.

——, and Sigmund, Paul. *The Political Economy of Income Distribution in Mexico.* New York: Holmes and Meier, 1984.

——; Dornbusch, Rudiger; and Obstfeld, Maurice, eds. *Financial Policies and the World Capital Market.* Chicago: University of Chicago Press, 1983.

Badie, Bertrand, and Birnbaum, Pierre. *The Sociology of the State.* Chicago: University of Chicago Press, 1983.

Bailey, John. "The Bureaucracy." In George Grayson, ed., *Prospects for Democracy in Mexico.* New Brunswick: Transaction Publishers, 1990.

——. *Governing Mexico.* New York: St. Martin's Press, 1988.

——. "Presidency, Bureaucracy, and Administrative Reform in Mexico: The Secretariat of Programming and Budget." *Inter-American Economic Affairs* 34, no. 1 (Summer 1980).

Banac, Ivo, ed. *Eastern Europe in Transition.* Ithaca: Cornell University Press, 1992.

Banco de México. *The Mexican Economy 1992.* Mexico: Banco de México, 1992.

Barenstein, Jorge. "Los administradores en el sector público mexicano." *Ensayos del CIDE* 1–2 (March 1982).

Barkin, David. *Distorted Development: Mexico in the World Economy.* Boulder: Westview Press, 1991.

Barry, Tom, ed. *Mexico: A Country Guide.* Albuquerque: Inter-Hemispheric Education Center, 1992.

Basáñez, Miguel. *La lucha por la hegemonía en México, 1968–1980.* Mexico: Editorial Siglo XXI, 1982.

——. *El pulso de los sexenios: Veinte años de crisis en México.* Mexico: Editorial Siglo XXI, 1990.

Bassols Battalla, Ángel. *Geografía económica de México.* Mexico: Trillas, 1982.

Beltrán y Puga, Tatiana Elena, and de la Torre Yarza, José Miguel. *El predominio de las presiones políticas sobre un ensayo de racionalidad en las decisiones gubernamentales.* Mexico: INAP, 1980.

Bennett, Douglas C., and Sharpe, Kenneth E. *Transnational Corporations versus the State: The Political Economy of the Mexican Auto Industry.* Princeton: Princeton University Press, 1985.

Benveniste, Guy. *The Politics of Expertise.* Berkeley: Glendessary Press, 1972.

Beristain, Javier, and Trigueros, Ignacio. "Mexico." In John Williamson, ed., *Latin American Adjustment: How Much Has Happened?* Washington, D.C.: Institute for International Economics, 1990.

Berle, Adolph, and Means, Gardner. *The Modern Corporation and Private Property.* New York: Macmillan, 1932.

Bermeo, Nancy, ed. *Liberalization and Democratization: Change in the Soviet Union and Eastern Europe.* Baltimore: The Johns Hopkins University Press, 1992.

Birnbaum, Pierre. *States and Collective Action: The European Experience.* Cambridge: Cambridge University Press, 1988.

Block, Fred. *Revising State Theory: Essays in Politics and Postindustrialism.* Philadelphia: Temple University Press, 1987.

Bourdieu, Pierre. "Cultural Reproduction and Social Reproduction." In J. H.

Karabel and A. H. Halsey, eds., *Power and Ideology in Education*. Oxford: Oxford University Press, 1977.

——. *Outline of a Theory of Practice*. Cambridge: Cambridge University Press, 1977.

Bowles, Samuel, and Gintis, Herbert. *Schooling in Capitalist America*. New York: Basic Books, 1976.

Brandenburg, Frank. *The Making of Modern Mexico*. Englewood Cliffs: Prentice Hall, 1964.

Bravo Aluija, Marcela, and Sirvent, Carlos. "La elite política en México." In Germán Pérez and Samuel León, *Diecisiete ángulos de un sexenio*. Mexico: Plaza y Valdés, 1987.

Breser Pereira, Luis Carlos. *A sociedade estatal e a tecnoburocracia*. Sao Paolo: Brasiliense, 1981.

Bright, Charles C., and Harding, Susan F., eds. *Statemaking and Social Movements: Essays in History and Theory*. Ann Arbor: University of Michigan Press, 1984.

Brito Lara, Tomás. *La sucesión presidencial de 1910 en 1988*. Mexico City: privately published, 1988.

Brittan, Samuel. "The Economic Contradictions of Democracy." *British Journal of Political Science* 5 (1975).

Brothers, Dwight, and Wick, Adele. *Mexico's Search for a New Development Strategy*. Boulder: Westview Press, 1990.

Brzezinski, Zbigniew. *The Grand Failure: The Birth and Death of Communism in the Twentieth Century*. New York: Charles Scribner's Sons, 1989.

Bustani Hid, José. "El presupuesto federal: Elaboración, aprobación, y ejecución." In José Bustani Hid et al., *La administración pública federal*. Vol. 2. Mexico: UNAM, 1973.

Butler, Edgar W., and Bustamante, Jorge, eds. *Sucesión Presidencial: The 1988 Mexican Presidential Election*. Boulder: Westview Press, 1991.

Calderón, José María et al. *Economía y política en el México actual*. Mexico: Terra Nova, 1980.

Callaghy, Thomas. "Towards State Capability and Embedded Liberalism." In Joan Nelson, ed., *The Politics of Economic Adjustment: Fragile Coalitions*. New Brunswick: Transaction Publishers, 1989.

Calvo Nicolau, Enrique, and Vargas Aguilar, Enrique. *Constitución política*. Mexico: Editorial Themis, 1989.

Camacho Solís, Manuel. "Los nudos históricos del sistema político mexicano." In Centro de Estudios Internacionales, *La crisis del sistema político mexicano, 1928–1977*. Mexico: Colegio de México, 1977.

——. "La reforma democrática." In Rolando Cordera Campos, Raúl Trejo Delarbre, and Juan Enrique Vega, eds., *México: El reclamo democrático*. Mexico: Editorial Siglo XXI, 1989.

——. "El poder: Estados o 'feudos' políticos." In Centro de Estudios Internacionales, *La vida política en México*. Mexico: Colegio de México, 1974.

——. "Los quehaceres de la renovación nacional." *Nexos* 86 (February 1985).

Cameron, David. "On the Limits of the Public Economy." *The Annals of the American Academy of Political and Social Science* 459 (1982).

Camp, Roderic. "The Cabinet and the *Técnico* in Mexico and the United States." *Journal of Comparative Administration* 3, no. 2 (August 1971).

——. "*Camarillas* in Mexican Politics: The Case of the Salinas Cabinet." *Mexican Studies* 6, no. 1 (Winter 1990).

————. "Losers in Mexican Politics." In James Wilkie, ed., *Quantitative Latin American Studies. Statistical Abstract of Latin America,* Supplement no. 6. Los Angeles: UCLA Latin America Center, 1977.

————. *Mexican Political Biographies, 1935–1981.* Tucson: University of Arizona Press, 1982.

————. *Mexico's Leaders: Their Education and Recruitment.* Tucson: University of Arizona Press, 1980.

————. "The Middle Level Technocrat in Mexico." *Journal of Developing Areas* 6 (July 1972).

————. "The Military." In George Grayson, ed., *Prospects for Democracy in Mexico.* New Brunswick: Transaction Publishers, 1990.

————. "The National School of Economics and Public Life in Mexico." *Latin American Research Review* 10, no. 3 (Fall 1975).

————. "The Political Technocrat in Mexico and the Survival of the Political System." *Latin American Research Review* 20, no. 1 (1985).

————. "A Re-examination of Political Leadership and the Allocation of Federal Revenues in Mexico." *Journal of Developing Areas* 10, no. 2 (January 1976).

————. "Role of the *Técnico* in Policy Making in Mexico: A Comparative Study of a Developing Bureaucracy." Ph.D. dissertation, University of Arizona, 1970.

————. "El sistema mexicano y las decisiones sobre el personal político." *Foro internacional* 27, no. 1 (July 1976).

Canak, William L., ed. *Lost Promises: Debt, Austerity, and Development in Latin America.* Boulder: Westview Press, 1989.

Cárdenas, Enrique. "A Reflection on Mexico's Contemporary Economic Problems in Historical Perspective." Paper presented at a Conference on Mexico's Search for a New Development Strategy, Yale University, April 6–8, 1989.

Carmona, Fernando et al. *El milagro mexicano.* Mexico: Nuestro Tiempo, 1974.

Carpizo, Jorge. *El presidencialismo mexicano.* Mexico: Editorial Siglo XXI, 1983.

Carr, Barry, and Anzaldua Montoya, Ricardo, eds. *The Mexican Left, the Popular Movements, and the Politics of Austerity.* La Jolla: Center for U.S.-Mexican Studies, University of California, San Diego, 1986.

Carrillo Castro, Alejandro. *La política y la administración pública en México.* Mexico: ICAP/PRI, 1980.

————. *La reforma administrativa en México.* 4 vols. Mexico: Porrúa, 1982.

————. "El sistema nacional de planeación." In Secretaría de Programación Presupuesto, *Aspectos jurídicos de la planeación en México.* Mexico City: Porrúa, 1981.

Casar, María Amparo, and Peres, Wilson. *El estado empresario en México: ¿Agotamiento o renovación?* Mexico: Editorial Siglo XXI, 1988.

*Censo de recursos humanos del sector público.* Mexico: 1975.

Centeno, Miguel Ángel. "Between Rocky Democracies and Hard Markets." *Annual Review of Sociology,* forthcoming.

————. "Electoral-Bureaucratic Authoritarianism: The Mexican Case." In Arturo Valenzuela, ed., *Politics, Society, and Democracy: Latin America.* Boulder: Westview Press, forthcoming.

————. *Mexico in the 1990s: Government and Opposition Speak Out.* La Jolla: Center for U.S.-Mexican Studies, University of California, San Diego, 1991.

————. "The New Científicos: Technocratic Politics in Mexico, 1970–1990." Ph.D. dissertation, Yale University, 1990.

————. "The New Leviathan: The Dynamics and Limits of Technocracy." *Theory and Society* 22, no. 3 (Summer 1993).

————. "The Press and Mexican Presidential Elections of 1988." Unpublished paper, Mexico City, 1988.

————, and Maxfield, Sylvia. "The Marriage of Finance and Order: Changes in the Mexican Political Elite." *Journal of Latin American Studies* 24, no. 1 (Spring 1992).

————, and Weldon, Jeffrey. "Small Circle of Friends." Paper presented at Latin American Studies Association meetings, Washington, D.C., April 1991.

Centro de Investigación para el Desarollo, AC (CIDAC). *Reforma del sistema político mexicano*. Mexico: Diana, 1990.

Chandler, Alfred D. *The Visible Hand: The Managerial Revolution in American Business*. Cambridge: Harvard University Press, 1977.

Cleaves, Peter. *Bureaucratic Politics and Administration in Chile*. Berkeley and Los Angeles: University of California Press, 1974.

————, and Scurrah, Martin. *Agriculture, Bureaucracy, and Military Government in Peru*. Ithaca: Cornell University Press, 1980.

Cline, Howard. *The United States and Mexico*. Rev. ed. New York: Athenaeum Press, 1963.

Cochrane, James. "Mexico's New Científicos." *Inter-American Economic Affairs* 21, no. 1 (Summer 1967).

Colegio de México. *Historia de la revolución mexicana*. Mexico: Colegio de México.

Collier, David, ed. *The New Authoritarianism in Latin America*. Princeton: Princeton University Press, 1979.

Collier, Ruth Berrins, and Collier, David. *Shaping the Political Arena: Critical Junctures, the Labor Movement, and Regime Dynamics in Latin America*. Princeton: Princeton University Press, 1991.

Collins, Randall. *The Credential Society*. New York: Academic Press, 1979.

Cordera Campos, Rolando, and González Tiburcio. "Percances y damnificados de la crisis económica." In Rolando Cordera Campos, Raúl Trejo Delarbre, and Juan Enrique Vega, eds., *México: El reclamo democrático*. Mexico: Editorial Siglo XXI, 1989.

Cordera Campos, Rolando, and Tello, Carlos. *México: La disputa por la nación*. Mexico: Editorial Siglo XXI, 1981.

————. "Prospects and Options for Mexican Society." In Clark Reynolds and Carlos Tello, eds., *U.S.-Mexico Relations: Economic and Social Aspects*. Stanford: Stanford University Press, 1983.

————, eds. *La desigualdad en México*. Mexico: Editorial Siglo XXI, 1984.

Cordera Campos, Rolando; Trejo Delarbre, Raúl; and Vega, Juan Enrique, eds. *México: El reclamo democrático*. Mexico: Editorial Siglo XXI, 1989.

Córdova, Arnaldo. *La política de masas del cardenismo*. Mexico: Ediciones Era, 1973.

Cornelius, Wayne. "Liberalization in an Authoritarian Regime." In Judith Gentleman, ed., *Mexican Politics in Transition*. Boulder: Westview Press, 1987.

————. *The Political Economy of Mexico under De la Madrid: The Crisis Deepens, 1985–1986*. Research Report Series, no. 43. La Jolla: Center for U.S.-Mexican Studies University of California, San Diego, 1986.

————, and Craig, Ann. *Politics in Mexico: An Introduction and Overview*. La Jolla: Center for U.S.-Mexican Studies, University of California, San Diego, 1988.

————; Gentleman, Judith; and Smith, Peter, eds. *Mexico's Alternative Political Futures.* Monograph no. 30. La Jolla: Center for U.S.-Mexican Studies, University of California, San Diego, 1989.

Cosío Villegas, Daniel. *El sistema político mexicano.* Mexico: Joaquín Mortiz, 1975.

Costa Pinto, L. A. *Nacionalismo y militarismo.* Mexico: Editorial Siglo XXI, 1969.

Crozier, Michel; Huntington, Samuel; Watanuki, Joji. *The Crisis of Democracy: Report on the Governability of Democracies to the Trilateral Commission.* New York: New York University Press, 1975.

Cumings, Bruce. "The Origins and Development of the Northeast Asian Political Economy." In Frederic C. Deyo, ed., *The Political Economy of the New Asian Industrialism.* Ithaca: Cornell University Press, 1987.

Cypher, James M. *State and Capital in Mexico.* Boulder: Westview Press, 1990.

Dahrendorf, Ralf. *Reflections on the Revolution in Europe.* New York: Random House, 1990.

de Schweinitz, Karl. *Industrialization and Democracy: Economic Necessities and Political Possibilities.* New York: Free Press, 1964.

Deyo, Frederic C., ed. *The Political Economy of the New Asian Industrialism.* Ithaca: Cornell University Press, 1987.

Diamond, Larry; Linz, Juan; and Lipset, S. M., eds. *Democracy in Developing Countries.* Boulder: Westview Press, 1989.

Dick, G. William. "Authoritarian versus Nonauthoritarian Approaches to Economic Development." *Journal of Political Development* 82 (1974).

DiMaggio, Paul, and Powell, Walter. "The Iron Cage Revisited: Institutional Isomorphism and Collective Rationality in Organizational Fields." *American Sociological Review* 48 (1983).

di Palma, Giuseppe. *To Craft Democracies: An Essay on Democratic Transitions.* Berkeley and Los Angeles: University of California Press, 1990.

Domhoff, G. W., and Dye, Thomas, eds. *Power Elites and Organizations.* Beverly Hills: Sage Publications, 1987.

Dresser, Denise. *Neopopulist Solutions to Neoliberal Problems.* La Jolla: Center for U.S.-Mexican Studies, University of California, San Diego, 1991.

Eckstein, Susan. *The Poverty of Revolution: The State and the Urban Poor in Mexico.* Princeton: Princeton University Press, 1977.

————, ed. *Power and Popular Protest: Latin American Social Movements.* Berkeley and Los Angeles: University of California Press, 1989.

Eisenstadt, S.N., and Lemarchand, René, eds. *Political Clientalism, Patronage, and Development.* Beverly Hills: Sage Publications, 1981.

Eisenstadt, S.N., and Roniger, Luis. *Patron, Clients, and Friends: Interpersonal Relations and the Structure of Trust in Society.* Cambridge: Cambridge University Press, 1984.

Evans, Peter. "Class, State, and Dependence in East Asia: Lessons for Latin Americanists." In Frederic C. Deyo, *The Political Economy of New Asian Industrialism.* Ithaca: Cornell University Press, 1987.

————. "The State as Problem and Solution." In Stephan Haggard and Robert Kaufman, eds., *The Politics of Economic Adjustment: International Constraints, Distributive Conflicts, and the State.* Princeton: Princeton University Press, 1992.

————; Rueschemeyer, Dietrich; and Skocpol, Theda, eds. *Bringing the State Back In.* New York: Cambridge University Press, 1985.

"The Exit from Communism." Special issue of *Daedalus* 121, no. 2 (Spring 1992).

Ezcurdia, Mario. *De la política*. Mexico: El Día, 1983.

———. *¿Hubo alguna vez un gobierno paralelo?* Mexico: INAP Serie Praxis no. 44, 1982.

Fernández Christlieb, Paulina, and Bejar Algazzi, Luisa. "La década de los sesenta." In Germán Fernández del Castillo, ed. *Evolución del estado mexicano, 1940–1983*. Mexico: Ediciones el Caballito, 1986.

Fernando, Juan. "Las elites." *Revista española de la opinion pública* 43 (January–March 1976).

Finzi, Claudio. *Il potere tecnocratico*. Rome: Bulzoni, 1977.

Flores de la Peña, Horacio et al. *Bases para la planeación económica y social de México*. Mexico: Editorial Siglo XXI, 1966.

Foweraker, Joe, and Craig, Ann, eds. *Popular Movements and Political Change in Mexico*. Boulder: Lynne Rienner Publishers, 1990.

Fox, Jonathan, and Gordillo, Gustavo. "Between State and Market: The Campesinos Quest for Autonomy." In Wayne Cornelius, Judith Gentleman, and Peter Smith, eds., *Mexico's Alternative Political Futures*. Monograph no. 30. La Jolla: Center for U.S.-Mexican Studies, University of California, San Diego, 1989.

Foxley, Alejandro. *Latin American Experiments in Neoconservative Economics*. Berkeley and Los Angeles: University of California Press, 1983.

Franco, Fernando. "La reforma electoral." In Diego Valadés and Mario Ruiz Massieu, eds., *La transformación del estado mexicano*. Mexico: Diana, 1989.

Frankel, Roberto, and O'Donnell, Guillermo. "The Stabilization Programs of the IMF." In Richard Fagen, ed., *Capitalism and the State in U.S.-Latin American Relations*. Stanford: Stanford University Press, 1979.

Frisch, Alfred. "Les Previsions à l'épreuve de la réalité: L'Exemple de la technocratie." *Analyse et Prevision* 16, no. 3 (September 1973).

Garrido, Luis Javier. "The Crisis of *Presidencialismo*." In Wayne Cornelius, Judith Gentleman, and Peter Smith, eds., *Mexico's Alternative Political Futures*. Monograph no. 30. La Jolla: Center for U.S.-Mexican Studies, University of California, San Diego, 1989.

———. "Un partido sin militantes." In Soledad Loaeza and Rafael Segovia, eds., *La vida política mexicana en crisis*. Mexico: El Colegio de México, 1987.

Gentleman, Judith, ed. *Mexican Politics in Transition*. Boulder: Westview Press, 1987.

Gereffi, Gary. *The Pharmaceutical Industry and Dependency in the Third World*. Princeton: Princeton University Press, 1983.

———, and Wyman, Donald L., eds. *Manufacturing Miracles: Paths of Industrialization in Latin America and East Asia*. Princeton: Princeton University Press, 1990.

Gil, Carlos B. *Hope and Frustration: Interviews with Leaders of Mexico's Political Opposition*. Wilmington: Scholarly Resources, 1992.

Gil, Jorge; Schmidt, Samuel; and Castro, Jorge. "La red de poder mexicana: El caso de Miguel Alemán." Mimeographed. November 1991.

Gilbert, Claude. "Le Mexique: Des hauts fonctionnaires introuvables?" In Daniele Lochak et al., eds., *La Haute Administration et la politique*. Paris: P.U.F., 1986.

Gilly, Adolfo. *La revolución interrumpida*. Mexico: Ediciones el Caballito, 1971.

Godau, Rainer. "Mexico: A Bureaucratic Polity." Master's thesis, University of Texas, Austin, 1976.

González Casanova, Pablo. *La democracia en México*. Mexico: Editorial Era, 1965.
————. *El estado y los partidos políticos en México*. Mexico: Editorial Era, 1982.
————, and Aguilar Camín, Héctor, eds. *México ante la crisis*. Vol. 2. Mexico City: Editorial Siglo XXI, 1985.
González Graff, Jaime. *Las elecciones de 1988*. Mexico: Diana, 1989.
Gooding, John. "Gorbachev and Democracy." *Soviet Studies* 48, no. 2 (April 1990).
Gordillo, Gustavo. "Estado y movimiento campesino en la coyuntura actual." In Pablo González Casanova and Héctor Aguilar Camín, eds., *México ante la crisis*. Vol. 2. Mexico City: Editorial Siglo XXI, 1985.
Gourevitch, Peter. *Politics in Hard Times: Comparative Responses to International Economic Crises*. Ithaca: Cornell University Press, 1986.
Granovetter, Mark. *Getting a Job: A Study of Contacts and Careers*. Cambridge: Cambridge University Press, 1974.
Grayson, George. "Oil and Politics in Mexico." *Current History* 82, no. 488 (December 1983).
————, ed. *Prospects for Democracy in Mexico*. New Brunswick: Transaction Publishers, 1990.
Greenberg, Martin. *Bureaucracy and Development*. Lexington: Lexington Books, 1970.
Grimes, C. E., and Simmons, Charles. "Bureaucracy and Political Control in Mexico: Towards an Assessment." *Public Administration Review* 29, no. 1 (January–February 1969).
Grindle, Merilee. *Bureaucrats, Politicians, and Peasants in Mexico*. Berkeley and Los Angeles: University of California Press, 1977.
————. "Policy Change in an Authoritarian Regime: Mexico under Echeverría." *Journal of Inter-American Studies and World Affairs* 19, no. 4 (November 1977).
————. "Power, Expertise, and the *Técnico*." *Journal of Comparative Politics* 39 (May 1977).
Gruber, Wilfred. "Career Patterns in Mexico's Political Elite." *Western Political Quarterly* 24, no. 3 (September 1971).
Guillén Romo, Héctor. *Orígines de la crisis en México*. Mexico: Editorial Era, 1984.
Habermas, Jurgen. *Toward a Rational Society*. Boston: Beacon Press, 1975.
Hafstadter, Dan. *Mexico, 1946–1973*. New York: Facts on File, 1974.
Haggard, Stephan. *Pathways from the Periphery: The Politics of Growth in the Newly Industrializing Countries*. Ithaca: Cornell University Press, 1990.
————, and Kaufman, Robert. "Economic Adjustments in New Democracies." In Joan Nelson, ed., *The Politics of Economic Adjustment: Fragile Coalitions*. New Brunswick: Transaction Publishers, 1989.
————, eds. *The Politics of Economic Adjustment: International Constraints, Distributive Conflicts, and the State*. Princeton: Princeton University Press, 1992.
Hall, Peter. *The Political Power of Economic Ideas: Keynesianism Across Nations*. Princeton: Princeton University Press, 1989.
Hamilton, Nora. *The Limits of State Autonomy: Post-Revolutionary Mexico*. Princeton: Princeton University Press, 1982.
————, and Harding, Timothy F., eds. *Modern Mexico: State, Economy, and Social Conflict*. Beverly Hills: Sage Publications, 1986.
Handelman, Howard, and Baer, Werner, ed. *Paying the Costs of Austerity in Latin America*. Boulder: Westview Press, 1989.

Hansen, Roger. *The Politics of Mexican Development.* Baltimore: The John Hopkins University Press, 1980.

Hart, John Mason. *Revolutionary Mexico: The Coming and Process of the Revolution.* Berkeley and Los Angeles: University of California Press, 1987.

Hellman, Judith Adler. *Mexico in Crisis.* New York: Holmes and Meier, 1983.

Hernández Rodríguez, Rogelio. "Formación y trayectoria de las secretarios de estado en México, 1946–82." Master's thesis, FLACSO, January 1985.

————. "Los hombres del Presidente de la Madrid." *Foro internacional* 28, no. 2 (July–September 1987).

Huntington, Samuel. *Political Order in Changing Societies.* New Haven: Yale University Press, 1968.

————, and Nelson, Joan. *No Easy Choice: Political Participation in Developing Countries.* Cambridge: Harvard University Press, 1976.

————, and Weiner, Myron, eds. *Understanding Political Development.* Boston: Little Brown, 1987.

Ibarra, David, and Alberro, José Luis. "Mexico." In Joseph Pechman, ed., *The Role of the Economist in Government.* New York: Harvester Wheatsheaf, 1989.

Ilchman, Warren; Stone Ilchman, Alice; and Hastings, Phillip K. *The New Men of Knowledge and the Developing Nations.* Berkeley and Los Angeles: Institute of Governmental Studies, University of California, 1968.

Johnson, Chalmers. *MITI and the Japanese Miracle: The Growth of Industrial Policy, 1925–1975.* Stanford: Stanford University Press, 1982.

————. "Political Institutions and Economic Performance." In Frederic C. Deyo, ed., *The Political Economy of the New Asian Industrialism.* Ithaca: Cornell University Press, 1987.

Johnson, Kenneth F. *Mexican Democracy: A Critical View.* Boston: Allyn and Bacon, 1971.

Juárez, Antonio. "La clase obrera y sus condiciones de vida en México." In *Democracia y condiciones de vida.* Mexico: Colección el obrero mexicano, Editorial Siglo XXI, 1984.

Kahler, Miles. "External Influence, Conditionality, and the Politics of Adjustment." In Stephan Haggard and Robert Kaufman, eds., *The Politics of Economic Adjustment: International Constraints, Distributive Conflicts, and the State.* Princeton: Princeton University Press, 1992.

————. "International Financial Institutions and the Politics of Adjustment." In Joan Nelson, ed., *Fragile Coalitions: The Politics of Economic Adjustment.* New Brunswick: Transaction Publishers, 1989.

————. "Orthodoxy and Its Alternatives: Explaining Approaches to Stabilization and Adjustment." In Joan Nelson, ed., *Economic Crisis and Policy Choice: The Politics of Adjustment in the Third World.* Princeton: Princeton University Press, 1990.

Katz, Friedrich. *The Secret War in Mexico: Europe, the United States, and the Mexican Revolution.* Chicago: University of Chicago Press, 1981.

Katzenstein, Peter. *Small States in World Markets: Industrial Policy in Europe.* Ithaca: Cornell University Press, 1985.

Kaufman, Robert. "Economic Orthodoxy and Political Change in Mexico." In Robert Kaufman and Barbara Stallings, eds., *Debt and Democracy in Latin America.* Boulder: Westview Press, 1989.

————. "Industrial Change and Authoritarian Rule in Latin America: A Concrete Review of the Bureaucratic-Authoritarian Model." In David Collier, ed., *The*

*New Authoritarianism in Latin America.* Princeton: Princeton University Press, 1979.

────. "Mexico and Latin American Authoritarianism." In José Luis Reyna and Richard S. Weinert, *Authoritarianism in Mexico.* Philadelphia: ISHI, 1977.

────. "Stabilization and Adjustment in Argentina, Brazil, and Mexico." In Joan Nelson, ed., *Economic Crisis and Policy Choice: The Politics of Adjustment in the Third World.* Princeton: Princeton University Press, 1990.

Kelley, Guillermo. "Politics and Administration in Mexico: Recruitment and Promotion of the Político-Administrative Class." Technical Paper Series no. 33, Institute of Latin American Studies, University of Texas, Austin, 1981.

Knight, Alan. "Historical Continuities in Social Movements." In Joe Foweraker and Ann Craig, eds., *Popular Movements and Political Change in Mexico.* Boulder: Lynne Rienner Publishers, 1990.

────. *The Mexican Revolution.* 2 vols. Cambridge: Cambridge University Press, 1986.

────. "The Peculiarities of Mexican History." *Journal of Latin American Studies* 24 (Supplement, 1992).

Kohli, Atul. "Democracy and Development." In John P. Lewis and Valeriana Kallab, eds., *Development Strategies Reconsidered.* New Brunswick: Transaction Publishers, 1990.

────. "The Politics of Economic Liberalization in India." *World Development* 17 (1989).

Krauze, Enrique. *Por una democracia sin adjetivos.* Mexico: Joaquín Mortiz, 1987.

Larson, Magali. *The Rise of Professionalism.* Berkeley and Los Angeles: University of California Press, 1977.

Laumann, Edward O., and Knoke, David. *The Organizational State.* Madison: University of Wisconsin Press, 1987.

Leal, Juan Felipe. *La burgesía y el estado mexicano.* Mexico: Editorial el Caballito, 1980.

Lerner de Sheinbaum, Bertha. "La tecnocracia en México: Ni embrión, ni garantía de profesionalismo." *Revista Mexicana de Sociología* 45, no. 2 (1983).

────. "La teoría marxista clásica y el problema de la burocracia." *Revista Mexicana de Sociología* 41, no. 4 (1979).

Levi Peza, Manuel. *Por donde empezar.* Mexico: Biblioteca Estudios Políticos, 1987.

Levy Daniel. "The Political Consequences of Changing Socialization Patterns." In Roderic Camp, ed., *Mexico's Political Stability: The Next Ten Years.* Boulder: Westview Press, 1986.

────, and Szekely, Gabriel. *Mexico: Paradoxes of Stability and Change.* Boulder: Westview Press, 1983.

Lieuwen, Edwin. "Depoliticization of the Mexican Revolutionary Army, 1915–1940." In David Ronfeldt, ed., *The Modern Mexican Military: A Reassessment.* Monograph no. 15. La Jolla: Center for U.S.-Mexican Studies, University of California, San Diego, 1984.

Linz, Juan J., ed. *The Breakdown of Democratic Regimes: Crisis, Breakdown, and Reequilibration.* Baltimore: The Johns Hopkins University Press, 1978.

────. "Totalitarian and Authoritarian Regimes." In Fred Greenstein and Nelson Polsby, eds., *Handbook of Political Science.* Vol. 3. Reading: Addison Wesley, 1975.

Loaeza, Soledad. "The Impact of Economic Crisis on the Mexican Political System."

In Susan Kaufman Purcell, ed., *Mexico in Transition: Implications for U.S. Policy*. New York: Council on Foreign Relations, 1988.

————, and Segovia, Rafael, eds. *La vida política mexicana en crisis*. Mexico: El Colegio de México, 1987.

Lomnitz, Larissa Adler, and Perez-Lizaur, Marisol. *A Mexican Elite Family, 1820–1980: Kinship, Class, and Culture*. Princeton: Princeton University Press, 1988.

Looney, Robert. *Economic Policymaking in Mexico*. Durham: Duke University Press, 1985.

López Gallo, Manuel. *El elegido*. Mexico: Ediciones el Caballito, 1989.

López Portillo, José. "La función de control en la administración pública." *Revista de Administración Pública* 22 (January–February 1971).

————. *Mis tiempos*. Mexico: Fernandez Editores, 1988.

Luna, Matilde. "La administración estatal y el régimen político." *Revista Mexicana de Sociología 50*, no. 3 (July–September 1988).

————. "Las transformaciones del régimen político mexicano en la década de 1970." *Revista Mexicana de Sociología* 14, no. 2 (April–June 1983).

Lustig, Nora. "The Mexican Economy in the Eighties: An Overview." Mimeograph. Washington, D.C.: Brookings Institution, June 1989.

Madrid Hurtado, Miguel de la. *A mitad del camino: 1985*. Mexico: Presidencia de la República, 1986.

————. *Cien días ante la crisis*. Mexico: Presidencia de la República, 1983.

————. *Cien tesis sobre México*. Mexico: Editorial Grijalbo, 1982.

————. *Cuadernos de pensamiento político*. Mexico: PRI, 1982.

————. *Diálogo presidencial, 1982–1983*. Mexico: Presidencia de la República, 1986.

————. *Estudios de derecho constitucional*. Mexico: Porrúa, 1980.

————. *Los grandes problemas de hoy*. Mexico: Editorial Diana, 1982.

————. *Informes I-VI*. Mexico: Presidencia de la República, 1983–1988.

Malloy, James, ed. *Authoritarianism and Corporatism in Latin America*. Pittsburgh: University of Pittsburgh Press, 1977.

Mares, David R. "Explaining Choice of Development Strategies: Suggestions from Mexico, 1970–1982." *International Organization* 39, no. 4 (Fall 1985).

Márquez, Vivianne, and Godau, Rainer. "Burocracia y políticas públicas: Una perspectiva desde América Latina." *Estudios Sociológicos* 1, no. 2 (May–August 1983).

Martínez de Navarrete, Ifigenia. "La distribución del ingreso en México." *El perfil de México en 1980*. Vol. 1. Mexico: Editorial Siglo XXI, 1980.

Maxfield, Sylvia. "Bankers' Alliances and the 'New Institutionalism': Macroeconomic Policy Patterns in Mexico and Brazil." Mimeographed. Yale University, 1988.

————. *Governing Capital: International Finance and Mexican Politics*. Ithaca: Cornell University Press, 1990.

————. "International Economic Opening and Government-Business Relations." In Wayne Cornelius, Judith Gentleman, and Peter Smith, eds., *Mexico's Alternative Political Futures*. La Jolla: Center for U.S.-Mexican Studies, University of California, San Diego, 1989.

————, and Anzaldua Montoya, Ricardo, eds. *Government and Private Sector in Contemporary Mexico*. La Jolla: Center for U.S.-Mexican Studies, University of California, San Diego, 1987.

Melgar Adalid, Mario. "Los grupos de presión." In Diego Valadés and Mario Ruiz Massieu, eds., *La transformación del estado mexicano*. Mexico: Diana, 1989.

Meyer, John. "The World Polity and the Authority of the Nation-State." In A. Bergesen, ed., *Studies of the Modern World-System*. New York: Academic Press, 1980.

———, and Scott, R. W. *Organizational Environments: Ritual and Rationality*. Beverly Hills: Sage, 1983.

Meyer, Lorenzo. "La democracia política: Esperando a Godot." In *Nexos, Mexico Mañana*. Mexico City: Nexos, 1988.

———. "El estado mexicano contemporáneo." In Colegio de México, *Lecturas de política mexicana*. Mexico: Colegio de México, 1977.

Michels, Robert. *Political Parties*. New York: Collier Books, 1962.

Middlebrook, Kevin J. *Political Liberalization in an Authoritarian Regime*. Research Report, no 41. La Jolla: Center for U.S.-Mexican Studies, University of California, San Diego, 1985.

———. "The Sounds of Silence: Organized Labor's Response to Economic Crisis in Mexico." *Journal of Latin American Studies* 21 (May 1989).

Migdal, Joel S. *Strong Societies and Weak States: State-Society Relations and State Capabilities in the Third World*. Princeton: Princeton University Press, 1988.

Mills, C. Wright. *The Power Elite*. New York: Oxford University Press, 1959.

Mirón, Rosa María, and Pérez, Germán. *López Portillo: Auge y crisis de un sexenio*. Mexico: Plaza y Valdés, 1988.

Mitchell, Christopher. "The Role of Technocrats in Latin American Integration." *Inter-American Economic Affairs* 21 (Summer 1967).

Molina Piñeiro, Luis J. *Estructura del poder y reglas del juego político en México*. Mexico: UNAM, 1984.

Molinar Horcasitas, Juan. *El tiempo de la legitimidad*. Mexico: Cal y Arena, 1991.

———. "Vicisitudes de una reforma electoral." In Soledad Loaeza and Rafael Segovia, eds., *La vida política mexicana en crisis*. Mexico: El Colegio de México, 1987.

Moreno Sánchez, Manuel. *Crisis política en México*. Mexico: Editorial Extemporáneos, n.d.

Morris, Stephen D. *Corruption and Politics in Contemporary Mexico*. Tuscaloosa: University of Alabama Press, 1991.

Nagle, John. *System and Succession: The Social Bases of Elite Recruitment*. Austin: University of Texas Press, 1977.

Needleman, Carolyn, and Needleman, Martin. "Who Rules Mexico? A Critique of Some Current Views on the Mexican Political Process." *Journal of Politics* 31 (November 1969).

Needler, Martin. *Politics and Society in Mexico*. Albuquerque: University of New Mexico Press, 1971.

Nelson, Joan, ed. *Economic Crisis and Policy Choice: The Politics of Adjustment in the Third World*. Princeton: Princeton University Press, 1990.

———. *Fragile Coalitions: The Politics of Economic Adjustment*. New Brunswick: Transaction Publishers, 1989.

Newell, Roberto, and Rubio, Luis. *Mexico's Dilemma: The Political Origins of Economic Crisis*. Boulder: Westview Press, 1984.

*Nexos. Mexico Mañana*. Mexico City: Nexos, 1988.

North American Congress on Latin America. "The Latin American Left: A Painful Rebirth." *NACLA Report on the Americas* 25 (5 May 1992).

Nuncio, Abraham, ed. *La sucesión presidencial en 1988*. Mexico: Grijalbo, 1987.

O'Donnell, Guillermo. *Bureaucratic Authoritarianism*. Berkeley and Los Angeles: University of California Press, 1988.

———. *Modernization and Bureaucratic Authoritarianism*. Berkeley: ISI, 1979.

———; Schmitter, Phillipe, and Whitehead, Laurence, eds. *Transitions from Authoritarian Rule: Prospects for Democracy*. Baltimore: The Johns Hopkins University Press, 1986.

Olson, Mancur, Jr. *The Rise and Decline of Nations: Economic Growth, Stagflation, and Social Rigidities*. New Haven: Yale University Press, 1982.

O'Malley, Ilene. *The Myth of the Revolution: Hero Cults and the Institutionalization of the Mexican State*. New York: Greenwood Press, 1986.

Ortiz Mena, Antonio. "Desarollo estabilizador: Una década de estrategia económica en México." *Trimestre económico* 37, no. 146 (April–June 1970).

Packenham, Robert. *Liberal America and the Third World: Political Development Ideas in Foreign Aid and Social Science*. Princeton: Princeton University Press, 1973.

Padgett, Vincent. *The Mexican Political System*. Boston: Houghton Mifflin, 1966.

Padilla, Remberto H. *Historia de la política mexicana*. Mexico City: EDAMEX, 1988.

Partido de la Revolución Democrática (Human Rights Commission). *Radiografía del fraude*. Mexico: 1988.

———. *Three Years of Political Repression in Mexico*. Mexico: July 1991.

Paul, Ellen Frankel. *Totalitarianism at the Crossroads*. New Brunswick: Transaction Publishers, 1990.

Paz, Octavio. "Burocracia y democracia en México." *Vuelta* 127 (June 1987).

Pazos, Luis. *Hacia donde va Salinas*. Mexico: Diana, 1989.

Pereyra, Carlos. "Effectos políticos de la crisis." In Pablo González Casanova and Héctor Aguilar Camín, eds., *México ante la crisis*. Vol. 2. Mexico: Editorial Siglo XXI, 1986.

———. "Las vísperas de las urnas." *Nexos* 87 (March 1985).

Pérez, Germán, and León, Samuel. "En busca de la legitimidad perdida." In Pérez and León, *Diecisiete ángulos de un sexenio*. Mexico: Plaza y Valdés, 1987.

Perrow, Charles. *Complex Organizations*. 3d. ed. Glenview, Ill.: Scott, Foresman, 1986.

Peschard, Jaquelina et al. "De Ávila Camacho a Miguel Alemán." In Germán Pérez ed., *Evolución del estado mexicano, 1940–1983*. Mexico: Ediciones el Caballito, 1986.

Pfeffer, Jeffrey. *Power in Organizations*. Marshfield, Mass.: Pitman Publishing, 1981.

Pichardo Pagaza, Iganacio. *Introducción a la administración pública de México*. 2 vols. Mexico: INAP, 1984.

Presidencia de la República. *Diccionario biográfico del gobierno mexicano*. 1st, 2d, 3d eds. Mexico: Fundo de la Cultura Económica, 1984, 1987, 1989.

———. *El ejecutivo ante el congreso*. Mexico: 1977–1978.

———. *The Mexican Agenda*. Mexico: 1991.

———. *Los presidentes de México: Discursos políticos*. Mexico: 1989.

———. *Primer informe de Carlos Salinas de Gortari, Anexo*. Mexico: 1989.

———. *Las razones y las obras*. Vols. 1–4. Mexico: CFE, 1983–1989.

*Proceso. Planes sin planificación*. Mexico: CISA, 1980.

Przeworski, Adam. *Democracy and the Market: Political and Economic Reforms in*

*Eastern Europe and Latin America.* Cambridge: Cambridge University Press, 1991.

————, and Wallerstein, Michael. "The Structure of Class Conflict in Democratic Capitalist Societies." *American Political Science Review* 76 (1982).

Purcell, John, and Kaufman Purcell, Susan. "Mexican Business and Public Policy." In James Malloy, ed., *Authoritarianism and Corporatism in Latin America.* Pittsburgh: University of Pittsburgh Press, 1977.

Purcell, Susan Kaufman. *The Mexican Profit-Sharing Decision: Politics and Economic Change in an Authoritarian Regime.* Berkeley and Los Angeles: University of California Press, 1975.

————. "Mexico: Clientalism, Corporatism, and Political Stability." In S. N. Eisenstadt and Rene Lemarchand, eds., *Political Clientalism, Patronage, and Development.* Beverly Hills: Sage Publications, 1981.

————, ed. *Mexico in Transition: Implications for U.S. Policy.* New York: Council on Foreign Relations, 1988.

Quick, Stephen A. "Mexico's Macroeconomic Gamble." Paper presented at the conference, Mexico: Contrasting Visions, Columbia University, April 1989.

Ramírez, Gilberto, and Salim Cabrera, Emilio. *La clase política mexicana.* Mexico: Edamex, 1987.

Ramos, Alejandro; Martínez, José; and Ramírez, Carlos. *Salinas de Gortari: Candidato de la crisis.* Mexico: Plaza y Valdés, 1987.

Reding, Andrew. "Mexico: The Crumbling of a Perfect Dictatorship." *World Policy Journal* 8 (Spring 1991).

————, and Whalen, Christopher. "Fragile Stability: Reform and Repression in Mexico under Carlos Salinas." Mimeographed. New York: Mexico Project, World Policy Institute, 1992.

Remmer, Karen. "Democracy and Crisis: The Latin American Experience." *World Politics* 42 (April 1990).

————. "The Politics of Economic Stabilization." *Comparative Politics* 18 (October 1986).

Rey Romay, Benito. *México 1987: El país que perdimos.* Mexico: Editorial Siglo XXI, 1988.

————. *La ofensiva empresarial contra la intervención del estado.* Mexico: Editorial Siglo XXI, 1984.

Reyes Esparza, Ramiro, et al. *La burgesía nacional.* Mexico: Editorial Nuestro Tiempo, 1978.

Reyes Heroles, Federico. *Transfiguraciones políticas del estado mexicano.* Mexico: FCE, 1986.

Reyna, José Luis. "Redefining the Authoritarian Regime." In José Luis Reyna and Richard S. Weinert, eds., *Authoritarianism in Mexico.* Philadelphia: ISHI, 1977.

————, and Weinert, Richard S., eds. *Authoritarianism in Mexico.* Philadelphia: ISHI, 1977.

Riggs, Fred. *Thailand: The Modernization of a Bureaucratic Polity.* Honolulu: East-West Center Press, 1966.

Ronfeldt, David. "The Mexican Army and Political Order since 1940." In David Ronfeldt, ed., *The Modern Mexican Military: A Reassessment.* Monograph no. 15. La Jolla: Center for U.S.-Mexican Studies, University of California, San Diego, 1984.

————. "Questions and Cautions about Mexico's Future." In Susan Kaufman Pur-

Spalding, Rose. "Welfare Policy Making: Theoretical Implications of a Mexican Case Study." *Comparative Politics* 12, no. 2 (July 1980).

Stallings, Barbara. "International Influence on Economic Policy: Debt, Stabilization, and Structural Reform." In Stephan Haggard and Robert Kaufman, eds., *The Politics of Economic Adjustment: International Constraints, Distributive Conflicts, and the State*. Princeton: Princeton University Press, 1992.

Staniland, Martin. *What Is Political Economy?* New Haven: Yale University Press, 1985.

Stenzel, Konrad. "Markets against Politics in the Chilean Dictatorship: The Role of Professional Economists, 1973–1985." Unpublished paper, Yale University, 1986.

Story, Dale. *The Mexican Ruling Party: Stability and Authority*. New York: Praeger, 1986.

Street, Susan. "Burocracia y educación: Hacia un análisis político de la desconcentración administrativa en la SEP." *Estudios Sociológicos* 1, no. 2 (May–August 1983).

Suárez, Luis. *Echeverría en el sexenio de López Portillo*. Mexico: Grijalbo, 1983.

Suárez Farías, Francisco. "La elite política." *Revista Mexicana de Sociología* 50, no. 3 (July–September 1988).

———. "Normas y prácticas del liderazgo político en México." Paper presented at UNAM, January 1988. Mimeographed.

———. "The Political Elite of Mexico under the Presidency of Luis Echeverría." Ph.D. dissertation, University of Essex, Department of Government, 1989.

Suárez Gaona, Enrique. *¿Legitimación revolucionaria del poder en México?* Mexico: Editorial Siglo XXI, 1987.

Suleiman, Ezra. *Elites in French Society*. Princeton: Princeton University Press, 1978.

Tannenbaum, Frank. *Mexico: The Struggle for Peace and Bread*. New York: Knopf, 1960.

Teichman, Judith. *Policymaking in Mexico: From Boom to Crisis*. Boston: Allen & Unwin, 1988.

Tello, Carlos. *La nacionalización de la banca*. Mexico: Editorial Siglo XXI, 1985.

———. *La política económica de México, 1970–1976*. Mexico: Editorial Siglo XXI, 1979.

Thompson, James D. *Organizations in Action*. New York: McGraw-Hill, 1967.

Trimberger, Ellen K. *Revolution from Above: Military Bureaucrats and Development in Japan, Turkey, Egypt, and Peru*. New Brunswick: Transaction Publishers, 1978.

Tucker, William P. *The Mexican Government Today*. Minneapolis: University of Minnesota Press, 1957.

United States Arms Control and Disarmament Agency. *World Military Expenditures, 1967–1976*. Washington, D.C.: U.S. Government, 1978.

Valadés, Diego, and Ruiz Massieu, Mario, eds. *La transformación del estado mexicano*. Mexico: Diana, 1989.

Vernon, Raymond. *The Dilemma of Mexico's Development*. Cambridge: Harvard University Press, 1963.

Villa Aguilera, Manuel. *La institución presidencial*. Mexico: UNAM, 1987.

Whitehead, Laurence. "Political Change and Economic Stabilization: The Economic Solidarity Pact." In Wayne Cornelius, Judith Gentleman, and Peter Smith, eds., *Mexico's Alternative Political Futures*. La Jolla: Center for U.S.-Mexican Studies, University of California, San Diego, 1989.

Wiarda, Howard, and Kline, Harvey F. *Latin American Politics and Development.* 2d ed. Boulder: Westview Press, 1985.

Wilkie, James. *The Mexican Revolution.* 2d ed. Berkeley and Los Angeles: University of California Press, 1970.

Williams, Edward J. "The Evolution of the Mexican Military and Its Implications for Civil-Military Relations." In Roderic Camp, ed., *Mexico's Political Stability: The Next Five Years.* Boulder: Westview Press, 1987.

Wionczek, Miguel. "Electoral Power: The Uneasy Partnership." In Raymond Vernon, ed., *Public Policy and Private Enterprise in Mexico.* Cambridge: Harvard University Press, 1964.

Womack, John. *Zapata and the Mexican Revolution.* New York: Random House, 1970.

Zaid, Gabriel. *La economía presidencial.* Mexico: Vuelta, 1987.

Zamora Millán, Fernando. *México: ¿Ahora hacia dónde?* Mexico: Publicaciones Cruz O., 1987.

Zaslavskaya, Tatyana. *The Second Socialist Revolution: An Alternative Soviet Strategy.* Bloomington: Indiana University Press, 1990.

# Index

abstentionism, within PRI, 56–58
administrative sector: career patterns in, 104n.11, 132n.58; corporatist-planning perspectives on reform of, 214–19; popularity of, among Mexican elites, 120
age cohorts: of bureaucratic elites, 108–10; career patterns of elites and, 133n.60; education patterns of elites and, 120n.37
agricultural policy: vs. industrial policy, as key to economic growth, 178n.8, 179; international influence on, 240; social welfare programs and, 205–6, 208–9; success of *salinastroika* and, 244
Agriculture, Ministry of: purge of personnel, 168n.75
Aguilar Camín, Héctor, 142n.73
Aguirre, Ramón, 160n.54, 163
Alemán, Miguel, 8, 49, 54–56, 80; *camarillas* system under, 149n.13, 150; regional political machine of, 112n.20; Stabilizing Development program, 178n.7
"Alliance for Production," 185
Andres de Oteyza, José, 187
*arribismo* concept, in PRI, 59–60
Asian countries ("Asian Dragons"): Global Development Plan and, 188–89; influence on Mexican economic reform, 194, 244–45; as models of economic reform, 31–33, 232, 234
Aspe, Pedro: on economic policies, 95–96, 141n.73, 143, 217n.21; on privatization, 195; role of, in Salinas's *camarilla*, 162n.60, 166n.71, 170; on social welfare policies, 206; teaching activities of, 220n.42
authoritarian regimes: centralization of bureaucratic power in, 46–47; decline of, 27; Mexican model of, 32–33; success of economic reform linked to, xi–xii, 30–33, 232–39. *See also* democratic theory
Autonomous Technological Institute of Mexico (ITAM), 107, 119
autonomy. *See* power, distribution of
Ávila Camacho, Manuel, 8, 48–49, 54, 149n.13

Baja, California (Norte), opposition electoral victories in, 17–18, 225
Baker-Brady debt agreements, 198
Banco de México, 151; Echeverría's economic policies and, 81–82, 182–83; López Portillo presidency and, 159–60; private-sector employees in, 130; role of, in government, 77–79
banking sector: bureaucratic elites links with, 129, 132n.58, 139–40; debt negotiations with, 71n.80; economic reform and, 25–26; growing privatization of, 193–94; nationalization of, in 1982, 9; state's autonomy and, 71; *técnicos* participation in, 105
Banobras agency, 96
Bartlett, Manuel, 148n.11; *camarillas* system and, 142n.77, 143n.79, 160n.54, 161n.59, 164; SPP and, 92
Basáñez, Miguel, 104n.11, 113, 132n.57
Basic Plan of the Government (Proyecto de Plan Básico de Gobierno), 86
birthplace of elites, importance of, 110–12
Borrego Estrada, Genaro, 92n.55, 166n.71
Brady plan, 71. *See also* Baker-Brady debt agreements
budget policies: control over as central political tool, 92–94; emergence of SPP and, 88–90; national planning programs and, 84–88
bureaucracy: age cohorts for, 108–10; ascendancy over party politics, 7–8, 39–40, 81–82; by representative agencies, 137; career specialization patterns, 135–40; de la Madrid's influence on, 141–44, 157–63, 168–69; educational levels among, 116–22, 117n.29; emergence of SPP and restructuring of, 88–94; hegemony of, during Cárdenas regime, 7–8; limits to autonomy of, 67–73; military controlled by, 47–51; mobility within, for elites, 135–39; national planning structure and, 81–88; nepotism patterns among, 113–15; "organizational" politics of, 122; party politics neutralized by, 39–40, 51–59, 125–28; personnel profiles by sector, 136; power central-